Savage Detours

Savage Detours

The Life and Work of Ann Savage

LISA MORTON AND KENT ADAMSON

FOREWORD BY GUY MADDIN

McFarland & Company, Inc., Publishers
Jefferson, North Carolina, and London

Lisa Morton is also the author of these works from McFarland:
The Cinema of Tsui Hark (2001; softcover 2009); *A Hallowe'en Anthology: Literary and Historical Writings Over the Centuries* (2008); and *The Halloween Encyclopedia* (2003)

Unless otherwise noted, all quotes from Ann Savage are taken from interviews conducted with her by the authors from 2000 through 2008. Some review quotes and press articles were taken from clippings included in Ann's personal scrapbook, where sources were frequently not cited.

Frontispiece: Tom Neal and Ann Savage in *Detour* (1945).

LIBRARY OF CONGRESS CATALOGUING-IN-PUBLICATION DATA

Morton, Lisa, 1958–
Savage detours : the life and work of Ann Savage / Lisa Morton and Kent Adamson ; foreword by Guy Maddin.
  p.   cm.
Includes bibliographical references and index.

ISBN 978-0-7864-4353-6
softcover : 50# alkaline paper ∞

1. Savage, Ann, 1921–2008. 2. Motion picture actors and actresses—United States—Biography. I. Adamson, Kent. II. Title.
PN2287.S2775M67   2010   791.4302'8092—dc22 [B]   2009040998

British Library cataloguing data are available

©2010 Lisa Morton and Kent Adamson. All rights reserved

No part of this book may be reproduced or transmitted in any form or by any means, electronic or mechanical, including photocopying or recording, or by any information storage and retrieval system, without permission in writing from the publisher.

Front cover: portrait of Ann Savage. Three boxed photographs: Columbia Pictures presents Ann the Savage, 1943; Ann fishing, 1947; Ann demonstrating her bowling skills, 1943. Film reel ©2010 Shutterstock

Manufactured in the United States of America

McFarland & Company, Inc., Publishers
Box 611, Jefferson, North Carolina 28640
www.mcfarlandpub.com

For Ann, the one and only.
She lived her life to its fullest,
by dreaming, hoping and loving with all of her heart
for each of her 32,087 days on earth.
She was quite a gal!

Acknowledgments

The authors gratefully acknowledge our collaborator, Ann Savage, not only because she lived it the first time around, but re-lived it for camera, microphone and notepad through endless hours—years, actually—of interviews and follow-up.

The authors also gratefully acknowledge the invaluable assistance of: Dan Weinstein and the Iliad Bookshop; Eddie Brandt's Saturday Matinee (truly the world's greatest video store); Arianne Ulmer Cipes for her many and varied insights; Randall "Cochise" Miller for his contributions to the archive, and for screening Ann's films so she could revisit and discuss them, many of which she hadn't seen in over 50 years; Lindsey Walker—archivist, organizer, and creative goddess of all things online and digital; Josh Caldwell, Jacob Vaughan and Bryan Poyser for their stellar work with cameras and microphones capturing Ann's great style and the music of her language; Guy Maddin for his generous insights and contributions while juggling not one but two festival tours, and two theatrical releases; Jody Shapiro for producing miracles; George Toles and John Gurdebeke for keeping her star shining; Ian Handford for giving the lady warmth and good cornering on ice; Eddie Muller and Alan K. Rode for their love and support of all things Savage, Detour and Noir; rad Brad Shuster, for graphics excellence; Ricky Lee Grove, a partner in crime; and finally, Don and Shirly Kennedy for a lifetime of encouragement, mutual love, and movie loving.

Table of Contents

Acknowledgments — vii
Foreword by Guy Maddin — 1
Preface — 5
Introduction by Kent Adamson — 7

Part One. Biography

1. Dixie Fried Roots — 16
2. West by Southwest — 23
3. Zero for Conduct — 28
4. The Miracle on Sunset Boulevard — 32
5. Strange Illusions — 41
6. Be-Boppin' the B's — 57
7. Detoured — 59
8. New York Renaissance — 70
9. Flying Solo — 74

Part Two. Filmography

Major Film Roles — 80
Minor Film Roles — 180
Television Appearances — 183

Appendix 1: Detour *Script with Ann Savage's Notes* — 185
Appendix 2: Detour *Pressbook* — 225
Bibliography — 231
Index — 233

Foreword
by Guy Maddin

In late 2006, when I had just completed the treatment for my feature film *My Winnipeg*, I was left with a painful, seemingly irresolvable regret. I had written the character of my real-life mother into the script knowing all the while that there had been only one woman in the history of Hollywood who could play this fiercely loving, ofttimes terrifying force of maternity, and that woman was Ann Savage. I hadn't noticed Ann in the credits of any movies made during my lifetime, nor encountered any mention of her in any of the trades, so I just assumed she was long gone from acting, if not from this earth. What a spot I'd put myself into by writing a part that could only be played by someone who no longer existed. With that highest grade of self-pity us solipsistic directors always indulge ourselves in, I tapped out my plangent lament to one of my few industry friends who might understand my agonies, Dennis Bartok, the former programmer at the American Cinematheque, at the historic Egyptian Theatre right in the heart of old Hollywood.

Dennis was happy to astonish me with news that not only did Ann still exist, but that she was a personal friend of his, that she had just been at his wedding, and that she was still as fiery as she was that long-ago week in 1945 when Edgar G. Ulmer captured her legendarily member-withering assault on the camera as Vera, a once-comely roadkill self-willed back to life and pried from the shoulder of the highway to wreak vengeance on all the cowardly men who ever played her cheap.

Not only was the most frightening femme fatale in the history of film noir still among us, Dennis seemed to think it plausible that she might act for me. I begged him to help me make this happen, so Dennis gave me the phone number of noir author, programmer and bon vivant Eddie Muller, and he in turn gave me the number of Ann's manager Kent Adamson. My ardent desires to reignite the Savage flame on screen must have come off as sincere to these three men—Dennis, Eddie and Kent (Ann's three trusted lines of defense against intrusions from the bat-winged vampiric opportunists that have flap-filled the night airs of Los Angeles ever since the movies arrived in town)—because they all put in a good word for me with Ann. Then the three guardians supplied her phone number and, as in an old chivalric tale of bravery tested, told me the rest was up to me.

Yes, now it was up to me to woo her back into pictures after a half-century of almost uninterrupted retirement. And never in a long life of ardently wooing would-be lovers have I pursued a beloved harder, with more fear and trembling, or with more at stake. Before working up the courage to phone I did some research. Her last period of steady activity was in '50s TV—a 1952 appearance alongside Cesar Romero in an episode of *Schlitz Playhouse of Stars* seemed to me her most intriguing credit of the time. I adored Romero from my childhood enthrallment with his Joker and thought I might be able to find some common ground with the long-retired actress in exchanged admiration of this long-dead super-suave, silver screen queen. Then I found myself researching Cesar Romero. And from Romero, my researches spun out of control till I found myself reading up on Ramon Navarro. I realized I was over-preparing, simply putting off the moment when I'd have to dial those fearsome numbers and take my chances with Ann herself — take my chances with whatever Fate had in store for me, my hopes and my precious film future.

I made the call.

Chilled by flop-sweat, I made the call.

Breathless as a Death Row inmate personally phoning the governor, I made the call.

After a few strident rings which gathered together for me all the shadows of all noir, a perfectly sweet woman's voice greeted me on the other end of the blower. Is it possible I was listening to Ann Savage? Could this mellifluously throated interlocutor be the same woman whose low-budget feral ferocity and castrating caterwauling triple-distilled every unhappy American marriage into the sixty-seven minutes of poison that is *Detour*? It was! But, disorientingly, this Ann Savage spoke so sweetly! In response to my diffident greeting she wafted out toward me a reply in the dulcet tones a woman would use while sliding fresh-baked cookies out of an oven. Suddenly, a grandmotherly gingham flashed before my swimming eyes. I found myself capable of breath. All my fears dispersed! I was talking to Ann Savage, and she was listening to me! We exchanged volleys of pleasantries and platitudes until, perhaps panicking and definitely mistiming myself, I launched into my passionate Cesar Romero encomium.

"What in Sam Hill are you talking about?" interrupted the puzzled retiree.

"I just wanted to let you know I would've thoroughly enjoyed your TV work had I been born when it was on," I stammered, "and that I understand thoroughly any second thoughts you may have about acting again after being away from movies for a while."

"All this talk about being away from movies doesn't cut any ice with me!" snapped *Detour*'s Vera, suddenly awakened by my clumsy step. "I've never been away from movies! Never! I'm in the movies **every** day! I go to them all the time, and when I go to them, I'm **in** them!"

God, I had really stepped in it. The conversation had quickly tipped into a graveyard spiral. I later learned what Ann meant by this statement about being "**in**" the movies every day. It turns out that even though Ann had left pictures for many decades, she still kept up with the state of film very passionately — Scorsese was a favorite — and she had never abandoned the craft of acting. Armed with a current SAG card, always ready for another chance to show her chops, she would often rise early to do her hair & makeup, don her furs and jewels, and embark on secret sorties onto the sidewalks of L.A. to make character studies of unwitting pedestrians. Or she would do her people studies riding on the bus for hours. She liked the mix of personalities there, but was threatened by the risk, so she'd carry her Louis Vuitton purse on one arm, and in the other hand would hold a small brown paper bag. In the paper bag she'd carry her wallet, any jewelry she was transporting to her bank vault, and her loaded .38 Smith & Wesson. She had prefigured that anyone who mugged her would go for the Vuitton handbag, and then be really sorry on account of the other bag.

Luckily, I recovered my dignity enough during the remainder of that phone conversation to receive permission to call this immortal fury again. Over the course of a few months I gained her trust. She had been approached about coming out of retirement before, apparently, but always by directors hoping to trade on her novelty power in some sort of neo-noir project in dire need of the boost it could get by transplanting the totemic strength of Ann's name directly from authentic Poverty Row posters onto their own sad, sad one-sheets. I had one thing going for me: I was not making a noir. Ann liked the idea of doing something outside this genre, of making something new. Once I figured this out I had plenty to say to her, because I really felt I had some pretty new filmic objectives in my crosshairs!

Ann and I became friends! We became partners in this project. She loved the mad idea of playing a woman, my mother, who thought she was playing herself in something that was supposed to be a documentary but really wasn't. She loved the challenges inherent even in the actor's approach to this character, the kind of meta-backstory that had more twists than most plots. She and I got a great kick out of all the prep we did together, rehearsing dialogue over the phone while I worked on preproduction in faraway Winnipeg, Canada, and she went through her own Los Angelino boot camp at home, readying herself for her close-up, reciting her lines ever more fiercely until she was spitting rivets into my avid ears!

When she landed in Winnipeg she hit the ground running. I like to think we worked as quickly, as immediately and as economically as she did with Ulmer on *Detour*. What a team! I dreamt of tying her up in a long-term contract. "Savage Signs Three Pic Deal with Maddin" the Variety headlines would read. She and I discussed making a documentary together. I spoke out loud of remaking with Ann her earlier war propaganda vehicle *Two-Man Submarine*. Alas, the titanic opportunities never arrived. As we all must, someday, she and I just ran out of time. Fate tapped her on the shoulder.

I miss Ann. I miss her terribly. But if you'd told me just a few years ago that I'd someday be in this state of sadness because I'd lost my friend Ann Savage, I would have been selfishly thrilled to know that I would someday get to know her. And so, here I stand, thrilled! But not selfishly. While I admit I shall always be proud to have my name forever tangled up in cross-reference with hers in that great movie database in the sky, I feel even more powerfully the genuine thrill at having known and loved my dear friend, Ann Savage.

Guy Maddin is an award winning screenwriter, director, actor and cinematographer. His 2008 movie My Winnipeg *featured Ann Savage as his mother.*

Preface

In a recent article by *Time Magazine* critic Richard Corliss listing the "Top 10 Greatest Villains," Ann Savage was one of only two women named, honored for her role as Vera in Edgar G. Ulmer's 1945 noir classic *Detour*.

The life and career of Ann Savage are worth exploring well beyond her most well-known film, *Detour*, because they reveal an entire underbelly to Hollywood that is too often overlooked or ignored: the B-film industry. Put under contract at Columbia in 1942 (at the age of 21), Ann learned the ropes cranking out cheap musicals, westerns, mysteries and comedies. She made 16 films for Columbia in two years, often working with the same actors, directors and set technicians over and over. Interestingly enough, many of those same actors and crewpeople—including Tom Neal, Sheldon Leonard, director William Berke, and producer Sigmund Neufeld—who worked with Ann on various Columbia productions would reappear with her in the credits of movies made at "Poverty Row" companies like PRC, Republic and Affiliated. The career of Ann Savage is a microcosm of this entire "other" Hollywood, a place where the movies were cheaper, faster and sometimes riskier. It was a world where women could become outlaw leaders or sexual schemers, while their A-picture counterparts were often little more than set decoration (or, at best, icy, aloof seductresses). In the B arena, novelists like *Detour*'s Martin Goldsmith might be allowed to adapt their own books into screenplays, and makeup men like Bud Westmore would be told to make their leading ladies look worse. It was a strange and yet compact arena, one in which the key players usually knew each other and accepted their lot with a shrug and a smoke.

For most of the 1940s, Ann was truly a queen in this empire, and so this book will present the career of this gifted performer in the larger context of the B-film industry.

Astonishingly little has been written about Ann (Eddie Muller's excellent chapter on her in *Dark City Dames* notwithstanding); one major critic, in fact (David Thomson), could only speculate about the origins of *Detour*'s protagonists.

The B industry is often difficult to study, since even good prints of the movies have vanished. Ann, thankfully, documented her career carefully, recording hours of interviews with the authors of this book and making available her amazing collection of film prints, posters, stills, clippings, scrapbooks, journals, and notes (most of which are now permanently archived at the University of Texas in Austin). She enjoyed talking about her career and her life, and was unusually candid and honest.

This book is divided into a biography, which incorporates extensive quotes from Ann and reveals the human being behind the actress, and how a childhood in the 1920s and '30s shaped a B-movie queen and pinup model; a filmography, discussing the films and television shows she appeared in; and two appendices which shed light on her most famous role—Vera in *Detour*. For the filmography, behind-the-scenes notes have been included to provide some idea of how careers frequently overlapped and branched off in the B-movie world. Because many of these films are difficult to see now, detailed synopses have also been provided, as well as some critical commentary.

Unless otherwise noted, all quotes from Ann Savage are taken from interviews conducted with her by the authors from 2000 through 2008. Some review quotes and press articles were taken from clippings included in Ann's personal scrapbook, where sources were frequently not cited.

If this book could serve one purpose, it would be in leading to the rediscovery of other films in Ann's career. Because — despite six decades' worth of praise for her mesmerizing and terrifying performance in *Detour*— there really was more to Ann Savage than just the undeniably great villainess Vera.

Introduction
by Kent Adamson

I first met Ann Savage in the early 2000s at a public function in Hollywood. I unknowingly sat in front of her, at a comic film. When it was over and we were filing out she said to me, "You're a laugher, I like that," and introduced herself. We chatted, she told me she lived locally, and she learned I was a writer. We exchanged phone numbers. Though I was delighted to have met her, it was a busy time and I neglected to call immediately. About two weeks later she phoned, asking, "How come you haven't called me?" This was my true introduction.

The eminent British film critic John Russell Taylor had been my professor at USC during the spring of 1977 with a class entitled "The History of the B Movie." Taylor was the authorized biographer of Alfred Hitchcock, but Poverty Row movies were his secret passion. He made a radical case for the times: that B movies deserved the same recognition as major studio genres like westerns, musicals, and war films. *The Kings of the Bs* served as our bible.

In the 1970s, before home video and cable exploded, old B movies were rarely shown, appearing hacked up and scratchy on syndicated television, and in a very few "revival" movie houses. Pop irony in cinema was limited to art houses with Warhol factory "Superstar" projects, and the glorious reign of Divine in John Waters' midnight movies. Mainstream distribution of old entertainment product in new packages as "Movie Classics," "Classic Rock," and even food products rebranded as "Coke Classic" et cetera, et cetera, et cetera, as though repetition determines classicism, had not yet been flushed into the pipeline. Cultural labels cum marketing hooks, like "Art Brut," "Outsider Art," and "Lowbrow Art" were also not yet applied to commercial film.

1977 was the year punk stole headlines, and fat Elvis died. It seemed as if the refined and kindly Taylor had curated an outburst of punk film, showing everything from Edgar G. Ulmer's *Detour* and Paul Bartel's *Private Parts*, to George Kuchar in *Thundercrack!* He introduced our class to the concepts of "independents" and "film noir." He traced the direct influence of American B movies on the French New Wave of the '60s. The B's were full of freedom, hysteria, and hot sex not found in A pictures. The best were fast, raw and intense, the perfect course of study for hormonally driven, late teenaged, punk loving "Cine Rats."

The pop cultural label Ann applied to herself and career was "Outsider." Ann had several more titles bestowed upon her in her lifetime, and they make an impressive list of credits. Always ahead of her time, Ann began her rise to infamy at the age of six, grabbing a name more commonly found attached to teenagers: "Runaway." She quickly added: "Street Fighter," "Hollywood Kid," "Hot Rodder," "Babe," "Cop Spotter," "Crack Shot," "Dropout," "Divorcee," "Actress," "Model," "Pinup," "Starlet," "Leading Lady," "Femme Fatale," "Fashion Plate," and "Lovely Wife" all before the age of 25. Subsequently, she also added "Television Pioneer," "Art Connoisseur," "Gourmet Cook," "Hostess," "Widow," "Has Been," "Speed Rated Pilot," "99," "Mistress," "Legend," "Icon," "Dark City Dame," and "Noir Goddess."

During her reclusive final year she became "A Garbo for Our Times," and ultimately (now that she is gone), "Immortal."

Back in the '70s, without any information about the perfectly named Ann Savage, we could only wildly imagine her story. Her character in *Detour*, Vera, was like a dark goddess set free from the underworld by a crack in the San Andreas Fault. An eruption from a hellish lava hole, she took human form in the blazing California desert to drive Tom Neal, and audiences, into insanity. The sexiest and scariest succubus ever filmed! There was no explanation for this spontaneous attack of acting. Nobody had seen anything like it. Evil and indelible. Let the other students find subtext in *Pillow Talk*; the only pillow in this B movie would be used by Vera to smother Doris Day.

The serenely lovely, beautifully groomed and well mannered woman who told me she was Ann Savage seemed to have nothing in common with my memory of Vera, except a slight hint in her amazing mezzo soprano coloratura voice. It was low, slightly husky, with perfect diction, evenly modulated, and lightened with sweet high notes. I wondered ... if I recorded her voice and sped it up, would Vera come flying out of my speakers?! I thought Vera must be lurking somewhere in those rich tones, at some other pitch, or in a different key. It didn't take me long to find out.

We were scheduled to work together as volunteers for charity. We would meet at an appointed time. It was a rainy day and I was 15 minutes late. As I drove up, I could see her pacing in high heels. My stomach fell; of course she had been perfectly on time in spite of the rain. When I got out of my car and began to offer my sincerest apology, the lady that barked the fast, clipped questions and waited for no answers was pleased to meet me. In spite of this, we had a wonderful day.

It rained all day long, and nobody showed up for us to meet or greet on behalf of our organization, so we talked movies, and *Detour*, and swapped travel stories. We had both traveled the world and wished to see more. We shared our favorite stories of our most beloved cities ... hers — Istanbul, Turkey; mine — Venice, Italy. We compared crazy adventures, hers driving from Finland into communist Russia with her husband during the Khrushchev era — trailed by the KGB; mine surfing nude beaches on a personal survey of fleshpots of the world.

At the end of the day she looked at the floor and said, "I like the way you keep your shoes polished." I told her, "My father was a Marine, we were taught to spit-shine before we were in school." She said, "Normally, I daren't look at the shoes ... almost always a disaster." I was struck by the word "daren't." It was new to me. I didn't realize that the significant words were "shoes" and "polish." I gave Ann a ride home; she invited me to lunch.

It was a Sunday and her favorite restaurant, Musso and Franks, was closed. She asked if I knew Canter's Deli in "the Fairfax." A mutual favorite. We shared meatloaf, another mutual favorite. When I helped her out of the car at her apartment building, she said, "Now you know one of my biggest secrets." I lamely tried to joke, "Only one?" "Yes, Vera is my angry voice." "Holy Heart Failure!" I thought. "The earth's core combusted before my eyes, and I've lived to tell the story." At this moment, the image of Vera made her final exit, and the brave, brutally honest woman Ann Savage actually was became a friend.

She planted a small kiss on her index finger, touched it lightly on my forehead, and said, "When are we on for Musso's?"

Getting to know Ann in her 80s presented an inspirational view of seniorhood as an ultimate state of personal anarchy. She had gotten away with a lot as a beautiful teenager in the 1930s. She knew, as a legendary octogenarian, she could get away with a lot more. She happily played the (as she called it) "age card" with anyone who dared to use the word "no" in her presence. She drew upon her acting skill for extra powers of persuasion. If that wasn't enough, she had the Devil's dictionary of profanity in one hand and her beloved .38 snub-nose always ready. Ever ahead of her time, Ann never waited to become empowered by federal law or women's groups; she had emerged powered at birth, and never took her foot off the accelerator.

Ann Savage was a born actress. Her instinct for the art began to show by the age of three. The legendary Max Reinhardt was her first acting coach. When they met in 1939, she was an unruly and stunningly beautiful 18-year-old Hollywood kid; he was a living legend, almost 70, with no intention of slowing down.

"Dr. Reinhardt," as she called him, had barely escaped Hitler's Germany in the 1930s and came to California to make movies and run an actor's workshop. He also had an eye for Hollywood blondes, the younger the better. He taught Ann the fundamentals of acting. They became instant friends, calling each other "Duck" (as in "Ducky"—a common 1930s pet name meaning "the best, the greatest"). Ann learned the Stanislavski acting doctrine of "spiritual realism," which involved being present in the immediate moment of life and the life of the character being created.

Ann at 21 (1942).

Ann practiced acting daily. During the periods when she was not employed in film or television, she studied everyday people and repeated their natural dialogue. She called it "rehearsal"; it put her in touch with her thoughts and emotions. Movies and television were "employment," which she was always eager to take on. Ann maintained her membership in the Screen Actors Guild without interruption from 1942 until her death at age 87.

Ann Savage was a very fine artist. Her pivotal performance as Vera in *Detour* was groundbreaking, decades ahead of its time. Her final performance in *My Winnipeg* showed that she still had power and impeccable timing more than sixty years later. Her pacing, inflection and emotion in her last scene in the film, the last scene that was shot, her final bow forever, are perfect. She did it in one take.

Ann made over 30 movies and a dozen or so TV shows. The slightly shy, sweet-natured woman behind the mask of "Ann Savage," first known to her friends as "Bernie" Lyon, lived a life that nearly encompassed the entire history of film—from the silent era to the digital age. She was a walking encyclopedia of actors and performance. When watching a movie she'd poke her sharp little elbow in your side and say, "Look what she's doing in this scene."

Ann Savage survived a harrowing childhood due to the unconditional love and plain hard work of her mother, Louise. Her early life was so challenging that she often said she never expected anything from anyone. This attitude gave her a true humility and made her later successes deeply gratifying.

In her last years, Ann attached herself to one feature script, three documentaries and Guy Maddin's *My Winnipeg*. She prepared extensively for her work, taking it very seriously. She would ask me to run lines with her, which I considered a great honor. Right from the start she was up on her feet, reading and pacing. Over several weeks she would write out her lines and pace them off, working on the voice and her body movement. Her character in *My Winnipeg* walked, talked, used her hands and arms, and sat on the couch entirely differently than Ann Savage in real life.

Ann loved the originality of Guy Maddin's vision. The balletic beauty of *Dracula: Pages from a Virgin's Diary* impressed her, and after several phone conversations she felt he was a director she could trust. Over the two years it took to shoot and complete *My Winnipeg*, Ann and Guy became loyal friends. She celebrated his mounting success at the Hollywood premiere of *Brand Upon the Brain!* in December of 2006. In the fall of 2007, prior to the world premiere of *My Winnipeg* at the Toronto International Film Festival, Ann reviewed the final cut of the film. She was delighted by, and very proud of, the result.

It was with deep appreciation for their work together, and their friendship, that Ann chose Guy to write the foreword to this book.

Trying to pack as much as possible into each day, Ann continued to travel to film festivals, record interviews, keep up correspondence with friends and fans, and play tennis weekly until she was over 86 years old. She was a busy person who never wasted time. When cautioned to slow down by her doctors or friends, she'd ignore them and say, "I'm already on borrowed time, honey," and keep going full steam ahead.

Ultimately, sadly, time began to catch up to Ann. Ever the pragmatist, she arranged for her collection to be housed at the University of Texas at Austin, and approved the shift in focus for this book from autobiography to a biography and filmography. She had recorded many hours of oral history, shot on-camera interviews, and sorted thousands of photos and archival papers.

Co-author Lisa Morton joined this project to share her considerable writing talent, as well as her insight from long experience in the film business. Ann was impressed with Lisa's working knowledge of professional film and live theater.

In counterpoint to her noir characters, Ann was an optimist. A legendary beauty in Hollywood circles, she had been groomed for glamorous roles at Columbia Pictures. Her pinup photos and fashion portraits were shot by the top photographers and are now collector's items. It is a tremendous irony that she is known today for her most deglamorized role, Vera.

Ann was a laugher herself. She loved to watch comedies and westerns. She had a home full of movie and still cameras, and several generations of video. Ann was the family filmmaker, in control of the movie camera, and her third husband Bert shot the slides. Her movie collection included 16mm, Super8mm, 8mm, VHS, Laserdisc, and DVD formats. She repeatedly watched the films of Tati, Chaplin, Laurel and Hardy, the early funny ones of Woody Allen, Clint Eastwood, Martin Scorsese, and, of course, Ulmer. She was mercurial and took personal exception to Alfred Hitchcock ("a bastard"), Orson Welles ("a blowhard") and Budd Boetticher ("a mean bastard"), and would not watch their work.

Ann was of the generation that viewed television as a communications marvel. She religiously watched James Lipton on *Inside the Actor's Studio* and simply tuned out the medium's misuse by greedy hucksters. She adored Robert Osborne on Turner Classic Movies, Oprah, and any western show, especially reruns of *Bonanza*—the early ones with Pernell Roberts.

She played down her own fame, saying that she "was never really a star." The day Ann discovered the internet was one that changed her life. She had stopped in the Apple Store at the Grove Mall, and began typing on a laptop. A salesman showed her Google and asked what she wanted to search. "Ann Savage" brought up over one million pages. Later she asked, "Who puts it there?" Surely not Columbia Pictures; they hadn't even put her movies on VHS.

The same people who had written to Ann for decades, blindly proposed marriage, asked for autographs, photos, and even dispensation for illness, were promoting her on the internet—her fans. She was especially grateful to her fans, and always generous with them. Ann corresponded with them regularly. They were not an abstraction to her, they were real people.

She had actually met them early in her career, while on the road with USO War Bond

Ann the filmmaker (in Athens, Greece, 1965).

tours in the '40s, and found a genuine mutual love. They invited her home for dinner, introduced their brothers, baked pies for her, drew her portrait, sent tapes of her films, asked her for beauty tips and always admired her loveliness. Her fans were like a huge international extended family, and having grown up as a lonely only child, she was grateful for, and humbled by, the love they showed her.

When she fell ill, staying inside more frequently, she used the internet to communicate with friends and fans. She loved to travel the world by searching for photos of her favorite foreign countries: Turkey, Spain and China. She reunited with people she hadn't seen in decades, made friends with children of old friends and dear ones now gone.

Ann accomplished much in her life, and still had much left to do. She wanted to visit New York again, see another season of the bullfights in Spain, and yearned to introduce audiences to more of her work. Most of all, she wanted to make more movies.

In spite of pain, her moods were usually good, though once in a while her sharp humor would fly out, catching me off guard. One morning I asked her a little too casually, "How are you feeling today?" She shot back, "How the hell do you think I feel?"

She never gave up. Though she struggled with several compound ailments, she wanted her hair done a week before she passed away, and made sure the hairdresser saw the Time Magazine article naming *My Winnipeg* as one of the top ten films of 2008. She had survived many hardships, and counseled me to "roll with the punches." She refused to be defeated by anything, including her own body. She said several times: "Never quit."

On her last day, Christmas, she listened to the rain on her window and the music of Artie Shaw, Barney Kessel, and Ray Charles, artists she never tired of hearing. She silently squeezed my hand and drifted into a peaceful sleep.

Nothing can replace her elegance and grace, her impulsive intuition, and razor sharp humor. A couple of years earlier, over lunch at Canter's, she suddenly turned serious and said to me, out of the blue, "You're going to miss me." I stopped stuffing my face, and swallowed. "Yes, absolutely ... I will ... but if I have a heart attack first, from all this meatloaf, you'll miss me." Silence. "I'll think about it, honey." We laughed.

One by one, over the last thirty years, the citizens of "Old Hollywood" have disappeared. They were unique to their time. Many were uneducated and grew up on the road in vaudeville. Very few had corporate experience or middle class backgrounds. They lived by their wit and talent, their charm and beauty. Ann went into a deep depression when Ray Charles died. She said she was sorry for the world that this "genius, this beautiful man, is no longer with us." She knew he was irreplaceable, and his time on earth was done. She couldn't stop crying and stayed in bed for three days.

After Ann was gone I felt like one of the aimless sleepwalkers in *My Winnipeg*. I was zombified; I couldn't find a door, or a key, or a trail of footprints in the snow to follow home. We had been through so much together, so quickly, it was overwhelming. Gradually, her words and stories began to come back into focus. I found notes she had written to me but never delivered. Pictures she had signed for friends and not sent. Notebooks with her dialogue lines written out. Scripts with character annotations. She received several heartfelt tributes, and many people offered their condolences and support. They described her sheer loveliness, even more powerful in person than onscreen. She was very beloved. Though my life will never be the same without her, Ann lives on through her inspiring strong will and her historic work on film.

Ann's beloved mentor, Max Reinhardt, did not live to see Hitler's defeat by Allied forces in the spring of 1945, nor the dawn of the Atomic Age later that summer. He also missed Ann's 1945 demolition of the limits of film acting with her nuclear femme fatale in *Detour*.

However, the spirit of Max Reinhardt is still felt today, like a radiant ghost in the cine-

Ann and Kent Adamson in 2006.

matic blowback of *Detour*. A public domain "orphan" film, it has persisted for more than half a century.

Detour has survived neglect, brutal cuts for television, the destruction of its camera negative, its nitrate prints turned to dust, careless transfers to video, and the lack of investment funds for a definitive restoration. *Detour* persists, based on its own strengths. That it still has a following is due to the hard work of many people, and in large part to the fearless, unnerving performance of Reinhardt's pupil for life, the immortal Ann Savage.

Part One
Biography

Chapter 1

Dixie Fried Roots

> My father was a mean bastard. The less said about him, the better. He had a violent temper, which I inherited. I've never been able to forgive him for the things he did to my beautiful mother. My mother grew up on a farm in Mississippi. She had a lovely southern accent which she never lost. It sounded like music in the air. My parents owned a jewelry store in Dallas, Texas. They worked very hard, and the only happy memories I have of them together are when we went to the movies downtown. We all loved the movies. The ride to the movies was a happy time, we would talk and laugh and we couldn't wait to get there.
>
> One of my earliest memories is being taken to a gigantic palace to meet a very important king. I realized years later, when I asked my mother about it, that we had gone to an ornate movie theater to see Valentino. The movies were silent then, and the theater was filled with beautiful music. I wanted to get up and dance for the king, it was so moving. I always had the same problem in church. I never liked to sit down. Still don't.
>
> The ride home from the movies was always quieter. Everyone was tired, and I guess my parents had started thinking about the next day's work. When we got home I would cheer them up by play-acting scenes from our favorite movies. I didn't know a damn thing about acting ... I didn't even know what acting was ... but it usually worked ... and was fun for all of us.
>
> — Ann Savage, 2006

Ann Savage spent her early childhood years in the deep American South of the 1920s. Her mother Louise was the last child of ten born in 1899 to Marcus Alonzo Carr and his wife Nancy in the Bear Creek area of Attala County, Mississippi. Bear Creek was not an incorporated town, or even a district, but a collection of large subsistence farms. Marcus Alonzo, a farmer known as Lonnie, was a deacon and occasional preacher in the Bear Creek Baptist Church.

The Carr family had settled in the area in the 1850s and, by the good fortune of their birth patterns, was largely unscathed by the Civil War. In the mid–1860s Marcus's father George Miller Carr was too old to fight in the war, and Marcus, who was born in 1853, and his brothers were all too young. Attala County was not a significant southern battleground, with life continuing much as before the war.

The Carrs were not known to own slaves, their farms being small enough to be tended by their large families. Slavery, however, was an accepted institution in Mississippi, and the social division between blacks and whites was total. Though raised in the ignorance and bias of the time, Ann Savage grew far beyond her early background. She was proud of her own accomplishment and was open in her recognition of others. Later in life she would marry a Jewish man, vote for Larry Flynt in his run for Governor of California, support Barack Obama's candidacy for the Presidency (living to see him win), and respectfully point out that Oprah Winfrey's family had also hailed from the humble soil of Attala County, Mississippi.

After the Civil War, during the era of reconstruction, the Carr family continued to expand their farms, and a few of Marcus Alonzo's brothers became merchants in the nearby town of McCool. Ann's mother Louise, who was named Louisa at birth, was born far later than her siblings and spent most of her childhood learning to cook, keep house, and look after her older brothers.

A naturally blonde beauty like her older sisters and cousins, Louise was married at a young age to Gohar Miller from neighboring Choctaw County. Gohar was killed in World War One, and Louise married again to another Army man, Hugh Lyon, also from Mississippi. After World War One wound down, Hugh Lyon was stationed at Fort Jackson in Columbia, South Carolina.

As the capital of South Carolina, Columbia had a significant Southern Confederate history during the Civil War. South Carolina was the first state to secede from the union in 1861, and one of the last battlegrounds at the close. After the burning of Atlanta, Columbia was also burned to the ground in 1865 by General Sherman during his long march to the sea. The city survived and

Ann's mother, Louise (1947).

rebuilt after the Civil War, but the economy did not begin to thrive until Fort Jackson became one of the largest Army bases in the U.S., and a departure point for soldiers headed to Europe to fight in World War One.

In the early 1920s, after the war, Fort Jackson was in the process of being decommissioned by the U.S. federal government as a base. Having provided basic training for thousands of young soldiers, the base was no longer a priority. One of the healthy survivors then being mustered out of the Army to return to civilian life, Hugh Lyon was among the soldiers passing through Fort Jackson during demobilization.

Ann Savage was born on February 19, 1921, to Hugh Lyon and Louise Carr Miller Lyon in the Fort Jackson base hospital — among the sick and wounded soldiers of World War One — as Bernice Maxine Lyon. By the end of 1921, Fort Jackson would be decommissioned, and it remained so until it reopened in the late 1930s in preparation for World War Two. It has never been closed since, and is a mainstay of the economy in Columbia. The Lyon family would return to Mississippi and then move frequently throughout the South until they settled in Dallas, Texas, in the mid–1920s.

Ann was raised by Louise in the charismatic, fiery Christian spirit of Baptist liturgy, and fondly remembered attending religious Chautauqua tent shows. Though she would later embark on a lifelong spiritual quest, embrace Judaism, and develop her own hybrid form of worship, Ann never forgot her early teachings of the Christian Bible. Steeped in the lessons of the balance between wicked sin and blessed redemption, Ann shared with her mother a profound love of church. She fully embraced sin, atonement, and forgiveness as the natural cycle of human existence, giving equal weight to all three. She had deep faith in the existence of a forgiving higher holy spirit.

Settling in Dallas, Texas, during the postwar boom of the "Roaring Twenties," Hugh Lyon opened a jewelry store and taught Louise the trade. As a toddler, Ann was attended during the day by the family maid. Spoiled with candy and treats, she was an overweight child. Her parents indulged her with toys, her favorite being a "singing dog" record player. This was a plush stuffed version of Nipper, the Gramophone "His Master's Voice" logo dog, with a player for 78 rpm records in its base.

As an only child, Ann spent many hours alone while her parents worked, listening to records and teaching herself how to dance. Both her mother and father were excellent dancers and taught her when they arrived home from work. She would pick up the rhythm of the music naturally, and follow her parents' feet to learn the steps. The family maid taught Ann the Shimmy, a "dirty" dance for the time, and Ann's father gave her a blistering spanking when she proudly showed it to him. Undeterred, Ann would later learn "racy" dances like the Black Bottom and Charleston, in the face of her father's punishment. As a child, Ann dreamed of becoming a dancer, avidly learning popular dance and ballroom. Late in life she'd demonstrate every dance trend from the '20s through the '60s, starting with the Black Bottom through the Rumba, Conga, Mambo, and ending with the Twist.

The Lyon household, though prosperous in Dallas, was filled with tension. Hugh kept his most expensive pieces of jewelry in a safe at home. Obsessed with fear of robbers, he had guns hidden around the house, and warned Ann and her mother not to touch them. Hugh liked to unwind with a glass of whisky at night and got meaner with each sip. He would slip into sullen silences, ignoring his wife and child for hours. He picked fights with Louise, accusing her of flirting with customers in the store and neglecting their child. One night while drinking, cleaning his gun, and verbally assaulting Louise, he dropped the gun on the floor. It fired straight into his foot. Hugh jumped a mile, hopping on one leg and cussing Louise at the same time.

Hugh would taunt his daughter by placing his gun on a windowsill and telling her not to touch it. He'd leave the room and wait for Ann to pick it up. When he returned, catching her holding the loaded weapon, he'd give her a vicious spanking and then lecture her never to play with guns. If Louise intervened in this punishment, Hugh would become violent while dressing her down verbally.

The family came together for dinner each night, usually an enjoyable event. Louise was an excellent cook, full of her own variations of traditional Southern dishes. Ann particularly loved her mother's meatloaf, cornbread, and chicken and dumplings. Hugh was a hearty eater and spent more time filling his mouth than talking at the table. For a special dinner, Louise cooked ham with red-eyed gravy, a mix of pan-fried ham fat drippings and Dr. Pepper soda. A beef roast would be served with black-eyed gravy, which was made from fat drippings mixed with coffee.

On Sundays Louise would make up a week's worth of dessert—fried pies. These were fresh fruit preserves poured onto a circle of flour dough. The circle was folded over in half and pinched shut around the open edges, then skillet fried in two inches of boiling lard. Louise kept a five-pound can of lard next to the stove for frying everything from bread slices to chicken breasts. Ann described her mother's cooking: "When my mother made country gravy, she used buttermilk in place of whole milk; she always put special ingredients in her cooking, and lots of love."

Louise had learned that her buttermilk pie was a man pleaser back on the farm when her brothers would finish an entire pie in one meal. Ann craved her mother's cooking her entire life. As an adult, she would develop a hunger pang for Southern fried food in the oddest locations—while crossing the Atlantic by ship or flying her plane to Mexico.

In 1927, at the age of six, an already headstrong Ann plotted her escape from the oppressive world of Hugh Lyon. She decided she'd had enough of his rants and rages. She felt thoroughly rejected by his stony silences, and, furthermore, she was displeased that the family maid was too busy cleaning to entertain her with more dance lessons. Ann opened her children's cardboard suitcase, carefully packed her favorite toys, and took off running from the house. The maid caught her a few blocks away, crossing a busy intersection. "I didn't have a plan, or know where the hell I was going.... I wanted out of that damn house. It felt great to be free! I was running and running and loving it! I've never forgotten that feeling," Ann said.

Another blistering spanking. Another knockdown fight between Hugh and Louise. This time Ann tried to intervene between her parents, hitting her father to break up the fight. Hugh picked Ann up off the floor, took her to the hall closet, and locked her in. Through the closet door, Ann could hear the argument between her parents play out. She felt she could see through the door, actually see what was going on in the living room, even though she was alone in the dark.

When she started attending school in Dallas, she loved playing sports and meeting other kids, but didn't get along very well with her teachers. "In those days, the teacher's word was law, and they enforced it." Ann remembered, and believed, "They were more interested in pushing little defenseless children around, and playing favorites than they were in teaching. I never had a good teacher, except in church and later when I met Max Reinhardt." Ann also developed a reputation as a fighter on the playground, one to beat. "I didn't pick fights, but if I got into one ... I got M-A-D and gave it everything I had. I guess I overdid it, because my parents had to answer for me several times."

In school, Ann was befriended by a strong Latin boy who walked her home:

> Roberto ... he was very good looking and tall, but had a club foot so the other kids wouldn't play with him. He was a good fighter too. We were much too young to go steady or anything like that, but we were good friends, and he kind of protected me. I would walk my bicycle home, and he would walk beside me, and the bullies would leave me alone. He never said much. I would chatter away about this or that, and all he would say was "dat's niiice." We bought wonderful spicy tacos from a stand for a nickel. After we moved away, I never had tacos as good as those until I went back to Texas almost 80 years later.

Roberto walked Ann to the front of her house every day after school. He never asked to go inside, and he never said goodbye. He was fascinated with her blonde hair; his dark eyes would stare through her and he'd rub his hand on top of her head, then turn and keep walking. She'd watch him walk far down the street and then reluctantly go into her parents' house. After school, the evenings came quickly and the black Texas night fell fast.

Ann started to spend more time with her mother. In a jealous rage at work one day, Hugh fired Louise and sent her home to fire the maid. Hugh was convinced that Louise was trying to start a romance with one of her regular customers. She began taking care of the house herself and looking more closely after their daughter. Louise was devoted to Hugh, and followed his wishes. She tried to please him and take good care of her family, as she had learned back on the farm in Mississippi.

Ann remembered many happy moments with her mother, especially watching the huge electrical storms that gathered over the Texas skies:

> We'd sit on the porch and watch enormous thunderclouds roll in. They were so large, it's hard to describe. They looked like gigantic ships sailing slowly through the sky. Electricity would flash silently over the face of the clouds and then seconds later you'd hear the thunder crack. They'd blow slowly into town, lightning would strike the ground all around you, hard rain would pour down, and then they'd sail slowly away. We loved it.

Hugh began coming home later and later from work. Once he arrived, he had less and less to say to Louise and Ann. They would watch for him on the porch. The bright red and blue Texas sunset would turn pitch black, and he'd saunter past with a grunt. One day Hugh didn't come home at all. Ann and Louise had dinner alone together, and then a neighbor came over to watch Ann while Louise went looking for her husband.

Ann was told by her mother that Hugh had been killed. She was scared and hysterical, thinking that robbers had gotten her father and were going to come to the house, kill them, and steal her father's jewelry. Though she didn't let on in front of Ann at the time, Louise's fear was even greater. The robbers had already come. They were Hugh Lyon. He had taken all of their money, all of his jewelry from the safe (including all of the jewelry he had ever given Louise), closed the store, and disappeared with another woman. He left Louise her wedding ring and Ann. She didn't know where to turn; her family was two states away in Mississippi. Broke and alone, without a job, a car, a phone, or many friends, she was devoted to caring for her daughter. Louise was only 29 years old, still a naïve, uneducated farm girl.

Volunteers from church and neighbors helped out, keeping food on the table and looking in on the distraught mother and daughter. Finally, one of Louise's cousins from Mississippi showed up in Dallas. He was on his way to California, and helped move Ann and Louise to a farm run by his friends in Waxahachie, Texas, where they would stay until he sent for them. All the furnishings of the house in Dallas were sold; Ann and Louise kept a suitcase of clothes each.

The farm family was kind and generous, sharing their home and food with the total strangers. Ann loved the open country and wandered for hours each day, glad to be out of school. Louise helped the family with laundry, house cleaning and cooking, making them meals and sometimes her special buttermilk pies.

The open countryside of Waxahachie, only 30 miles south of Dallas, is a completely different environment from big city life, and free of urban pressures. Looking more like the grassy Great Plains, it is farming and ranch country. Great Texas longhorn bulls roam the fields, and lazy herds of cows dot the low rolling hills. Ann had to learn to navigate carefully through the fields past the bulls, and loved to help out with the cow herding.

The family would go fishing often. They taught Ann how to dig for worms and prepare stink bait to catch the fat and tasty local catfish. Catfish hunt by smell, and are lured by the stinkiest bait one can put on a hook. "The family we stayed with prepared their stink bait very seriously," Ann remembered.

> They would take flour, chicken livers, and old cheese that had become green with mold, wad it together and fry it up in little balls to keep it on the hook. The catfish loved it. The men would clean and filet the fish, and the women would fry it and make hush puppies. I learned how to find a good fishing hole, reel in the fish, clean, prepare, and cook 'em. What an education!

While exploring the fields around the farm, Ann was caught far from the house when a huge tornado blew in. The family found her, and she helped them quickly herd all the livestock into the barn. They all went down into a basement cellar to ride out the storm:

> It was so dark down there. Spooky. The only light was from small oil lamps. The floor was loose dirt, and the walls were carved out of the dirt as well. Long wiry roots were growing out of the walls, they looked like long witches fingers, bent and craggly with curled hairy ribbons growing out of them.

The memory was still chilling to Ann, almost 80 years later.

> We could hear the storm blow over the farm. The ceiling started to groan, and strange and painful creaking and whining sounds were coming from far away. It sounded like the whole town was dying right over our heads. I have never been so scared in my entire life.

The father had a guitar and started to play. "He sang, too. Then others would join in. I was too scared to sing. I hugged my mother tight and tried not to cry."

When they got out of the cellar, there was a giant tree uprooted and lying near the front

Ann, still fishing as a grown-up, catches a big one (1947).

of the house. The farm looked fine, with no serious damage. Ann heard the mother laugh and say, "All that fuss for some extra firewood." The next day the men inspected the farm and met with the neighbors. The following Sunday everyone dressed up in their finest and attended church together, giving thanks for their survival.

Louise's cousin was making progress in Los Angeles as a law professor, and sent a pair of train tickets for them to move west. When the train tickets arrived, Ann wanted to run away and hide:

> I didn't want to leave. I loved life on that farm; the family was wonderful to us. I realize now, looking back ... it was the only time in my entire life that I lived with a large happy family. There was no fighting. They worked together, helping each other, and they helped us too.

Chapter 2

West by Southwest

The train ride to California was a revelation to Ann. "Having nothing to compare it to, I had no idea how lucky we were to travel to California by train." Ann roamed the hallways of the long cars, and became a favorite of the conductor. She followed him like a shadow while he performed his duties, and saw parts of the train that were off limits to others. "I thought it was thrilling. I peeked in the baggage car, the kitchen, and even the men's bathroom!"

When Ann could sit still in the coach, she became fascinated with the passing countryside:

> The desert was new to me. It was so barren and endless, beautiful. I remember a section where the plateaus were streaked with colors, as though someone had sat on top of the cliffs and dripped paint down the sides. Beautiful. We weren't on the train for more than a few days, but it seemed like weeks to me. It was also where I learned how to play cards and bet on poker for the first time in my life. We played for peanuts. Unshelled.

A long, comfortable passenger train was a busy playground for a nine-year-old girl, and soon Ann began to enjoy the journey and forget about where they had been and where they were going.

Los Angeles was already a sprawling city in the late 1920s. Rail tycoon Henry Huntington had launched the Pacific Electric Railway, an interurban transit system in Los Angeles in 1901. Rapid development followed the rail lines wherever they were installed. By the 1920s it was possible to travel from the beach to the mountains of Southern California cheaply and efficiently. Eventually, this rail grid would provide the right-of-way for much of the freeway system in the Los Angeles area, and connect the hundreds of small cities, districts and villages that are called L.A. Huntington's plan still defines Los Angeles County.

Louise's cousin helped them find a small apartment and showed them around the city. He had been a law professor and was just starting his own practice. He didn't own a car, and gave them a streetcar map that covered the entire city and county of Los Angeles. They all went to see the Pacific Ocean and take in the sights of Santa Monica.

The tall cliffs of the Palisades looked out over the long natural bay that stretched from Redondo Beach on the south up to Malibu on the north. Ann and Louise watched their first sunset over the Pacific. "It stayed light a long time. Nothing blocked the sun as it came to rest in the water. The clouds were gorgeous, lit up like they were lined with gold." A crowd had gathered on the cliffs to watch the sunset. "When the last little dot of sun disappeared into the ocean, everyone applauded." Louise's cousin explained that Californians were sun worshippers. "My mother thought they were kooks, and I thought they must be heathens."

The earliest impressions Ann formed of Los Angeles were of time and space rather than specific scenery or landmarks. "It took a long time to get across town by Red Car." The Red

Car was the nickname for the Pacific Electric Railway. All the distances were measured in the time of a streetcar trip: "10 minutes on the Red Car," "45 Minutes on the Red Car," etc.

The communities of Los Angeles were spread out into a vast city that seemed open and mobile. The central City of Los Angeles continually expanded its boundaries in every direction. It was governed by a strict set of legal restrictions on land ownership, which were also reinforced by the legal covenants of communities and land developers. Within the city many races were restricted from owning land; they were forced to settle in the unincorporated sections outside of city limits.

Jewish settlers in the 1800s created a community in the Boyle Heights district, east of the city limits. By the early 1930s, the Fairfax district, then also outside city limits, had become a middle class development for prosperous Jewish families on the west side of town. Beverly Hills was developed as its own city, with high real estate values aimed at the post-industrialized movie colony, with no restrictions toward the Jewish faith. Blacks were confined to a long, narrow strip south of downtown on Central Avenue. Mexican, Central and South Americans lived east of downtown, and spread from there to the south. Watts was a multi-ethnic community consisting of blacks, Italians, Czechs, Hungarians and many other immigrant families.

Many of the individual cities had their own city services and law enforcement, but not all. The City of Sherman, in the heart of Los Angeles, on the eastern border of Beverly Hills, was too small to have its own police force and city services, so it was served by the County of Los Angeles. So a call to the police in Beverly Hills would get a response from the Beverly Hills Police Department, and a call in Los Angeles would bring LAPD, but in Sherman and other unincorporated areas, law enforcement was left to the understaffed County Sheriff's Department.

As Southern whites, Ann and Louise were not faced with legal restrictions, and could, and did, move freely all over the Los Angeles area. However, socially and economically, they experienced the lines of discrimination that still subtly rule the population. Having thick Southern accents branded them as "Okies," even though neither had ever set foot in the state of Oklahoma.

They lived in small apartments and rented rooms in boarding houses in the unincorporated areas. Ann remembered that most of the elementary schools she attended were mixed race. Almost all of her school friends had two parents who both worked. The wives did not go out of their way to invite Louise to school functions. Even though Louise was a working woman with a respectable job, Ann felt they perceived single women as a threat to their men, and quietly cut them out of activities.

"We initially lived near Hoover Avenue, a little west of downtown." It was an older district with grand Victorian houses that had been sliced into apartments. "I had a long walk to school." Louise sought work as a jewelry saleswoman, and moved frequently with Ann if she found a job paying more money, or an apartment with cheaper rent. Home ownership was a dream that seemed far beyond their reach. They liked the ocean and found an affordable apartment down south in Long Beach.

Living in the Long Beach area, they were near the epicenter of the 1933 earthquake on March 10. Ann had left school to meet Louise after work, and they were walking home. The quake hit at 5:55 pm, a strong 6.4 magnitude, which immediately toppled buildings and threw electric poles and wires to the ground:

> We ran out into the street. We didn't know what the hell was going on! I watched the side of a building just fall over. We had never heard of earthquakes. It rolled quickly though without warning. Buildings shook and things exploded, or fell in every direction. The street came up higher than the sidewalk, it was tough to stay on your feet, and then it was gone.

Ann and Louise carefully made their way home. They found their apartment building was still standing. "The building right next door collapsed, and one of mother's friends was inside, she was killed," Ann remembered. Many buildings lost their concrete facades, and most brick construction was heavily damaged. The Long Beach quake forced a total revision of building codes in the Los Angeles area. At the time, there was very little information about earthquakes, and recovery was slow. Louise took Ann out of school and moved away as quickly as possible. "Many of the schools were heavily damaged, and people were living in the streets, afraid to go back inside their homes."

The Long Beach earthquake seemed to shape Ann's view of life in Southern California.

> We knew it was different than anyplace we had ever lived. The city was very pretty; the towns weren't built up much in those days, and were separated by long stretches of country with beautiful flowers and trees. People rode horses down Sunset Boulevard through Beverly Hills. Things happen fast in Los Angeles, they turn on a dime. Changing all the time. You could have a nice house one minute, and the next second, it was gone.

Louise found a new job in Los Angeles, and they moved north near the Baldwin Hills district. They lived in a small garden court apartment, and Ann went back to school. She and her mother developed a new routine, and once again put shocking change and tragedy behind them.

> I got a cat named Snookie, she was the first pet I ever had. She was a beautiful marmalade tabby, and looked like a little orange tiger. She was a determined climber and got herself into the strangest places. We'd come home and find her up in a cupboard, or on top of the fireplace mantel yowling because she was afraid to jump down.

Ann and her friends in the neighborhood liked to dress Snookie up in doll clothes and give her rides in a baby carriage. "Snookie was adorable. She had a lace bonnet and a little smock; she was my best pal ... we did everything together."

Louise had met a new man at work and started to bring him home for dinner. At first he and Ann got along very well, but as he lingered longer with each visit, Ann started to resent him. "I started telling him to leave, and my Mother wouldn't go along with me, so she'd send me to the front closet for punishment." Ann would take Snookie and her dolls, and play in the closet, making up stories for them, losing all track of time:

> I never really minded it in there because I had plenty to do, and nobody interfered with my games. I talked to the cat and the dolls and explained everything in the world to them. I was the boss, Snookie was my assistant, and the dolls had to put up with us.

Louise's new boyfriend suddenly moved into the apartment, and life became difficult once again. "It was too small for all of us, we should have moved to a larger place but couldn't afford it. I was a demanding child, used to having my own way. I wanted this guy to leave us alone, but my mother liked having him around." The man started to drink after dinner, which Louise objected to. He ignored Louise's wishes, which set off a round of regular arguments between them.

When the boyfriend's drinking got out of control, Louise finally asked him to move out of the apartment. He refused. One night an argument became heated between them, and Louise tried to throw the man out the front door. It turned into a free-for-all shoving match, with Ann joining in. The man succeeded in pushing Ann and Louise out the door, and locked them out. A neighbor across the court had witnessed the event and invited them into her home. When the man got tired of being by himself in the apartment, he walked across the way and drunkenly shouted for Louise to come home. The neighbor went outside and met the man on her porch with a brick to his head. She chased him back to Louise's apartment and ordered him to take all of his belongings and get out. Once again, Louise and Ann were alone. "We never saw him again. Good riddance."

At the same time, a neighbor in the next unit got a small bird in a cage and hung it on her porch during the daytime. Snookie became fascinated with the bird next door, one time getting herself stuck on the neighbor's roof. The bird became an obsession for the cat, until one day Snookie managed to scale a pillar on the porch, claw the bird in the cage and kill it.

Snookie disappeared not long after that. Ann was heartbroken and went looking for her everywhere.

> Some of the kids told me our neighbor had killed Snookie as revenge for her dead bird. I went crazy. I wanted to kill that lady! I went over and banged on the door and raised hell. Another neighbor came and got me and had to watch me until my mother came home.

Louise decided it would be best for everyone if they moved. She found another job in the jewelry district of downtown Los Angeles, and they moved into a boarding house a little north of the Mid-Wilshire area.

"My poor mother had a hard life. She'd get up very early, feed me, dress us both and get on the streetcar at sunrise." At work, Louise stood on her feet all day, selling jewelry and precious stones. Hugh Lyon had taught her well, she knew her business and how to negotiate. A pretty woman of petite build, Louise became a favorite of her customers wherever she worked. In the evening she'd catch a nap on the streetcar home and then make dinner for herself and Ann.

Ann also got an early start every day, walking herself to school. She often was the first student to arrive, and would busy herself playing handball against a school wall. A fierce competitor in sports, she liked to play against the other kids. If her opponent cheated, Ann's temper would rise quickly and a fight would break out. If she attacked viciously enough, Ann would be sent home before school had started. "I was glad not to sit in those dull classrooms." Ann had not yet learned the concept of playing hooky, eluding truant officers and police. She simply walked herself straight back home. "I was a good kid and stayed inside. I loved having the whole day to myself."

Saturday was Ann's favorite day of the week. Her mother would take her on the streetcar downtown to work. She loved the stones and jewelry that Louise handled in her job, and quickly soaked up her mother's knowledge of gems and the tricks of the trade. The Los Angeles jewelry district located at 7th and Broadway downtown was one of the largest in the world. Retailers, wholesalers and manufacturers were part of a thriving industry that was still busy during the economic stress of the Great Depression of the 1930s. As customers fled the stock market, and bankrupt brokers committed suicide, commodities dealers held on. Investments in gold, silver and jewels were considered safe during hard times.

As a young teenager, Ann envisioned a glamorous future life as a jewelry buyer. The men in the store advised Ann that a pretty girl could travel the world, inspecting and buying the finest stones. The stone-cutter in the basement loved his work, but told her it was a filthy job. She had seen the brutal pitfalls of retail sales from her mother's perspective, but a buyer got to travel, had the best clothes, and enjoyed an exciting life.

After helping her mother open the store, Ann would go around the corner to Broadway and spend the entire day in one of the lavish movie palaces. Movies had always been a part of her life, but since she'd arrived in Los Angeles, with its huge theaters, Ann practically lived at the movie houses:

> I went to every theater on Broadway and sat through the movie several times. I loved everything they showed — newsreels, cartoons, musical shorts, travel documentaries, it didn't matter what it was. As long as it moved, I loved it!

She loved the silent films she had seen as a young child, and was a fan of almost any western, but when sound came in she was entranced by the stars and kept tabs on the way they dressed, and imitated their patterns of speech:

> I loved Carole Lombard, and taught myself her laugh. She had a wild laugh, and she was so beautiful. She was elegant. Funny. I loved her in *Twentieth Century* with Barrymore, and *My Man Godfrey* with William Powell — he was another favorite, such a beautiful man, and so funny! I also loved Barbara Stanwyck — a great actress, the greatest, I think. I had followed her since I was little; she made a deep impression on me. I didn't imitate her, but remembered her style, how she could be tough and warm at the same time. I loved Harlow, so glamorous. I'd watch her and dream of wearing those clothes and jewels with something snappy to say.

Ann was a fan of the "great actors" like George Arliss, Paul Muni and John Barrymore. "Arliss was a big star, he played historical characters, he was historic. I loved him in everything. Muni was the most serious, perfect for movies ... Arliss and Barrymore had more Broadway in them." She also adored western heroes like Tom Mix and Jack Holt, but it was the larger-than-life women and their wardrobes that held her attention.

On Sundays, her mother's only day off from work, Ann would press for a special streetcar excursion to Hollywood, or even further west to the magnificent Carthay Circle Theater. "The Carthay was my favorite. It had a beautiful park around it and looked like an old Spanish mission." Located right off the Pacific Electric "Red Car" line, the Carthay Circle drew fans from all over Southern California. It was a premiere first-run house and screened expensive roadshow movies. "We couldn't go all the time, but when we did it was special."

Ann was thrilled when Louise would take her to Hollywood; she loved the dramatic style of Grauman's Egyptian and Chinese Theaters.

> Mother and I both had the movie bug, as fans. In those days you could see movie stars having lunch at C.C. Browns on Hollywood Boulevard, or waiting for their cars at the Brown Derby on Vine Street. It was so exciting to be in this wonderful part of the world called Hollywood. I always felt like a little of it rubbed off after a visit.

Chapter 3

Zero for Conduct

Come Monday, it was back to the hard grind of work for Louise and school for Ann. "As I got older, I started to receive more attention from boys. I was still too young to date and didn't have much of an idea about what this actually meant, but I loved the attention!"

Ann also noticed that she was receiving more attention from the girls in school — in the form of jealousy:

> One morning I had played handball with a young black guy, and his girl thought I was trying to steal him. She called me all sorts of ugly names, and I called her a goddamned nigger. Boy, did she teach me a lesson! She kicked the shit out of me. We had a huge fight and she ripped a hank of hair out of the crown of my head, scalp and all! I still have a bald spot there. It hurts now to even talk about it.

Ann responded to the heart of her opponent. "It was the only time I ever appreciated losing a fight. It was wrong and low of me to throw that name at her, and I never used that word again." Louise had to take time off work to meet with school officials after Ann's latest fight. As Ann entered her teenage years, new tension developed with her mother.

Louise had bought a goldfish and kept it in a bowl on the dining room table. Ann wanted nothing to do with a pet fish. "I don't know why, but I thought fish were disgusting pets; guess I'd filleted too many of them." When Louise came home from work, she would be sure to feed the fish immediately. "She talked to that fish like it was a child or something." Louise ignored her daughter and devotedly cared for the fish. When Ann heard her mother talking baby talk to the goldfish, she'd had enough. "One day when she was still at work I threw the fish on the carpet and left it for her to find when she came home." Looking back, Ann was shocked at her extreme reaction. "I was jealous of a damned fish." Louise was beside herself, in tears. "I tried to comfort her, and told her I was sorry. I said 'Don't cry mommy, don't cry,' but she was too hurt."

Not long after, Hugh Lyon showed up in Los Angeles. Ann was shocked that her "dead" father was still alive, but there was no joy in seeing him again. "He was still a manipulative bastard, and he tricked me into moving into his house." Hugh had promised to teach Ann to drive, which he followed through on, even though she was underage. After a short while, Ann moved back in with Louise. "I had nothing in common with my father except his temper, and that didn't make a good relationship."

Ann entered high school at Los Angeles High, south of the Larchmont area. She walked to school, living just west of the campus. She had begun to date, and met a boy a few years older who owned his own car. He had a fulltime day job. "He was a nice guy, but I really liked his car. It was bright red, which was an unusual color in those days."

Ann convinced him that since he didn't use his car while he was at work, she should drive it. She was underage, without a license, but had a great time racing at break-neck speed all over Los Angeles. "I discovered driving and hooky both on the same day. I skipped school to drive the car, and realized that no cops or truant officers would be looking for a kid driving a car!" This went on for weeks, until the day Ann ran over a traffic cop. "I only ran over his foot in an intersection — he wasn't hurt — but that was enough. I lost the car and my boyfriend."

Entering the world of dating was challenging for Ann, even though she had grown from a chubby tomboy into a very attractive girl. There was no lack of male attention, but she didn't like the approach of most boys her age. "If a boy tried talking dirty to me or whistled, I let 'em have it right then and there. I put up with nothing, and walked home alone from many dates." Ann tried her hand at makeup. "I thought I had done a wonderful job of painting my face; later when I worked for Columbia I learned what an art makeup really is." Ann was very proud of herself one day in a class on grooming, when the teacher asked her to stand up as an example. She thought she was picked to show how hair and makeup should be worn, but the heartless teacher said she was an example of what not to do. Ann ran home in tears. It was getting more difficult for her to find any reason to attend L.A. High.

Ann's senior high school photo, 1938.

One morning before class, Ann was visiting with a friend in a soda shop on Melrose Avenue. As they were talking, teenaged movie actor Mickey Rooney came into the shop with some of his friends. He gave the girls a long look, then came over and spoke with them.

It turned out that Mickey was attending Fairfax High, just across the street.

> I quit L.A. High on the spot, right then and there. I walked across the street and started taking classes at Fairfax. I followed Mickey's schedule as much as I could. When they asked me where I lived, I gave them my girlfriend's address in the district.

Ann had a natural affinity for Fairfax High:

> I thought it had a better class of people. Even though it was a longer walk to Fairfax than L.A. High, I was happy to be there.
>
> Mickey was a hero to everyone at school. I also discovered Canter's deli and have been going there ever since.

After years of being a nomad in Los Angeles, Ann started to feel at home.

There was a large group of kids at Fairfax who liked to do things together. "Nobody had any money, so we'd pool our change for gas and off we'd go." One day while they were at Will Rogers State Beach, Mickey Rooney showed up:

> He did some hilarious routines for me and my girlfriends. We loved it, and felt so honored. Mickey was one of those rare people who had it all, he was funny, smart, great looking, and most of all he was nice to everyone. Even though he was so talented and getting to be really famous, he was regular. We all loved him.

Louise and Ann were living in an old house that had been sectioned into apartments. The tenants shared a common kitchen and dining room. Ann met Clark Tenneson at dinner one night. "He was handsome, and he had a good job as a mechanic in a gas station. He looked so smart in his uniform, and was the fastest racer on Venice Boulevard." Clark took Ann to parts of Los Angeles she hadn't seen before. "We went for drives out to the ocean, fishing in Malibu, we'd feed the sea lions that were everywhere north of Santa Monica. We had a nice time dating."

Clark was the first serious boyfriend Ann had dated. He was older and looked after her. Through some of his friends, she found work as an extra at MGM. She had lived near the studio for a short time and was impressed with the big-name movie stars who worked there. Her friend from Fairfax High, Mickey Rooney, was a contract player at MGM and had started to move into leading roles in the Andy Hardy series and A-list features like *Boys Town* (1938). Ann stepped onto her first soundstage at the age of 17 as an extra in *The Great Waltz* (1938), a big-budget musical full of crowd scenes and large ballroom dancing sequences.

During the time Ann worked on *The Great Waltz*, MGM dominated the film business around the world. The MGM Studio lot was the pinnacle of industrialized motion picture production. Metro-Goldwyn-Mayer was founded in 1924 out of a large-scale stock merger between the Goldwyn Company, run by Edgar Selwyn, and Metro Pictures and the Loews theaters, both owned by Marcus Loew.

The Goldwyn Company was originally founded by Edgar Selwyn and Samuel Goldfish, who combined their names into Goldwyn. Goldfish then adopted the name as his own. They built the largest and most modern physical plant in Hollywood, actually located in Culver City. Before the Metro merger, Edgar Selwyn had forced Samuel Goldwyn out of the company, allowing him to continue to use their amalgam corporate identity as his personal name. Originally known as Metro-Goldwyn, the production company was financed by the Chase Manhattan Bank in New York. The parent company, Loews Inc., was also based in New York, and managed the distribution and exhibition side of the business all over the world, including large studios in England and Germany.

Louis B. Mayer, and his production chief Irving Thalberg, produced a number of profitable films for the studio in the 1920s, resulting in Mayer's name being added to the company. MGM transitioned from silent to sound films in the late 1920s, held steady during the Depression of the early 1930s, and survived the death of Irving Thalberg, a genius of filmmaking, in 1936.

Designed to run as a modern 20th-century assembly line, MGM aspired to create popular entertainment in an environment structured as a factory. For its time, it worked very well as a vertically integrated corporation that could feed films manufactured in Culver City through a pipeline spread across the world. By the time *The Great Waltz* was in production in the late 1930s, MGM was producing feature films, short subjects, newsreels, cartoons, and public information films at a furious pace. Rivaled only by Paramount and Warner Brothers, MGM set the creative and business standard of the time, and pioneered the mass production of mass communication.

Ann Savage walked onto the huge MGM lot and was swept away by its size, complexity and beauty:

> There were thousands of people working there. An empty stage was just a huge empty barn. Dusty. Smelly. Nothing to look at. The geniuses that worked in those studios could turn them into any place, any time. We were dressed in large frilly ball gowns and were whirling around in lovely old Vienna!

This view of life behind the walls of a major studio focused Ann's drive to act. "MGM had bigger stars, and made more movies than anybody. The people who worked there were special. They seemed to own the town."

At home, tension in the boarding house increased. Ann and Clark were spending more and more time alone together, and Louise was concerned that the relationship was getting too serious. Strange things started happening around the house. The food Louise and Ann kept on hand began to disappear. Louise caught a woman a little older than Ann stealing the food and confronted her. Ann walked in just as a loud argument broke out. The woman shoved Louise, who was much smaller. Ann shoved her back. The woman refused to back off, and a vicious fight followed. "I beat the shit out of that woman! She was tough, and needed to be taught a lesson. After my father, if anybody laid a finger on my mother, they paid for it. Believe you me!"

Wanting to move again, Louise began looking for another apartment. Ann was still attending Fairfax High, though missing many days of school to work as an extra at MGM. The school sent a note to the false address Ann had used, and the family reported that she did not live there; Ann had neglected to get their permission for her ruse. When confronted, and instructed to return to L.A. High, Ann walked out of Fairfax and never went back to school. Rather than make another move with Louise, Ann and Clark decided to get married.

The newlyweds learned immediately that they knew nothing about running a household or keeping a marriage together. "We were too damn young! We didn't know a damn thing. I loved my mother's cooking but never learned how to do it. I didn't like sitting around an empty house waiting for my husband to come home, and my husband didn't seem to like coming home." Clark kept racing, and liked to have a beer with the guys to celebrate a victory. "He came home with booze on his breath one too many times. I left and moved back in with my mother."

Chapter 4

The Miracle on Sunset Boulevard

Ann had grown up fast, and though she was underage, returning to school was of no interest, so she began to search for work. "My mother had started working with a Japanese man, Mr. Ishii, who imported pearls and gifts. He had a small shop downtown and didn't need any extra help." Ann started a couple of film related jobs that didn't work out, and then kept looking. "I found a job working at the desk at the Wilshire La Brea Bowl, a popular bowling alley, and then got another part-time job at the Beverly Hills Bowl."

The owner of the Wilshire La Brea Bowl liked Ann and trusted her working the bar when he stepped out. "It was mostly pouring beer and making change. Easy. I was underage, but nobody cared." She became a fulltime waitress, serving the lanes as well as the lounge. Working the bowling alleys also gave her an opportunity to practice her game. She had a great time until a federal agent showed up, wanting to verify her age. "The bartender tipped me off, and I hid out upstairs." The agent searched for Ann; he knew she was illegal. "The bartender fixed it by telling him I'd be back soon. He poured the fed a beer and slipped him a Mickey Finn." Chloral hydrate was most commonly used for this purpose. "He went out like a light, and I went back to the front desk."

While working at the bowling alleys, Ann played in several celebrity tournaments. Meeting famous actors like Harold Lloyd stoked her desire to act. Surprisingly, a pinsetter had been taking acting classes at the Max Reinhardt Workshop. He suggested to Ann that she apply for a scholarship that allowed students to work in the office for their tuition. When Ann interviewed at the workshop, the only position open was secretarial.

With no office experience and no training, she faked her way through the meeting and got the job. She quickly figured out how to perform her duties and reported for work. She kept her part-time job at the Beverly Hills Bowl in case things didn't work out. Most significantly, she began auditing classes with a legendary master of acting. "Meeting Max Reinhardt changed my life in every way. I saw that acting wasn't a dream, but hard work, and I could do it. I loved it!" For the rest of her life, on any application that asked her occupation, Ann listed only one word: Actress. It was her true life's work.

Along with her new beginning at work, Ann also began dating a new beau. Russell Selwyn was a scion of the MGM patriarchy. Known as "Rusty," he was the adopted stepson of Edgar Selwyn, still a major stockholder of the company. Rusty's mother Ruth was an actress whose sister Patsy was married to the chairman of the board of Loews, Nicholas Schenck.

A serious cadet in a military academy, and a popular regular among the "Hollywood Kids" of MGM, Rusty loved to bowl. He was impressed with Ann's technique, and kept signing up for lessons with her at the Beverly Hills Bowl. On their first date Rusty took Ann to a star-filled party at his stepfather's house and announced to everyone that she was studying acting with the world famous Max Reinhardt. This introduction was an instant icebreaker, and Ann met more movie people in one night than she had previously in her entire life.

At the Reinhardt workshop Ann was assigned to work with the manager of business affairs, Bert D'Armand. He was a middle-aged man with a tremendous sense of humor and a sharp head for finance. Bert had helped Reinhardt get established in the United States after he had emigrated from Austria. He carefully recruited paying students for the school, and kept operations running with workers, like Ann, who would accept tuition in lieu of pay. Bert had been involved in the stage production of the Reinhardt spectacles *The Miracle* and *A Midsummer Night's Dream*, and knew how to manage the master's extravagance against the reality of tight funding.

Bert D'Armand was married to Jane Randolph, his second wife, who had been an early student of Reinhardt's Hollywood Workshop. Jane worked, with increasing success, as a contract actress for Warner Brothers and RKO Radio Pictures. Bert understood the movie business and took the time to explain the politics of studios, casting and agents to Ann. Once again her life had changed quickly and significantly, this time for the better. She knew she was on the right track.

The entire Selwyn family embraced Ann and graciously made sure she was invited to their social functions. This put her in the middle of the MGM family, and once again her path crossed with Mickey Rooney's and his friends. At MGM, Mickey had been teamed with Judy Garland by producer Arthur Freed, to astounding success. Mickey and Judy were the first teenaged movie idols, and their dazzling popularity created excitement everywhere they went. Ann was delighted to be in the company of successful actors her own age. Among the others under contract at the time were Lana Turner, Jackie Cooper, and Ann Rutherford.

Edgar Selwyn decided to give Ann a screen test. He asked her to get her teeth fixed, and Rusty loaned her fifty dollars for the dentist. She was nervous during the test, but was assured that it had gone well. Assigned to the talent department, Ann met Lillian Burns, the resident acting coach, who was in charge of preparing the contract players for their scenes. The second Ann sat down she was corrected. Ann's skirt had hiked up, and she pulled it down over her knees. "No, no, no," Burns hollered, "never pull your skirt down!" Burns worked her over, objecting to almost everything Ann did.

"Lillian Burns was a frustrated actress, and wanted you to imitate her every move. Until you did exactly as she had done when running your dialogue lines, she wasn't happy." This approach contradicted both Ann's instinctive approach to character and the initial instruction she was beginning to receive at the Reinhardt Workshop. When she tried to discuss the character with Lillian Burns, she was haughtily dismissed. Sensing the authority of the talent department on the MGM lot, Ann tried to follow her instructions. The chemistry was not working, and Ann was not hired for the job. Years later, Ann's friend Audrey Totter, who had her own battle with the talent department at MGM, gave her some perspective. "Audrey said Lillian went out of her way to undermine any new blondes on the lot. She was very protective of Lana Turner and made it her mission to reduce competition."

The Selwyn family kept tabs on Ann's development with Reinhardt, and offered advice and reassurance. Her relationship with Rusty was becoming serious, and they welcomed her presence in their home. "Edgar Selwyn became like a friendly father to me, something I never had growing up. He was kind and understanding, and talked to me like a human being. He was a wonderful man; I was grateful for his advice." Selwyn also knew a great deal about acting, having been a performer himself on Broadway in New York before becoming a producer.

Max Reinhardt had become a source of fascination for Ann. He was a towering, intimidating historical figure in the acting world, and yet she found him sweet-natured and almost innocent — but not quite. "He was direct, like a child. Emotional. You could tell he'd been hurt by life but still had his dreams. I was 19 when I began to get to know him, and he was in his late 60s."

Ann was eager to learn the history of Reinhardt and his work in Germany and Austria. An expatriate, forced to flee Hitler, he didn't talk much about the world he left behind. Ann picked up information and stories from the other teachers at the workshop, including Reinhardt's wife, Helene Thimig, who was also an expatriate. Thimig conducted many of the

Ann demonstrates her bowling skills to four other Columbia starlets (left to right): Ann, Jeff Donnell, Adele Mara, Marguerite Chapman, and Leslie Brooks (1943).

background classes at the workshop, along with Natasha Lytess, who would later gain fame as Marilyn Monroe's acting coach prior to Monroe's meeting Lee and Paula Strasberg (and joining the Actor's Studio).

Max Reinhardt was one of the most influential actor/directors in the history of the world. He had developed his techniques of realism and naturalism over decades of study and practice in Austria and Germany. He was personal friends, and compared professional notes, with Constantin Stanislavsky, the great Russian actor/director whose writings and teachings have influenced performance for over 100 years.

Bert D'Armand was instrumental in helping the Reinhardt family get settled in Los Angeles and structuring workshop tuition for paying students, and endowments from motion picture companies to help the family stay afloat. While Reinhardt was in North America, Hitler and the Nazis had confiscated all of his personal and business property in Austria and Germany.

Bert D'Armand in his office at the Reinhardt Workshop, 1940.

Max Reinhardt had begun building his theatrical empire as an actor in the 1890s. Born in 1873, and raised in Austria, he made his mark on Viennese audiences while in his 20s, and later conquered the capital of German culture, Berlin. He pioneered the role of the director in theater and was renowned for creating vast spectacles that played to audiences of thousands. He also owned a small theater and became equally well known for intimate, character-driven experimental dramas. Reinhardt was later a founding father of the Salzburg Festival in Austria, and directed several popular stage productions of Shakespeare that toured the world. He made his first film in 1910. With phenomenal success and notoriety came vast wealth, which he used primarily to buy and build theaters and castles in Germany and Austria.

The theater work of Max Reinhardt was noted for its naturalistic performances in bold expressionist settings. With the electrification of theaters came groundbreaking experimentation in lighting and special effects. Reinhardt's achievements in direction and theatrical effects were applied by his students to silent German cinema. Among his many followers were F.W. Murnau, Ernst Lubitsch, William Dieterle, and Otto Preminger. In Europe, working and studying with Reinhardt was the highest pedigree in theater. The German film work of Murnau in the 1920s profoundly advanced expressionism in cinema, and resulted in his coming to Hollywood to make his silent masterpiece, *Sunrise*, in 1927.

As Hitler came to power in the 1930s, the Nazis began to attack successful Jewish businessmen, and started to chip away at Reinhardt's world. They began by levying large taxes on his personal real estate holdings, and then confiscated his theaters through nationalization. Reinhardt retreated from Berlin, spending most of his time on projects in Austria and abroad. When Hitler's Germany unified with Austria in 1938, the last hope of maintaining his life in Europe was lost, and Max Reinhardt became a naturalized citizen of the United States in 1940.

Making an initial impact on Hollywood with his staging of Shakespeare's *A Midsummer Night's Dream* at the Hollywood Bowl in 1934, Reinhardt was rewarded with a contract for a three-picture deal at Warner Brothers. The sellout crowds at the Bowl had convinced studio boss Jack L. Warner that Reinhardt knew the secret to bringing Shakespeare to the masses. *A Midsummer Night's Dream* was put into production as a feature film, with a lavish budget and the biggest stars on the Warner lot. James Cagney played Bottom, Olivia de Havilland was cast as Hermia, Dick Powell as Lysander and Mickey Rooney as Puck.

William Dieterle had been a leading actor under Reinhardt's direction in Germany, and was his long-time student. By the mid–1930s Dieterle had emigrated to Hollywood and launched a very successful career as a feature film director. Under contract to Warner Brothers, Dieterle was assigned to show Reinhardt the Hollywood ropes as co-director of the film version of *A Midsummer Night's Dream*. As a team, Reinhardt and Dieterle created a unique fantasy realm for their mix of mainstream stars and Shakespeare. The film is a rare opportunity for a slight, modern glimpse into Max Reinhardt's lifelong achievements in directing technique and effects.

Warner Brothers committed over one-and-a-half-million dollars to the production, and gave it first priority among its various studio departments and stars. Its style is a magical mix of theatrical fantasy and 1930s Hollywood high-key glamour. The actors deliver sensitive ensemble performances well beyond the scope of their other Warner Brothers screen roles. Cagney is particularly cast against type, showing a gift for light comedy in his part as Bottom that is a sharp contrast to his previous gangster parts.

Popular with critics, the film was nominated for an Oscar as Best Picture. It won for Best Cinematography. Given a full roadshow release, with special walk-in music as an overture composed by Erich Wolfgang Korngold, every effort was made to properly present the film as a special event to audiences. Unfortunately, it was not accepted by the public upon its release in 1935.

Though he remained in America until his death in 1943, Max Reinhardt never made another film. Warner Brothers did not exercise their option on his services for the remaining two films of his contract. Then, as now, and perhaps ever more, a high stakes public death at the box office means the death of someone's Hollywood career. In this case Reinhardt took the fall, while Warner, Dieterle, Cagney et al. went on to greater filmic glories. Reinhardt concentrated on theater production and teaching in Hollywood and New York. He began a new theater company, working with Harold Clurman (who had founded Group Theater in Manhattan with Lee Strasberg) and Stella Adler (who later achieved prominence teaching at the Actors Studio).

As a teacher in Austria, Germany and at his workshop in Hollywood, Reinhardt firmly believed, and continually espoused, that acting could *not* be taught. He stressed practice and performance, believing that acting was a continual process of self-discovery and the discov-

Max Reinhardt (seated at center of table on left side of photo) conducts a rehearsal in his workshop while Bert D'Armand (seated, center, precisely at the corner) looks on (1940).

ery of a character. It could only be achieved by doing and being, not by lecture and textbook. His method as a teacher was to direct plays in which his students performed. He rehearsed closely with each actor, and the resulting plays were produced by the workshop in public theaters. Reinhardt's method forced an acting student to search for truth over theatrical effect in performance.

Character truth — or, in Stanislavski, spiritual realism — is the core of believability for an acting performance. An actor in tune with a character can transcend the limitations of a script, weak collaborators, the artifice of theater and the physical limitations of film. Audiences will connect with the power of a true performance ahead of any other aspect of film or stage presentation.

In teaching the process of understanding and developing a character, Max Reinhardt stressed inner exploration of feelings and thought, tested through practice and rehearsal. This approach gave definition and support to Ann Savage's natural approach to acting. It set her free. By providing context, critical study, and acceptance for feelings she had struggled with in vague and instinctive ways, she had found work she loved, and an environment that developed her skills. She knew not only that she wanted to act, but that she couldn't help acting, and had to act to understand the people and world around her.

Ann Savage incorporated the Reinhardt tradition in the development of every character she ever created. Her style was a mix of Reinhardt, Stanislavski, her own personality and observation, and her unique assumptions of the truth of a character's identity. She began to study the people around her relentlessly, sometimes writing notes or making mental notes, and practicing ("rehearsing" early in the mornings) in the same way some practice meditation, chanting, or yoga. Once she mastered these mechanics of acting, she never let them slip away. Practicing her art grounded her. "It kept me sane in a crazy world."

Max Reinhardt told Ann she took to acting like a duck takes to water, and that this had been his own experience back in Vienna in the 1890s. She worked hard under Bert D'Armand in the office at the workshop, still held down her job at the Beverly Hills Bowl, continued to date Rusty Selwyn, and began to spend more time rehearsing with Reinhardt. Their mutual admiration led them to refer to each other as "ducky" (or "the best"), and they nicknamed each other "duck" in mutual recognition of their incredible early natural attraction to the powerful force of acting.

Extravagant by nature, and lacking his substantial income from motion pictures and theater by the late 1930s, Reinhardt began to depend on the acting workshop for personal income. Bert D'Armand began to increase enrollment of paying students. Introductory classes, which were conducted by Natasha Lytess and Reinhardt's second wife, Helene Thimig, were increased to handle the additional students. Ann studied with both teachers, picking up fundamentals in voice and body movement. Her natural ability as a dancer gave her the vision of stage blocking as choreography. She often worked out a character's movement before she had learned the dialogue.

Helene Thimig came from a distinguished Viennese acting family, and had achieved success as an actress prior to meeting and marrying Reinhardt. She was most noted for her performances in plays by Goethe, Shakespeare and Shaw. Jewish, she had also fled Vienna to escape the Nazis, and devoted her energy to teaching and promoting the work of her husband. Thimig and Lytess often clashed in the office, in full view of the students.

During an argument between the two in front of her secretarial desk, Ann tried to break them up so the students wouldn't witness the display. Lytess turned on Ann, venting her rage at the young student. "She started calling me names, so I let her have it!" Ann said. At that moment Bert came out of his office. "I wanted to deck her. She was way out of line! Bert had to hold me back." He broke it up and took Ann into his office. Talking the situation over, he cautioned her not to fight with any of the staff, telling Ann that even though she would probably win any contest, she would ultimately lose because she would be expelled from the school. "Bert had a nice way of helping me to see things more clearly. After I calmed down, he said to me 'You're a savage when you get mad.' This got us laughing, because it was too true."

In the early 1940s it became clear that war with Germany was inevitable. After Hitler invaded Poland and then France, many of the expatriates in Los Angeles made sure to establish that they were Austrian and not German. The Reinhardt family had deep roots in Austria, and Bert and his mother had emigrated from Poland when he was a child. His bond with the Reinhardts grew even closer as Bert tried to keep the Workshop afloat financially. He was also called upon more increasingly to help resettle the flood of talented immigrants who had fled Europe for Hollywood.

After the Japanese air force bombed Pearl Harbor in December of 1941, Japanese Americans on the west coast were relocated to internment camps. Louise had worked in Mr. Ishii's store for several years by this time. "Mother and I loved Mr. Ishii and his family." They felt he was the kindest man Louise had ever worked with. "The government shut down his store and moved his entire family away." Louise began looking for another job.

Rusty Selwyn was finishing as a student at the Military Academy. America had declared war on Japan, Germany and Italy. "We began to realize that Rusty was going to be sent away to war." The young couple faced an uncertain future. "His family wanted us to get married, but we weren't ready." They both felt it wasn't the right time to start a marriage. Ann had continued her work with Max Reinhardt, eventually winning a leading role in a Reinhardt Workshop production of Clifford Odets' *Golden Boy*.

"Barbara Stanwyck had played the part in the movie; she was terrific! I felt like I was jumping off a cliff; nobody could come close to her." Stanwyck had also been an early idol of Ann's, which made it a serious challenge. The Reinhardt Workshop used its productions as both a way to attract new students and to showcase its talent to the movie studios. Though the production values were bare bones on rented stages, Reinhardt treated each play as a serious professional project. After much study, he felt Ann was ready for a leading part, and he coached her carefully through long rehearsals for the play.

Her position as a secretary for the Workshop had given her a privileged view behind the scenes of the Reinhardt Workshop. "I worked with Bert's files every day and knew how the school kept running, and who paid for it." One of the students at the Workshop was Joan Barry. She was a great beauty who seemed to be more interested in her tennis game than acting. Ann was impressed with Barry's stature. "I thought she was a showgirl or a model; she was quite striking." Ann had been trying to develop her skill at tennis but lacked a court to play on. "Joan and I talked about tennis; she invited me to play. She seemed to be able to get on any court in town.

"When I asked around, I was told she had been the girlfriend of J. Paul Getty." At that time, Getty, an oilman, was considered the richest man in the world. "So I looked her up in Bert's files and found that her tuition was paid by Charles Chaplin." Ann asked Joan about her interest in acting. Chaplin had put Joan under contract for a film role, and she had left J. Paul Getty for him. Joan lived with Chaplin in Beverly Hills in a mansion with a private tennis court.

"Joan asked me if I would like to meet 'Charles.'... Would I ever! I went up to the house and we played tennis for a while with nobody around. The place seemed deserted." They completed several sets and met at the net after a fouled serve. "Joan spoke to me very quietly and said, 'Don't look, but Charles is over in the bushes watching us'; then we went back to playing." Sure enough, Ann caught a glimpse of Chaplin peeking through the shrubs as they worked up a sweat in the sun. Later, after the game, Joan offered Ann lemonade in the house. They sat in the living room, chatting. Chaplin came into the room and made his introduction. "Tennis was never mentioned, and he asked if we would like to hear some music he was working on." Chaplin put on a record and began to dance around the living room. "He acted out the parts of both a butterfly and a bee fluttering around a garden; he was perfectly in time with the music, and had them competing with each other for attention from the flowers. It was a wonderful afternoon."

As her performance in *Golden Boy* drew near, Ann felt she had created her own approach to the character. "I couldn't get Stanwyck out of my head, so I worked and worked to not be her but still be good." Bert had made certain that talent agents and studio scouts were coming to the showcase. Ann's performance was impressive and won her two offers from studios. "I tested at Fox and Columbia." Bert accompanied Ann to the meetings and tests to make sure the offers were legitimate. The head of the talent department at Columbia Pictures, Max Arnow, seemed to be the most serious, offering Ann immediate work in B pictures for producer Irving Briskin.

Chapter 5

Strange Illusions

Max Arnow had personally attended *Golden Boy* and was struck by Ann's beauty and her acting ability. Ann was instructed to sign her contract directly with agent Frank Orsatti, who had been appointed by Columbia to represent her. The Orsatti agency was one of the largest in Hollywood and controlled many of the actors' contracts at MGM, as well as Columbia Pictures. Arnow arranged a screen test with a new young director, William Castle. The word got out that Ann was on her way in Hollywood. On August 24, Ann received a telegram from her acting mentor, Max Reinhardt. It read: "Here's to a new star — good luck Duck." It was signed "Duck."

Ann signed the Orsatti agency contract on August 26, 1942, and shot her test at Columbia on August 31. She played opposite cowboy actor Tom Keene. The test went smoothly, and Ann won the approval of the studio executives, company founder Harry Cohn and his right-hand man, Sam Briskin, the brother of Irving, her new producer.

When it came time to sign the contracts, the screen name Ann Savage was made her legal name. After her fight with Natasha Lytess, Bert had begun to address her as "Savage." She liked it. Her best friend was a bit player named Ann Lester, so she borrowed her first name.

As proud as she was of her new name, Ann was not happy to be dressed up by the publicity department as a savage in a fur bikini carrying a shield and a spear. Photos of the savage Ann were printed around the world, much to her dismay. "I was embarrassed, it was so stupid that I hoped it would go away, but it caught on. I gave the publicity man at Columbia a piece of my mind!" He taught Ann her first lesson in promotion and public relations:

> He said I was green. The only thing people would remember was the name. They'll see another picture next week and one after that. All that mattered was how many inches of newspaper the picture and words used up, and that they spelled the name correctly.

She didn't agree with him at first. "I found it difficult not to take the things that were written about me very personally. After a few stories, I got the pattern."

Her agent called her into the office for a meeting. "Frank Orsatti gave me a scrapbook with my name embossed on the cover. He said 'I hope you fill a hundred of these.' It was a nice way to let me know I was out of line. Don't make waves, kid." She realized she had a lot to learn. "Orsatti then asked me if I would give him a kiss, and I told him not for a lousy scrapbook."

Columbia immediately put Ann to work with still photographers — shooting pinups, fashion layouts, human interest, portraits and holiday art. Some of the best still photographers in the movie business were on staff for Columbia at the time. Initially, Ann worked most often with George Hurrell and Robert Coburn. She was a favorite of the still department because she was versatile, a visual chameleon who projected character and situation in her modeling work. Every time the hair and makeup department changed her hair color, and she was given a new wardrobe, she looked like a different person. She projected character very easily, so Ann the cool icy blonde could easily turn into Ann the hot-tempered redhead.

George Hurrell loved to change his settings and backgrounds frequently to see what kind of character Ann would project. They did a lot of location work together, shooting around Los Angeles at hotels, swimming pools, apartment buildings. In the studio, Robert Coburn took a high-key approach, creating a series of moody fashion stills, then switched things up for a girl-next-door image. When the publicity department ordered calendar art, Ann threw herself into scenes from the four seasons and all the holidays. If they wanted to put her in snowshoes in front of a cardboard igloo for winter, she was happy to oblige. She could dress up as a glamorous high-fashion plate, or wear a straw hat as a country hick. One of her all-time favorite photos was for the wartime newspapers at Halloween, with Ann carving a pumpkin decorated with a moustache to look like Hitler.

Columbia Pictures presents Ann the Savage (1943).

As soon as her photos were carried in the press, Ann began to generate fan mail. The public liked her and asked for more. She struck a nerve as a beauty who was down to earth, looking like she was having fun shooting her pictures. For her, it was a thrill. "Imagine getting paid to be photographed! It was hard work, but it didn't seem real. Off to work ... we're celebrating Christmas in July!"

Ann's look was so versatile that the hair and makeup department used her to experiment with new styles. "They loved hair extensions and wigs. Wigs on top of wigs. The pompadour was in fashion; they stacked as many spit curls on my forehead as they could!" She wore every color and style of hair.

Columbia Pictures was very well organized. "They didn't waste one minute of time! That's one thing I learned from them — how to budget time." She'd report to the talent department every morning and they would give her assignments for the day. "When I wasn't shooting stills, I was rehearsing scripts, taking classes, or making an appearance." Columbia used its starlets to promote the war effort and sell bonds. "They sent us to rallies, to meet soldiers, and cheer people up. It was the best job in the world."

The studio ran six days a week. The talent department was in charge of acting classes, poise and grooming, and public appearances. "When you signed a contract with a studio in those days, they owned you. Not just your picture and voice, but your life. They wanted to know who you were dating, where you were going, and what you had for dinner!"

Max Arnow was the conduit of information from management to the actors. Most people lived in fear of the talent department, not wanting to do anything to upset the bosses.

Columbia's photo department finds a way to combine Ann, Halloween and World War II in this popular 1943 pinup.

I listened to everything they had to say as politely as possible. Then I would do whatever the hell I wanted. What the hell did they know? If I wanted someone to run my life, I would've gone to work for Howard Hughes.

The acting classes at Columbia Pictures were taught by former Broadway actress Josephine Hutchinson. "She was a great lady. Always working to help bring out the best in you, make

Four of Columbia's starlets (from the 1943 film *Dangerous Blondes*). Clockwise from upper left: Evelyn Keyes, Lynn Merrick, Anita Louise, and Ann Savage.

your performance sharper, but never yelling or talking down to you." Josephine Hutchinson was the opposite of her counterpart at MGM, Lillian Burns:

> She was a fine actress, and a lovely, kind woman. We all looked up to her and wanted to please her. After Max Reinhardt, I learned the most about acting from Josephine. She'd made a few movies herself, and really understood how to act for the screen.

Josephine Hutchinson taught Ann how to judge the camera angles and modulate her performance for each shot:

> When you're in close up, every movement of an eyelash shows up on the screen, so you have to be very still, but keep the rhythm of your dialogue going. What you do in a close-up and a medium shot are two different things. The camera reads movement differently from each angle; it's up to the actor to make adjustments for this.

After months of study and training, Ann was ready to shoot her first movie. Columbia produced a number of film series; new talent was often given a start in these episodic pictures. It was considered a bulletproof training ground for new actors. The series had been established with audiences, the leading actors were familiar, and a new face freshened up the formula. Ann was assigned to *One Dangerous Night* in the Lone Wolf series, starring Warren William as detective Michael Lanyard.

Warren William began his long acting career in silent movies. A tall and commanding presence with a deep, rich voice, he was a strong personality onscreen. He was also a shrewd investor and inventor, among the wealthiest and most respected of Hollywood citizens. It was a challenge to debut opposite such a polished performer. Ann knew if she could hold her own with William, his presence would help her performance look good.

The screenplay had a terrific scene where Ann's character, Vivian, pulls a gun on the Lone Wolf and ties him up. There was a slight hint of a former relationship between the two in the dialogue. Ann decided to play the scene with a smile, indicating that she's still attracted to William's character, but has to do her job. Viewed today, it's still an impressive debut. Ann takes charge of the scene immediately, laughing while she pulls the gun, and playing with William's hair seductively while he's tied up in a chair. Ann registered so strongly in the scene that it quickly became the buzz of the Columbia lot, drawing an audience at the dailies screening. Ann was immediately scheduled for her next eight films.

Ann in her debut, opposite Warren William in *One Dangerous Night* (1943).

After signing her contract with Columbia Pictures, Ann had quit her job at the Beverly Hills Bowl. She rented a spacious apartment in the Hollywood foothills at 2270 No. Beachwood Canyon Drive, and moved Louise in. They had always been compatible, and Ann was glad to be able to help her mother. Rusty Selwyn had entered the military and transferred to Washington, D.C., for additional training. The Selwyn family was gracious to Ann, keeping her on their social list, still making her feel at home and part of their family. They hoped she and Rusty would be back together again after the war.

As her time allowed, Ann kept up with Bert and the Reinhardt Workshop. The school was having trouble bringing in new students now that the war was gearing up. Young men were joining the military, and more women were going to work in factories. Max Reinhardt was spending most of his time in New York trying to run another acting workshop and planning theater projects. He had sold his house in Los Angeles, and the Warner Brothers prop department bought all of his furniture.

As the war effort built up, Hollywood saw more European expatriates come into town looking for work. Actors, directors, writers, and artists of all kinds moved to the United States, settling mostly in Los Angeles and New York. Many of them were Jewish, looking for refuge from the Nazi Holocaust.

Bert D'Armand was able to help resettle many families, as he spoke several languages fluently. He and his mother had emigrated slowly through Europe on their way to New York in the early 1900s. Bert knew German, Polish, French, Russian, and some Italian, and was a quick study in other languages. As a young man he grew up on the lower east side of Manhattan, among many other Jewish European immigrants. His mother traded jewelry, art, guns and knives to survive. Bert developed his trading skills early, becoming expert at international shipping and managing merchandise through the docks of New York.

In his twenties Bert had moved to England, where he traded in art and jewelry and began working in the English stock market. Riding the economic boom of the 1920s, Bert made significant profits through his trading, and got out of the stock market in 1928, a year before it collapsed. When it became clear that the effects of the crash were going to last a long time, Bert returned to the United States in 1930. He considered Manhattan his home, and reconnected with many of his old friends from the lower east side.

The federal prohibition of liquor throughout the 1920s had been a wildly successful marketing tool for increasing liquor sales at nightclubs in New York and Los Angeles. As the professional classes earned more money during this period of prosperity, they sought more exclusive ways of spending it. Illegal gambling was often a key profit center for any serious establishment selling bootleg liquor.

In Hollywood, the unincorporated area known as Sherman crossed Sunset Boulevard into the Hollywood Hills. This created a significant stretch of Sunset between Hollywood and Beverly Hills that was outside the jurisdiction of the Los Angeles Police Department. It became known as "the strip," and developed into an entertainment zone filled with nightclubs, restaurants, illegal bars and gambling clubs. It was policed by the underfunded Los Angeles County Sheriff. The heyday of the strip ran from the 1930s through the 1950s, when top headlining entertainment and cabaret acts were booked into the clubs, drawing audiences from all over the world. The strip also drew trouble and the occasional gun battle in broad daylight.

Bert moved to Hollywood in the mid–1930s. In addition to his work with Max Reinhardt, he operated as a talent agent and continued to deal in art. As European artists moved to New York and Los Angeles during the war years, they took their art collections with them. Bert helped broker passage for both, and raised money for resettlement from art collectors in the U.S. He also managed the film career of his wife, actress Jane Randolph. On friendly terms with the owners of many of the clubs on the strip, Bert loved Hollywood nightlife, and was a regular customer.

As Ann's career at Columbia Pictures accelerated, the Reinhardt Workshop was winding down. Reinhardt was still hoping to receive income from the Hollywood classes, but with the master based in New York, unable to give personal instruction, he undercut Bert's efforts to bring in new students. As he tried to launch new theatrical enterprises in New York, Reinhardt pleaded with Bert to find production funding, but it was not forthcoming.

Onscreen, Columbia was giving Ann the full glamour treatment in her 1943 B-movie appearances. She played a gorgeous spy in another Lone Wolf episode, *Passport to Suez*. She was a sunny ingénue in *After Midnight with Boston Blackie*, and did a hilarious comedy turn as a spoiled rich girl in a Blondie serial, *Footlight Glamour*.

The A-list feature *The More the Merrier* (also 1943), starring Jean Arthur and Joel McCrea, was shooting, and every contract girl at Columbia appeared in a bar scene. The director, George Stevens, picked Ann out of the group and gave her a bit of dialogue with Joel McCrea and Charles Coburn. At the end of the day's shooting, Stevens asked Ann out to dinner. She begged off, telling him she had an early call the next morning. The dialogue was cut out of the film, but Ann can be seen sitting next to McCrea and getting the eye from Charles Coburn.

Having a bit part in an A movie allowed Ann access to the closed set. She spent as much time on the set as possible, watching Jean Arthur shoot her scenes. The publicity department asked Arthur to model her wardrobe from the film as a still fashion layout. Studio boss Harry Cohn and Arthur had a standing feud over her salary demands and his efforts to get her into bed. They had long ago stalemated, and all that was left to them were constant battles. Arthur refused to do the fashion shoot, and suggested that Ann wear the outfits for the still photographers. Ann eagerly modeled the wardrobe and received international fashion coverage in the press.

Watching Jean Arthur on set provided an excellent lesson in comedy timing. Ann realized that much of Arthur's comedy effect was based on carefully regulated control of her breath. With apparent ease, she would blurt out long stretches of dialogue that seemed rushed or even dizzy onscreen, yet she was actually carefully pacing each word so she had enough breath for emphasis on the key words in the script.

Not all of the comedy was onscreen. Ann tried to unobtrusively enter the darkened stage to observe the shooting. Invariably, someone would see her and say "Hello, Ann," earning a reproachful *"Quiet"* from the assistant director, Budd Boetticher. Boetticher carried a riding crop with him that he would snap when displeased. Ann felt that he was itching to snap one of the contract girls with it, as he corralled them for their scene. He continually threatened to toss her off the set, as she observed the actors at work. One day, as she snuck onto the set in the dark, she passed a row of actors. One of them said, "Hi, Ann," and another pinched her behind. She let out a loud *"Yelp!"* Boetticher yelled *"Quiet!"* and Ann turned to smack the pincher, only to find a laughing Charles Coburn. He told her, "I'm sorry, I thought you were Ann Sheridan."

The publicity department put Ann under increasing pressure to date and make the rounds of nightclubs to get in the press. She was still loyal to Rusty Selwyn, but wanted to enjoy the benefits of her new career.

> I tried to wait for him, but I'm just not that kind of girl. I wanted to get out on the town, and he was three thousand miles away for who knew how long. I don't like long distance phone calls; how the hell can you carry on a long distance relationship? It was over.

Though she was still on the list, she attended the Selwyn family parties less often.

While she was making the B western *Saddles and Sagebrush* (1943), she started dating leading man Russell Hayden. "Columbia kept pushing me to get out on the town with an actor, so I went out with Russell." As soon as it hit the papers, Max Arnow called Ann in for a meeting. He told her she couldn't date Hayden because he was married. "I told him to go to hell," Ann said. Hayden was separated from his wife, so they continued to go out. She loved making the western outdoors, shooting on location, away from the nosy studio.

Ann and Russell Hayden became serious very quickly. "He had a huge ranch out by Palm Springs, thousands of acres. He asked me to marry him. He wanted to get his divorce, quit pictures and develop the ranch, work the cattle." Arnow kept pressuring Ann to date other men. "He said Hayden was headed for divorce court, and that I would be named as the other woman in the newspapers." The negative publicity could get her contract dropped by Columbia. "They had just told me that there was no such thing as bad publicity, you just measured the coverage with a ruler. Their crap didn't add up." It was an obvious game of control, and Ann refused to give in.

As she began another picture, Ann continued to see Hayden. *Two Señoritas from Chicago* (1943) was a musical. Ann was surprised she was cast: "I was a good dancer, but I couldn't sing a note." Columbia kept telling her she was going to play the lead in a big swing musical comedy called *What's Buzzin', Cousin?* "They told me it would make me a bigger star than Betty Hutton! I kept saying Betty Hutton can *sing*! She was in big swing bands! They'd say: 'You're a better dancer.'" As a first step, the executives would see how things went with *Two Señoritas*. Cast opposite New York cover girl Jinx Falkenburg, and vaudeville and radio star Joan Davis, Ann felt challenged. "Joan had toured and made movies with Eddie Cantor, and Jinx was the hottest model of the year; but I was the blonde!"

Joan Davis was a very acrobatic comedienne. She could take pratfalls and do stunts, and had made her fame as an eccentric dancer. "Joan had this move where she could skid on the edge of her high heel and not fall. It looked easy, but I tried to do it ... impossible!" Davis saw Ann practicing and showed her how to balance. "She said it was all in how you swung the other leg for movement and balance. Same thing with a pratfall. What you do with your legs as you fall is what makes it funny and safe." Eddie Cantor was a frequent visitor to the set. "He loved to watch Joan work; everyone was in awe of her moves."

Assigned to design the wardrobe on *Two Señoritas*, William Travilla became fast friends with Ann. Ann loved his work: "Billy could design high fashion gowns and crisp suits, but he was the best with sexy outfits." His feathered extravagance for the "Moon Dance" number steals the show.

Ann had played mostly bit or featured parts in her early movies. She showed her range from a dark femme fatale in *Passport to Suez* to broad comedy in *Dangerous Blondes*, and Columbia was ready to launch her in a leading role. *What's Buzzin,' Cousin?* (1943) was rewritten, with more emphasis on dancing than singing, but the part was given to tap dancer Ann Miller. "Ann Miller was a wonderful girl; perfect for the movie. I was happy she got it. I have no idea why they kept trying to put me in musicals!"

Columbia owned the rights to the autobiography of *Klondike Kate*, a legendary character of the Alaskan gold rush. The real Klondike Kate came to Hollywood from Alaska, reviewed all the contract actresses at Columbia, and picked Ann to play the part. It was her first leading role. In less than a year she had gone from bit parts with no dialogue to a leading lady.

Klondike Kate (1943) co-starred Tom Neal, who was also working his way up through B movies at Columbia. Neal had made a promising start as a contract player at MGM in the late 1930s. He had been personally thrown off the lot by Louis B. Mayer after openly offending Joan Crawford. He found work at B studios like Republic, mainly interested in trading off the press build-up he had received at MGM. Neal steadily rebuilt his career, gaining leading man parts and a contract at Columbia in the B-picture unit.

Ann Savage and Tom Neal first met on the set of *Klondike Kate*. Ann had taken her mark on stage, and had to remain perfectly still while being lit; then Tom Neal introduced himself. He said to her, "Come here, I have something to tell you," and as she leaned slightly over to him, Tom stuck his tongue in her ear. Ann smacked him as hard as she could with one hand, knocking him down.

For a B movie, *Klondike Kate* was a large production. It had period costumes, fully dressed backlot sets, a large cast and hundreds of extras. It was one of the first films directed by William Castle, who had worked at Columbia in the talent department, preparing actors for their roles. Tom Neal never let up on Ann, constantly trying to get her to break up on cam-

Ann finally gets the lead: *Klondike Kate* (1943).

era or blow her lines. When they were in a shot together, he was completely professional, but if he had to feed her lines off camera, he would purposely change the words around or talk gibberish to throw her. Ann mostly ignored him after their initial meeting. Though she thought he was both talented and handsome, she found his behavior childish. She was glad to meet and work with actress Glenda Farrell, who would become a lifelong friend.

Klondike Kate opened at the Egyptian Theater in Hollywood with the fanfare of an A-list premiere. It was a glamorous night, one of the happiest moments of Ann's life:

> I took my mother to the premiere. I was so proud of the film, we could hardly believe it was real. We had been to Hollywood Boulevard so many times to see movies and taken the streetcar home. That night we were driven home in a studio limousine.

Russell Hayden was getting closer to divorcing his wife. Even though the talent department had forbidden her to go out with him publicly, they still met privately. "I was close to marrying Russell, but his divorce was taking a long time to work out." In the meantime, the studio had booked Ann on a national war bonds tour.

Taking a month off from filming and publicity work, Ann barnstormed across the United States, selling war bonds in a new city each day. It was a tough schedule. She would travel at night, do a show in the afternoon, and then hit the road again. Edmund Lowe and Blackstone the Magician were also on the tour. The Columbia publicity department dropped notices in the press that a romance had blossomed between Ann and Edmund Lowe. "They made it up out of nothing! I liked Eddie Lowe but didn't date him, but it was good publicity; it drove Russell Hayden crazy." The studio constantly encouraged Ann to find a new boyfriend. "The more they bugged me about him, the more I liked him; I'm just that way."

The tour ended in New York, and Ann was given a few days off for a layover in Manhattan. She was told Harry Cohn was in New York and wanted a meeting with her. Her contract option was up for renewal, and though things had been going well with Columbia she had butterflies when she was told to meet Cohn. His reputation was fierce, and he was well known for chasing the women under contract to Columbia. Ann had met him briefly when she was signed to the studio, but he left her completely alone. "Harry Cohn never chased me. He was too busy fighting with Jean Arthur and Rita Hayworth to bother with me."

Cohn did tell Ann that her option would be renewed, but what he really wanted to talk to her about was personal business. His sister-in-law was in New York with her family and was unattached. Cohn asked Ann to chaperone his wife's sister, take in some Broadway shows, and help her see the town — all expenses paid. Ann borrowed fifty dollars from Cohn for pocket money and had a terrific time in Manhattan, courtesy of Columbia Pictures.

When it came time to leave New York, Cohn invited Ann to ride back to Los Angeles with his party on the Santa Fe Super Chief. The studio boss had a lavish private rail car that was the center of a nonstop party. Ann was given her own private room in the next car and allowed free access to join the family for meals — and a three-day, 'round-the-clock card game. She had never known such luxuries in her life. During the ride home Harry Cohn let Ann know that he had heard the rumors that she was through with Russell Hayden and had taken up with Edmund Lowe. Cohn gave his full approval for Lowe, expressing disdain for Hayden and calling him a "dusty cowpoke."

Ann found Harry Cohn to be "clear and direct." "He was a handsome man, expertly tailored, and a perfect gentleman. Of course, I first got to know him in the presence of his wife and sister-in-law." She felt his reputation as slovenly and abusive has been exaggerated since his death:

> I'll tell you one thing Cohn and those studio guys were — *Tough*! Tough, *strong, men*! Believe me, nobody called them names while they were alive, and they built businesses that gave work to thousands of people! They had to be *tough*! But Mr. Cohn was very nice to me.

Hayden had arranged with Ann to meet the train at the Pasadena station; they'd been apart for over a month. During a layover in Chicago, Ann wired Hayden to stay away from the station and Cohn; she'd meet up with him later.

When the train pulled into Pasadena, Russell Hayden was there to meet it. He made a display of greeting Ann with a large kiss, then went over and said hello to Harry Cohn. Ann never got over her anger at him for ignoring her wishes. "That was the end of Russell Hayden. What a stupid move. We shot another picture together, but it was over over over."

Back at Columbia, Ann went into another film with Tom Neal. The studio experts decided they had chemistry together and looked good as a couple in publicity photos. They had both received good press coverage and drew lots of fan mail. As they were preparing for *Two-Man Submarine* (1944), Ann began to realize that Tom Neal was interested in dating her. His approach was direct and crude, which offended her, and she turned him down. "The most difficult part of dealing with Tom was that I liked him. He could be lots of fun and very charming, but he had a devil inside of him, and was also capable of the worst, most embarrassing behavior." Ann knew in advance it was going to be a rough shoot.

Columbia began a new round of publicity for Ann. The war was going full blast, and the studios were supplying the troops with an endless number of pinup photos. Ann was one of the most popular, receiving large amounts of fan mail from soldiers stationed overseas. She was voted the "V Mail Female" by the U.S. Post Office for writing the most letters to soldiers overseas. Her fame as a pinup star seemed to be growing even larger and faster than her career in movies.

Ann tried to work up enthusiasm for *Two-Man Submarine*, but nothing seemed to go right during the shoot. After she had returned from New York and gotten paid, she immediately went to the production office and paid back the fifty-dollar advance Harry Cohn had given her. About a week later he called her while she was on the set:

> The entire company got worked up because a call from Mr. Cohn was coming through. When I answered the phone, he was friendly but asked me if I hadn't forgotten something. I played dumb and asked him what he meant. He reminded me of the loan and said I should come up to his office to repay him. When I told him I had already repaid the production department, he got gruff. I asked him if I had done something wrong to make him angry at me. He said, "Oh no, I could never be angry with you, you're too nice a girl." Then he hung up on me!

The shoot for *Two-Man Submarine* turned out to be worse than Ann had imagined. "Tom gave me a rough time all the way through. It was impossible to make that corny dialogue come to life, and the hairstyle they gave me looked like an airport runway!" The only bright spot for Ann was meeting and working with J. Carrol Naish. He'd had a distinguished career in theater and movies, and stuck up for Ann amid the disruption on the set. He showed her several screen tricks of the acting trade:

> Naish was very generous and interesting; he loved acting. He believed that acting in films was creating the illusion of a character and emotion from shot to shot. More technical than spiritual. He showed me how to be vulnerable onscreen by leaning forward in a close-up and looking up at the camera with the eyes. I used it later in *Detour* when Tom shoved me down on the couch, I said, "You hurt me," looking up in the close shot.

The worst days of the shoot involved the scenes in the water tank. "There we were with a bunch of Nazis and the Japanese Navy, up against a plywood submarine, and Tom Neal still trying to trip me up." The company waited for long periods while the director blew fake fog around the sub to disguise it. "It was a cold night shoot, I was already feeling a chill. We had several swimming shots left and I asked to do them later, it was too cold. The assistant director told me they had heated the water tank." The company had to get the shots, so the actors dived in the water, which was cold as ice. The rest of the shooting went slowly, taking longer than expected. "I could feel myself getting sick while I was still in the water."

Ann caught a serious cold that developed into pneumonia. She missed weeks of work, was replaced in films she had been assigned, and was taken off salary. The studios did not have sick pay or any medical benefits. Louise nursed Ann through the illness while holding down her fulltime job. "Our neighbors helped out; when I was feeling better, we threw a rent party." Louise cooked a big dinner, and neighbors and friends would come by and contribute whatever they could.

Back on her feet, Ann went into the production department, found the assistant director who had worked on *Two-Man Submarine*, and bawled him out. "I called him every name in the book, and made up some new ones." She was so harsh that Max Arnow called her into the talent department, letting her know that her tantrum was unforgivable.

Bert D'Armand contacted Ann to let her know that Max Reinhardt had passed away. She felt a loss that never left her. When Ann talked about Reinhardt, she would begin to tear up, something that never happened (even when discussing her beloved Bert or her mother).

> I learned so much ... everything. Such a brilliant mind, I could listen to him talk forever. I didn't care what he was going on about — acting, history or math. He made primary numbers sound beautiful ... infinite ... eternal ... that was Max Reinhardt. I never met another one.

At Columbia Pictures the men had more immediate earthly concerns. Almost any wartime drama was profitable; they couldn't make them fast enough. Ann was already scheduled for a reteaming with Tom Neal, and she began production on another musical, her third.

Ever Since Venus (1944) was a film Ann enjoyed making immensely. The script was light and made little sense, but she loved the cast and the music. Glenda Farrell had worked with Ann in *Klondike Kate*; joining them were Billy Gilbert, Fritz Feld, Hugh Herbert, Ross Hunter and swing bandleader Ina Ray Hutton. Ann and Glenda Farrell became good friends on this picture, and remained so for life. "Glenda was a master at inventing fun forms of trouble. She had grown up on the road in a vaudeville family, so she knew every prank in the book."

Being on set with established comedy character actors like Herbert, Gilbert and Feld was constantly hilarious. Ann thought Ina Ray Hutton and Ross Hunter had great senses of humor, too, and made the project a breeze.

> Ross had been a school teacher, but was movie struck and got into acting. We were about the same age and had grown up on the same movies. We loved to compare our favorite actors and actresses, and remember their scenes. He was a kind man, very handsome, but unsure whether he'd make it as an actor. It turned out he was a born producer and became one of the biggest.

As a producer, Ross Hunter had a string of hits at Universal Studios from the early 1950s through the 1970s, including *All That Heaven Allows* (1955), *Imitation of Life* (1959), and *Airport* (1970).

Ann began dating more seriously, and began to see Bert D'Armand. His second wife, Jane Randolph, had left him. She had attended a high school reunion, met up with a former boyfriend, and decided to rekindle the romance. Bert began actively dating again, asked Ann out, and showed her around the nightclubs and after-hours bars of Los Angeles. They were welcome everywhere, in any part of town. Bert knew the club owners on the strip, and in the gambling clubs. He took nightlife seriously and was on good terms in such out of the way places as Central Avenue and Malibu.

Though Bert was almost twice her age, she was having more fun with him than most guys she had ever gone out with. He liked to carouse, explaining to Ann that he had left his first wife, Helen, when she had a baby and wanted to stay home at night. Her friends approved of Bert (Glenda loved to join them for an evening out); he had a way with women that seemed to charm them immediately. Though she liked him, Ann was annoyed that Bert was juggling several women at once. Jealous in the extreme, she saw red whenever she realized he'd been out with another woman.

The "V Mail Female," 1943.

Columbia pushed the production of *The Unwritten Code* (1944) quickly forward to get another wartime home-front drama into theaters. "The script never made a damn bit of sense. It wasn't ready." Ann felt, "They took a good idea and turned it into mush." The plot concerned spies in a prisoner of war camp for German soldiers, set in the American heartland.

Ann and Bert at a party on the strip (1946).

The company shot the script without revision, and it was rushed out to the public. Tom Neal was still pulling his pranks on Ann, trying to break her up while filming, but the tone was friendlier. After three movies together they had settled into a grudging respect. Their onscreen relationship in *The Unwritten Code* is the warmest and most conventional of their work together.

As much fun as she was having doing the town with Bert, Ann was still frustrated that he kept playing the field. She decided to see what he'd do if she started dating right under his nose. At one of the late nightclubs, Ann met and danced with a handsome fellow who seemed to be close to her age. She thought a younger guy might finally make Bert jealous. He ignored her.

Catching a glimpse of the huge, immaculate Lincoln Continental he drove piqued Ann's interest in Cleland Huntington, known as Lee. She asked about him around the clubs, finding out that he was a film editor at Warner Brothers. She started dating Lee, and learned that he was a scion of the Huntington family. The same Huntington family that owned the Red Cars she had ridden as a child, the ones her mother still took to work downtown every day. Lee was quieter than Bert, but a much better dancer and a terrific tennis player. They had much in common, and received compliments for being such a lovely young couple.

Lee introduced Ann to the society families of Pasadena and San Marino. They lived on estates with full staff and long driveways. Even the opulence of the Selwyn or the Mayer homes, which she had visited at Sunday gatherings, were no match for the old-money eastside set. They also had the most severe and longest lasting property restrictions in Los Angeles County. The dress code was more formal than what she was used to, and the parties a little stuffier, but Ann was accepted warmly as Lee's regular date.

On her second War Bonds tour of America, Ann barnstormed the country with five war heroes. The schedule was tight as they hopped from base to base, sometimes taking the train, sometimes driving by car. Being in a new town each day meant little time for sleep, or anything else. In Texas the hotel that had been booked overnight for the troupe refused to admit Eddie "Rochester" Anderson, who was on the tour, claiming it was a "whites only" hotel. When management wouldn't make an exception and back down, all the performers refused to stay in the hotel, staying up all night at the train station with Rochester. Ann and the others made a party out of it: "What a great time we had, staying up, telling stories, singing, dancing, anything but give in to those ignorant fools!"

It was on this tour that Ann saw her father for the last time. "I found him in Mississippi. I had grown up, and knew more about relationships and people, and wanted to give the man a chance." Hugh Lyon met with her and almost immediately began his verbal attacks. "There was no point in talking to him. He was 100 percent J-E-R-K. I never saw him or spoke to him again."

Back in Hollywood, Ann felt that juggling between Lee and Bert was going nowhere. When she talked it over with Lee, he impulsively proposed marriage, and she quickly accepted. They eloped in Las Vegas, with Ann's best friend, Ann Lester, as maid of honor, skipping a formal Pasadena wedding.

Busy establishing a household and attending to her social duties as Mrs. Lee Huntington, Ann's thoughts momentarily retreated from her film career. Lee's mother and sister were very gracious about showing Ann the social ropes, hoping to help her succeed in her new role. Once they were settled in, it quickly became apparent to Ann that Lee had practically no interest in married life. The social whirl she had been enjoying was routine to him; he preferred the late nightclub life they'd enjoyed while dating. Ann felt like she had repeated the same mistakes she had made in her first marriage, leaping in and setting up a life without really knowing her mate. She suddenly felt trapped and uncertain, so she began looking for a new film.

Ann was glad to be starting a new movie with her good friend Jeff Donnell. Jeff played the sweet, innocent girl; Ann was a bad girl involved with a con man. Ann was very proud of her work in *Dancing in Manhattan* (1944). She despised the script, but liked the character she was assigned and dug into her part. For a light comedy, Ann's part has very dark undertones:

> For one thing, this lady needed the money she was trying to steal. She didn't think much of the guy she was with, but was sticking with him till payday. When their deal fell apart, she got very serious with the people around her.

Ann concentrated on the boundaries within the character and ignored the rest of the movie. It's a disturbing experience to see Ann Savage implode a film that is supposed to be pure wartime B-movie fluff. Rather than walk through a lousy part, as many actors would, Ann worked through her character to turn the film inside out and make some piece of it her own. The dinner table sequence is remarkable. Ann, in character, turns on the group, tossing them a little slice of realism that throws the rest of the table off.

As newer contract players began to appear on the Columbia lot, the production department grew more distant and unclear about her next assignment. Ann realized her days at Columbia were coming to an end. "I wasn't fired, or dismissed ... I wasn't anything. I received a little note in my paycheck that it was the final one." She was still with Frank Orsatti, and asked him for an explanation. He offered none and told her to relax,

1944 elopement photo of Ann and Lee Huntington.

he'd quadruple her price next week. Ann pondered the reason Columbia dropped her option; it upset her tremendously, she felt like she'd worked very hard for them and been rejected. "It could've been any one of ten reasons — my temper, the men I dated, the men I didn't date; they never said."

It also could have been as simple as a studio economy wave. Columbia laid off several others at this time. Ann had done a good job and was a sensation in the press, but had never established a firm screen identity at Columbia. They had no plans to move her into A-list features or give her a series of her own. In a film factory, it didn't make sense to accountants to keep giving a contract player like Ann the raises she was guaranteed at each option period when her parts could be played by a new contract actress at the base price of $75 a week.

The following week Frank Orsatti sent Ann to the Paramount lot. She signed a deal with Pine-Thomas Productions, a successful B unit there, and quintupled her salary. Ann had started in 1942 at Columbia for $75 a week. She had survived two six-month option periods and another one-year option period before Columbia dropped her, bringing her price after two years and nearly twenty movies to $150.00 a week. Orsatti got her $750.00 a week. Pine-Thomas also gave her a clothing budget for each film as part of their deal.

Ann's marriage to Lee Huntington had not improved, despite his reassurances and the good will of both their mothers. Feeling the need for something more solid in her life, she sought a divorce. With money of her own from Pine-Thomas/Paramount, Ann bought a complete new wardrobe and started dating with a vengeance.

Chapter 6

Be-Boppin' the B's

Paramount was one of the top three studios in Hollywood, along with MGM and Warner Brothers. They turned out dozens of films every year, had a large studio lot, and tremendous ranch facilities for location work. They had some of the biggest stars in the business, including Bing Crosby, who was the number one box office star in the world for 1944, '45, '46, and '47.

Ann was given the full glamour treatment and publicity buildup. Her stills were personally shot by Whitey Schaefer, the head of the photography department. He developed a softer focus, sexier look for her than she had been given at Columbia. She flew through the production of *Scared Stiff* and *Midnight Manhunt* (both 1945). Ann loved life as a freelancer. "You worked hard while you were on a production and then had some time to yourself. As a contract player at Columbia, you had to punch in every day or they wouldn't pay you."

During the downtime periods between films, Ann concentrated on her social life. She began dating Bert again, and decided that the best way to handle his casual approach was to give him a taste of his own medicine and not be exclusive. She met "Doc" Merman, a producer at Pine-Thomas. He earned his nickname because he could fix any production problem and kept the filmmaking machine well oiled. "Doc" liked to give his girls jewelry as a way to remind them of their time together. Ann made sure she wore her new gifts when she was out with Bert. No matter what she did, Bert wouldn't react or show any signs of slowing down in his own dating department.

Nightlife was always an adventure with Bert. He was tireless, staying out long after the bars closed. He drove a big black Cadillac, and though there were wartime shortages and rationing, he seemed to have no problem filling his gas tank and driving all over town in search of fun.

Bert took Ann places nobody else had. A typical evening would start with a showy dinner and dancing at the Coconut Grove, or a cabaret supper club like Ciro's or the Mocambo on the strip. They might take in a movie at one of the first-run Hollywood theaters like the Chinese or Egyptian, or see the strippers at Florentine Gardens, or a big production show like Earl Carrol's *Vanities*. After the night's entertainment, Bert would take her for a late drink at a private club in the hills. Usually, they gambled. Ann liked to roll the dice, and Bert was a fan of card games, but neither played for high stakes. Then the real fun would begin.

At the point where most of Ann's dates started to wind down, a night with Bert was just kicking into gear. In search of more music, dancing or action, they would go downtown or into the canyons to the type of establishments that required a password to gain entry. Ann's favorite club was called Brothers. It was at the north end of the Central Avenue district, almost in old Chinatown near Union Station. After hours, Brothers had it all: live jazz, gambling, big-name guest stars; and it served as a crossroads where white culture and black culture met. Ann heard many rumors about who owned Brothers, but was surprised that Bert never greeted an owner, as he always did in every other club they visited. When she asked him about it, he wouldn't talk.

Beyond risqué, Brothers offered themed nights of entertainment. Boys' night, girls' night, and black and white night usually included a well-rehearsed live musical act accented with heavy nudity. There were male and female drag competitions. It was very visual — and exclusive. The dancers at the club were among the best Ann had ever seen.

"If any big bands were in town, we could find them, after their show, still playing at Brothers or at a club on Central Avenue." It was also the place to find a late night supper of homey southern cooking. Ivie Anderson's Chicken Shack was open all night, as was Jack's Chicken in a Basket. Both restaurants were famous for their fried chicken, homemade pies and their all-night jazz chopping contests, where visiting musicians on tour would play toe to toe against local talent.

The music played on Central Avenue, especially after hours, in the mid–1940s was unique and different. Ann and Bert were intrigued. "It was improvisational. Loose, but good. Those guys went at it hard; it never got dull." When asked if it was bebop music, Ann got feisty:

> Who the hell cares what you call it! It was good! These were the best musicians in the world. They could improvise anything. It was genius music! Bebop schmeebop! You know what the music was called at the time? *Reefer music*. Ever heard of that?

There were plenty of drugs available on Central Avenue, but Ann and Bert preferred alcohol. "Bert would knock back a shot of whiskey, and I drank vodka. Still do. Give me a strong Bloody Mary and I'm happy." When asked if marijuana was smoked openly, she said:

> I'm sure it was, but not widely, not like the sixties when it was everywhere. Mostly, it was smoked in the alley, behind a club or something. People would be on the street, the doors were open, and you could hear music up and down the street. They weren't charging for music, they were charging for food and drinks, and whatever they ran under the table. We weren't interested in that, we liked the music.

Asked about her favorite musicians, Ann answered, "Ray Charles, Lester Young and his brother Lee, and Barney Kessel. Lee Young taught Mickey Rooney how to play the drums, by the way. All geniuses. Kings. They were the absolute best, bar none." Asked if she ever saw Charlie Parker in L.A., she said:

> No. I'm sure he was around, and I might have seen him play late at night, but we didn't see him on the bill. We missed Billie Holiday, too. I loved her music. We were supposed to catch her in a club, but she'd stabbed a heckler with his dinner fork the night before, and they cancelled her. She came right off stage, picked up this guy's fork and stabbed him! I bet *that* shut him the hell up for life!

After a great start at Pine-Thomas, her work seemed to be slowing down a little. Though she was enjoying cutting a complete path across Los Angeles society, she decided to take her work more seriously. Ann came to the conclusion that Orsatti was not handling her properly, and bought her way out of her contract. "It cost me a thousand dollars to buy that bastard out, but it was worth it. If they're not pushing you, time to move on. Fast."

Ann asked around for a new agent. Bert offered to represent her, but since they were still dating, she didn't want to put all of her business in his hands. Ann met with Tom Neal, who said he would talk to his agent — and then asked her out.

CHAPTER 7

Detoured

After Columbia, Tom Neal worked freelance and ended up with a multiyear deal at PRC. By 1945, Producers Releasing Corporation was a wholly owned subsidiary of Pathe Laboratories Inc., just as Republic Pictures was owned by CFI Laboratories. For the most part, the parent companies viewed film production as grist for their lab mills. They used the exposed footage from their production divisions as a way of keeping the film labs running at maximum efficiency round the clock, whenever they faced gaps in processing runs from paying clients. Their production budgets were very tight by big studio standards, as were profits.

Though PRC is often called a Poverty Row studio, it is a misnomer. More accurately, PRC was a very low budget independent production company with deep pockets at the corporate level. Pathe was an extremely wealthy parent company, having been a strong presence in the film business since the late 1890s. PRC had over two-dozen distribution exchanges around the United States, and also distributed through Pathe's foreign operations around the world. World War Two had been disruptive to international distribution, but the overall foreign network was in place and operational.

PRC produced many of their films at "poverty row" levels of production budget, sometimes shooting westerns quite quickly (in a week or less). However, this was not true for all their films. If a project had the potential of wide domestic or international appeal, the level of budget and quality of production was increased. After producer Leon Fromkess came to Hollywood from Pathe in New York to run PRC, he established several small production units that worked at different levels of budget and pace, the most creative being headed by Edgar G. Ulmer.

Tom Neal was in production at PRC with *Club Havana*, and was already assigned to the upcoming production of *Detour* (both 1945). It had a good script and a strong female role, which Tom had described to Ann. She signed with Tom's agent, who set up a meeting with Fromkess. At their first meeting, Fromkess offered Ann the part in *Detour* as the first film in a five-year deal. He also offended Ann by telling her that his primary interest was to reunite her with Neal onscreen and trade off the publicity that Columbia Pictures had generated for them. Ann promised to read the script and consider his offer.

When she began reading *Detour* she immediately knew it was a well-written script. She felt "the dialogue was sharp, even the narration was good. When I got to Vera's lines, and her blackmail, I knew it was a *great* script. I wanted to play it more than anything." Even more than her immediate dislike of Leon Fromkess, Ann also didn't like the five-year deal; she wasn't comfortable being tied up with a studio again, especially with one run by Fromkess:

> The French have a saying for a man like him: "Il pet haut quand leur cul"—"one who farts higher than his ass!" He was graceless, just blurted things out at you — half-accountant, half-car salesman. He was married to an obnoxious woman who had ambitions to be an actress, but had never done a damn thing and never would. She liked to offer her acting "tips." They were a horrible couple. Horrible!

Fromkess wouldn't budge on his five-year deal, and Ann wouldn't accept. Fromkess promised Ann first-class star treatment, with her makeup done by Bud Westmore of the famous Westmore Hollywood dynasty, who had set the standard for Hollywood makeup, and also promised to use her friend Benjamin Kline as cinematographer.

Ann loved Benny Kline; she had shot *Saddles and Sagebrush* (1943) and *Ever Since Venus* (1944) with him at Columbia. A film veteran since the early 1920s, he had helped her when she was a newcomer, explaining lenses and camera angles. He was also the one who gave her a set nickname—"Annie Pannie," using slang for face ("pan") to signify how beautiful and easy she was to light. He told her she didn't have a "bad side"; her face looked good from every angle. Kline was already working on the PRC lot and had shot the Edgar G. Ulmer masterpiece *Strange Illusion* (1945), and was currently working with Ulmer and Tom Neal on *Club Havana*. Eventually, Ann and Fromkess agreed to a two-picture deal, with the option to extend when it was completed.

Leon Fromkess took Ann to the *Club Havana* set to say hello to Tom and Benny and meet Edgar G. Ulmer. There was no audition or reading—Ulmer took a quick look at Ann and said, "She'll do." The deal with PRC was concluded—two pictures with an option for a third, each with escalating raises for Ann. Fromkess gave her a leatherbound copy of the *Detour* script with her name embossed on the cover as a thank you for the deal.

After a long ordeal in divorce court, Ann was happy to forget her troubles by plunging into the challenge of *Detour* and bringing Vera to life. She had moved back to the Beachwood

"Do I rate a whistle?" Ann and Tom Neal in *Detour* (1945).

Canyon apartment and was living with her mother. After writing her dialogue lines out to help commit them to memory, she started practicing them in motion. She liked to rehearse while doing housework and vacuuming:

> My mother, my husbands, and even my dog all thought I was nuts when I'd rehearse. They'd stare at me in the strangest ways. I'm sure I looked ridiculous, but it's really the best way to learn your lines. If you memorize and practice in motion, you're on your toes, and ready to be on that stage and anything they throw at you.

PRC worked fast, often shooting their westerns and prison dramas in one week. A more complex film like Ulmer's psychological thriller *Strange Illusion*, or *The Wife of Monte Cristo* (1946), would have a substantially bigger budget and a longer schedule. Occasionally, one of the larger-budgeted projects, like *Hitler's Madman* (1943), had been bought out and picked up for distribution by a major studio like MGM.

Director Edgar G. Ulmer was an A-list talent who, by the mid-forties, had been blackballed by the major studios for over a decade. He had come to Hollywood from Germany with F. W. Murnau in the 1920s, working as an art director on *Sunrise* (1927). Originally, in his home country of Austria, he had studied theater under Max Reinhardt. While at Universal he had fallen in love with, and eventually married, a woman who was married to a favorite nephew of the head of the company, Carl Laemmle. The Hollywood movie business of the golden age was so small and incestuous that a perceived transgression against a studio boss was considered a breach against all of them. The price was banishment from the realm. Ulmer never worked at a major studio again for the rest of his career. At PRC he was the in-house artistic director, and was first choice for the larger-budget, most creatively challenging projects.

Originally, director Lew Landers had been attached to the *Detour* script. Ann and Tom had worked with him at Columbia on *Two-Man Submarine*, an unpleasant experience. "Lew was a good guy, and I liked him personally, but he painted by the numbers," Ann remembered. Landers' name was on the first draft of the shooting script, but Ann crossed it out when Fromkess announced that Ulmer was going to direct *Detour* and that it would receive special treatment.

Ann's PRC contract for *Detour* called for three weeks of shooting. When she finished her work on *Detour* and left the set to begin *Apology for Murder* (1945), the company shot for an additional week. In the forties, Ann worked six-day weeks on every show. *Detour* was shot in a total of 28 days. When asked about this, and how the impression was formed that *Detour* was made in one week, Ann said:

> Edgar just threw that out offhand in an interview before he died. He wasn't serious, but it stuck. Edgar said all kinds of things. When they asked him what had become of me, he told them I owned the Mint Casino in Las Vegas! Hardly.

Over the years, since Ulmer's death in 1972, as *Detour* grew in prominence and gained recognition as the classic B noir, the myth grew. Ann observed: "It's a better story. What the hell difference does it make? Listen, I've seen a lot of crappy movies that shot for a year and a half."

The *Detour* shoot started on location in the high desert. Ulmer and the crew shot back plates for the rear screen projection driving sequences. Tom Neal shot his hitchhiking montage shots, then Ann joined the location.

Shooting the long shots in the gas station where Vera meets Al Roberts, Ann was ready to go out on the road to hitchhike, when Ulmer stopped her. She had received her first fresh-faced, Hollywood-style full makeup from Bud Westmore. Ulmer told Westmore that she needed to be dirtied up to match the character description in the script. Dirt and dark eye shadow was applied to Ann's face, cold cream was run through her hair to make it greasy and stringy, and dirt was thrown on her sweater and skirt.

Ann headed back out on the road for the wide hitchhiking shot and looked so convincing that a real car stopped in the middle of the shot and offered her a ride. She tried to shoo the car away, but the driver was insistent. "I wondered what the hell was wrong with that guy! I looked so lousy, he must've had a screw loose to want to pick me up so bad!" The shot was blown; Edgar and the crew were in tears laughing. The rest of the desert shooting went smoothly, and the company returned to Los Angeles for the interior and process shots.

Ulmer had worked the entire film out with an elaborate set of storyboards. With his background as an art director, he did all the drawing himself. Ann commented: "When he was on stage, Edgar must've been a very fine actor; he understood all the characters in *Detour* very deeply, and if you watch his other films, he always has respect for his characters as people."

During the shoot, Ulmer gave Ann many specific character directions that heightened both the madness of Vera and her intense sexuality. He suggested very slight and subtle movements that indicate what's on her mind. In the apartment when she stands in front of the Murphy bed with Roberts, Vera pulls her sweater down tight, heightening her figure. When she's lying on the couch with her legs spread out, she squeezes her thighs together. Her final pass at Roberts is a light hand on his shoulder, which he shrugs off.

The incredible voice of Vera was brought out by Ulmer's direction. Ann's voice went naturally into a gruff lower register when she became angry or tense. In some of the process shots she was also sitting in a position that squeezed her diaphragm and midrange. Finally, after a few lines were shot in her early scenes with Roberts in the car, Ulmer gave her a speeded-up pacing tempo by snapping his fingers quickly. When she hit that rhythm, Ann had Vera's voice, and she employed it throughout the rest of the shoot.

The production moved quickly from setup to setup, slowing down only twice. During one section of dialogue, Tom Neal went off his lines repeatedly, requiring over fifty retakes. As the numbers climbed higher, Ulmer started changing the slate numbers so the actual amount of film used couldn't be guesstimated by Fromkess during the screening of dailies. The only other time the crew slowed down was during the shots where Vera threatens to turn Roberts over to the police, half drunkenly wailing and running away with the phone. As Ulmer yelled cut, the crew broke into spontaneous applause across the set.

> It was the highest compliment I've ever received. Those guys are the toughest audience in the world; they know their stuff, and they've seen it all. Plus, they are under the gun and have to get the next shot going. It meant a lot to me.

It meant everything to Ann. Though *Detour* would be well received by reviewers and audiences when it was released, it took almost forty years for the film to receive true recognition. The memory of the crew's approval sustained her through the many years her work was neglected.

Ann's only regret with *Detour* was that she finished her work on the film a week before the production wrapped, went immediately into her next project, and missed the wrap party. She wanted to spend more time with the company. The shoot had been one of the best creative experiences she'd ever known. She hoped to work with cast and crew again.

Apology for Murder, her second project for PRC, was a three-week shoot she also enjoyed. The director, Sam Newfield, was one of the most prolific PRC regulars, working for his brother Sigmund Neufeld. Co-starring with Ann was Hugh Beaumont, who was a PRC regular. Long before he achieved TV fame as Wally and Beav's dad on *Leave It to Beaver* (1957–1963), Beaumont played noir heavies and detectives in B movies. Ann and Beaumont were a terrific

Tom Neal and Ann in *Detour* (1945).

match, with an immediate onscreen sexual chemistry. Beaumont was studying for the priesthood, and asked Ann to stop swearing on the set. She liked him so much she actually made an attempt to tone down her language. She loved the part of heartless husband killer Toni Kirkland, a sexy black widow. It was a huge disappointment when *Apology for Murder* was pulled from distribution under threat from Paramount over its similarity to *Double Indemnity* (1944).

The word of mouth around Hollywood on her PRC movies was positive, and Ann's phone began to ring more often. She started to get back out on the town once her production obligations to PRC were fulfilled. Bert was still one of her regular dates. She longed for him to see her exclusively, but after her marriage to Lee had failed, she gave up devising strategies to make Bert jealous and concentrated on enjoying the time she spent with him.

Detour did not result in the immediate offers Ann had hoped for; she was asked to test, and her interviews increased. She went over to the Selznick lot and performed a full screen test. Her meeting with David O. Selznick went splendidly; she thought him "wonderful! He was a big movie fan at heart. We talked movies much longer than we should have; he'd actually met Valentino, and told me he'd had a crush on Olive Thomas when he was young. I hoped we'd work together."

Fox gave her a small part in *The Spider* (1945) to serve as a screen test. She interviewed with George Cukor and came close to winning the female lead in *A Double Life* (1947), an A-list film starring Ronald Colman at Universal. She was cast as the female lead in the Universal B political comedy *The Dark Horse* (1946), with Philip Terry and a terrific cast of veteran character actors, including Allen Jenkins and Jane Darwell. Her time spent studying Jean Arthur's technique at Columbia came in handy on *Dark Horse*, as she played a fast-talking political campaigner with a heart of gold.

Herbert J. Yates was impressed with *Detour* and wanted to bring Ann over to the Republic lot. Ann did some preliminary wardrobe and hair tests for Republic, and was promised a part in an upcoming picture. "Bert and I went out on a double date with Herbert Yates and his wife Vera. They were both beautiful dancers, and enjoyed each other's company. It was clear they loved each other very much." Vera Hruba Ralston was the reigning queen of the Republic lot, and the source of much gossip in Hollywood. Ann found her "a peach!"

Once the war ended, Bert began to concentrate his efforts on developing a bigger roster as a talent agent. He scouted nightclubs and began looking for live performers to represent, in addition to actors and actresses. Bert was out on the town nearly every night of the week. There were luxury hotels being built in Las Vegas, with huge showrooms for live entertainment; Bert and his partners planned to book the new venues.

One of Ann's favorite cabaret acts was the solo artist Hildegarde. Ann said, "She was slick! Hildegarde could do more at Ciro's with two white gloves, a long-stemmed rose and her piano than a full orchestra, a chorus and six dancers!" Hildegarde was in Los Angeles with her longtime manager and close friend Anna Sosenko for a long run on the strip. One of the most popular and hardest working supper club acts, Hildegarde was usually on the road up to 40 weeks a year, earning as much as $17,000 a week. Her biggest wartime hits had been "The Last Time I Saw Paris" and "I'll Be Seeing You," both outselling Sinatra's versions. She was also a big international act, popular in Europe, able to sing and speak in French and German. Her first hit record in the early 1930s had been "Darling Je Vous Aime Beaucoup," written for her by Anna Sosenko.

Ann and Bert attended Hildegarde's opening night and sat ringside at Ciro's. Hildegarde was famous for picking men out of the audience, having a short dance with them and giving them one of the long-stemmed roses she kept in a vase on top of her piano. When she came down front and picked Bert out for her dance, and left him with two roses, it was a signal that their deal for Las Vegas was on.

During the run, Bert continued to negotiate terms with Anna Sosenko, and he asked Ann to accompany him another time to Ciro's. After the show, Hildegarde and Anna dropped by Bert's apartment just off the strip for a nightcap. They were all having a good time together, and the nightcap turned into several rounds. As Hildegarde and Bert discussed the various nights of the show, Ann began to feel herself seethe with jealousy when she realized Bert had attended many nights without inviting her. At one point Hildegarde asked Bert about one of his other dates, and Ann realized they were talking about her best friend, Ann Lester.

Ann had suspected them in the past but never had any proof. Hildegarde confirmed it! Full of jealousy and feeling betrayed, Ann picked a fight with Bert. He tried to calm her down, but his words had the reverse effect. Anna tried to reason with her, but Ann accused them all of being in on it, and turned her fire on Anna and Hildegarde. They quickly left the apartment, and when Bert tried to restrain her, she lashed out and began destroying his furniture. Ann smashed his lamps first, then she threw every piece of crystal and china at him, chairs, books, art, his full bar and decanters, then slapped him and walked out. Her performance had gathered a crowd from the building, but she left just before the police showed up.

Housing was still very tight in Los Angeles following a construction moratorium dur-

Posed publicity photo for *Detour* (1945).

ing the war, and Bert was thrown out of his apartment for the disturbance and destruction Ann caused. He called her up, saying he had no place to go, so he had to move in with her. Ann and Bert met and ironed out their problems. He moved in with Ann and Louise, enjoying the home life, and found he loved southern cooking. "Bert was a true New Yorker whose favorite dish was stuffed cabbage. It turned out he *loved* fried chicken with buttermilk gravy, and all of mother's desserts. I wish I'd brought him home for dinner two years earlier!"

Ann shot her third film for PRC, *Lady Chaser* (1946), to fulfill her original contract. Initially intended to be a crime thriller, it was eventually marketed as a man on the prowl sex comedy.

Leon Fromkess was no longer at PRC. He moved on after he'd generated bad blood with Edgar Ulmer over a loanout deal on *The Strange Woman* (1946). United Artists borrowed Ulmer from PRC, where he was still under contract, paying a high weekly rate for his services on the Hedy Lamarr big-budget historical drama, none of which was passed back to the director. Fromkess became head of production at Samuel Goldwyn Studios and was involved in the production of *The Best Years of Our Lives* (1946) and every other Goldwyn film until 1951. He then got into the new medium of television for a decade, with many successes, including the long-running show *Lassie* (1954–1974). When he returned to features in the

1960s, it was as a producing partner with Samuel Fuller on *Shock Corridor* (1963) and *The Naked Kiss* (1964).

Ann and Bert eloped to Yuma, Arizona, in early 1946, and eventually bought a house together on Schuyler Road in Beverly Hills. Bert brought home one of the first television sets in Los Angeles, looking to learn the new medium, and continued to expand the agency business. The prospects of growth in Las Vegas were good, as the Flamingo Hotel was getting ready to open and plans were being made for rapid construction of many more venues. As Bert explored opportunities in Nevada, he encouraged Louise to move to Las Vegas and helped her open a jewelry counter in a store on Fremont Street.

Herbert J. Yates made good on his promise to star Ann in a Republic Pictures feature with *The Last Crooked Mile* (1946). It was another femme fatale role with a nice double-cross and some gunplay. Costarring in the film was Donald Barry, who had gained fame as the hero Red Ryder in Republic's western series. Yates was trying to turn Barry into a star of crime thrillers, a B version of James Cagney. From the beginning, Ann and Barry did not get along. "He was the vainest and most egocentric man I ever met. He was constantly challenging me on set and finally told me to stop upstaging him. I told him, 'How can I help it, honey, how can I help it?'" Though the film turned out well, Ann was glad to be finished with the shoot.

Ann then began production on *Renegade Girl* (1946). She loved the script and the part of Jean Shelby, but was reluctant to make a western that required a great deal of riding. The director, William Berke, was a friend and had previously worked with Ann on *Saddles and Sagebrush* (1943) and *The Last Horseman* (1944) at Columbia. To make the riding easier on Ann, Berke asked her to practice with him at the stables in Griffith Park. Ann went to Abercrombie and Fitch, picked out a new western riding wardrobe, and met Berke. At the stable she was put on a horse that seemed friendly and tame; as she began to ride, she realized she had absolutely no control over the horse. "I got nervous and tried to stop him, but must've done the wrong thing and the poor horse bolted!" The horse took off with Ann right out of the entrance to the stables and into traffic on busy Alameda Boulevard! She was panic-stricken. The horse trotted down the street a bit, then slowed down. Berke and a stable hand were able to catch up and lead the horse back into the park. "I walked back — enough of that, to hell with him!"

A stunt double was hired for the riding action sequences. Ann practiced, and was comfortable in the medium and close shots.

Renegade Girl had a large cast of longtime cowboy actors. "I loved meeting and getting to work with Jack Holt, who had been such a big star, one of my favorites as a kid." She also worked with Claudia Drake of *Detour*, stunt hero Ray Corrigan, and American Indian legend Chief Thundercloud. William Berke went on to help create the Jungle Jim series with Tarzan legend Johnny Weissmuller, and would hire Ann again in 1950 for *Jungle Jim in Pygmy Island*.

By the late '40s the film business began to undergo a slump in box office attendance. Looking to the future, Bert had taken over Ann's career as agent and wanted to steer her into the growing opportunities in television. They were spending more time in Las Vegas, as Bert continued to expand his business there as the town grew.

The Flamingo Hotel project had been started by Billy Wilkerson and his investment partners. Wilkerson had founded and run the *Hollywood Reporter* trade paper, owned famous nightclubs like the Trocadero and Ciro's, the restaurant LaRue, and Vendome Liquor and Fine Food. Ultimately squeezed out of the Flamingo project by Benjamin Siegel, representing financial investors from New York, Wilkerson took a long vacation to Paris, France. Wilkerson was a popular character in Hollywood, and Bert was surprised when he left the project.

Newly-married Bert and Ann Savage D'Armand on the set of *Renegade Girl* (1946).

Through the *Hollywood Reporter*, and his successful nightclubs, Wilkerson had ties to all the major talent in Hollywood who would either be appearing at or visiting the Flamingo.

As the hotel geared up for its opening, all the different suppliers working on the project met and celebrated the new venture. Bert had considered moving to Las Vegas, but he and Ann were in love with their house in Beverly Hills and still enjoyed an active social life. Also, many of their Las Vegas friends had moved to Los Angeles or built second homes there. Though there was much tension at the upper management level of the hotel, for suppliers it was a happy event. Bert believed in the future of entertainment in Las Vegas and wanted to be part of the expansion he felt was coming. In the meantime, he and Ann were happily settled.

The house on Schuyler Road was an unusual design. It was sited on a knoll at the foot of the steep hills, and was terraced. It had a large yard with lovely gardens and a long dog run on the side. Ann had fallen in love with a beautiful Irish setter puppy, took her home and named her Lass. Ann loved to work in the garden; she was the only person on the street who did her own work. The neighbors would stop on the street and talk to her over the fence while she was outside, but not one would touch their own yard. Ginger Rogers lived further up the hill, and Mickey Cohen was nearby. Ann said, "Ginger Rogers was too stuck up to say hello, but Mickey stopped by frequently. He was a talker, just loved to chat."

After the Flamingo Hotel opened, it ran into trouble keeping its doors open. There was a lot riding on its success, and talent in the showroom was critical to attracting customers. Many established nightclub stars were unwilling to book dates there until a regular audience was proven. The operation was not earning much in the way of profits, and the hotel was behind on paying its bills. Bert was encountering such strong reluctance from talent who did not wish to appear at the Flamingo that he realized it was going to take a while for Vegas to pay off. He began to shift more and more to TV operations.

A few months after money had gotten tight at the Flamingo, Ben Siegel was shotgunned to death in his girlfriend's Beverly Hills house. New management was in place in advance of the killing, and the debts of the hotel were settled either in cash or with stock. Wilkerson returned to Hollywood from France immediately after Siegel's death. Bert decided the hotels in Las Vegas were too volatile and not well established; after Siegel's death he worked in Las Vegas and Reno only on a consulting basis.

Ann continued to interview for work in features but realized that she was not breaking out of B movies into the major studios. *Detour* was out of step enough with the prevailing styles of filmmaking and feminine standards of beauty that it turned some off. Director George Stevens admonished Ann's husband for letting Ulmer "destroy" the look of "such a beautiful girl." Only Harry Cohn stepped up in defense of Ann's performance as Vera. He was quoted to Ann as telling his production and talent departments, "You didn't know what to do with her when you had her — look what she can do!" Ann began to meet television producers and find work on series, sometimes with old friends from Columbia days, like Edmund Lowe and Tom Neal. When an occasional film part was given to her, she accepted and did her best in routine B features like *Jungle Flight* (1947), *Jungle Jim in Pygmy Island* (1950), *Pier 23* (1951), and *Woman They Almost Lynched* (1953).

Bert had gotten old friend and fellow part-time art collector/dealer MGM producer Arthur Freed to give Ann a small part in his Clark Gable movie *Any Number Can Play* (1949). Though she enjoyed being back on the MGM lot, and loved working with Gable and Freed, it was a dispiriting experience when the "experts" gave her a makeover. They changed her signature makeup, her hairstyle, darkened her hair, and even dubbed her low voice with a sweeter sounding MGM-style female. She found herself almost unrecognizable in the role.

Early television production hit Hollywood quickly, and B stars were in demand because they could easily handle the fast pace that TV demanded. As the major studios began to lay off their contract stars and use them on a freelance basis only, television was signing stars and growing rapidly. Both Ann and Bert were able to make the transition to TV without missing a beat. Bert and some partners had gained control of the rights to the old Buck Rogers serials and were able to syndicate them, and sell the rights for new productions. Ann found guest appearances to her liking, and often was able to earn as much on a day shoot as she had in a week on a B movie. Creatively, she found it unfulfilling, yet kept interviewing. She would occasionally snag a good feature call.

At first she was excited to meet with Alfred Hitchcock for a part in *Strangers on a Train* (1951), but the interview went so badly that she was relieved not to have to work with him. He had kept her waiting almost an hour past their appointment.

> He sat there, looking down his nose, and had the nerve to say, "Well, Miss Savage, why aren't you working more?" I was stunned and asked him to tell me what he thought! Then he had the stupidity to do so. It was clear his set would be daily torture.

Finally, Bert and Ann decided to sell their house on Schuyler Road. "I loved that place and didn't want to give it up, but it was too large for the two of us." Working in television was completely different; it moved so fast, with one or two day shoots, and offered little of the camaraderie and social life of the film business. Ann and Bert had decided against having a family; plus, the real estate market had gone up significantly, and they were able to realize a nice profit on the house. Once the house was sold and settled, they moved into a small apartment at Shoreham Towers, which they kept through the 1960s.

European production was opening up to American companies in the 1950s, and the stock market had recovered from the Depression and World War Two. As the great movie empires tightened their belts, TV was expanding, and the parent companies were mostly based in New York. After Ben Siegel's death, Las Vegas had also come under the tight control of investors in New York. There were growing opportunities in Cuba and the Bahamas, as both banking and gambling resorts with live entertainment expanded offshore. Bert felt that it made the most sense to move east and make New York their base of operations.

TV work was consistent, it paid well, and was produced at a fast pace. With a busy social life and a compatible marriage, Ann could relax in her search for the next movie. Trying to find a feature with depth had become purely frustrating, and film interviews and auditions felt like punishment and rejection rather than the beginning of artistic collaboration. Ann said, "After a while I just couldn't take it, and I didn't have to."

CHAPTER 8

New York Renaissance

After an extended break and long automobile tour of Mexico, Ann and Bert began to establish themselves in New York. They made immediate contact with Jeff Donnell, who Ann had stayed friends with since their days together at Columbia Pictures. Ann also fell back in step with Glenda Farrell, who had married Park Avenue doctor Henry Ross. Though Glenda still booked an occasional acting job, she maintained a busy social life in Manhattan and spent weekends on her large farm in upstate New York. Ann and Glenda loved to attend the auctions at Sotheby's together, and talked gardening and Hollywood gossip.

Bert began working on Wall Street, and continued to deal in art on the side. New York was at a peak in the 1950s, both socially and culturally, and the couple was glad they'd made the move. Even their dog Lass seemed happier with daily walks in Central Park and the stimulation of the city.

With the resources of New York libraries and museums close at hand, Ann began to study art history, architecture, and geography. She had learned from her travels that these were things she was fascinated with but hadn't learned about in school. She attended classes at the Museum of Modern Art and the Metropolitan Museum during the daytime, and often went to seminars in the evenings. Bert would join Ann and Glenda at afternoon auctions if there were pieces he was interested in.

Bert continued to represent art that was coming into the United States from Europe. New York had become the world capital of art trading and collecting by the mid–1950s. After the exodus of art and artists from Paris in the anticipation and wake of Nazi invasion, and the repeated shelling of London by Nazi bombs and rockets, Manhattan grew as a safe harbor and repository.

New York–based artists had a long and rich history of development that was still growing and changing rapidly in the 1950s. During the time Ann and Bert were in New York, the contemporary art world shifted from abstract expressionism to pop art to op art. The auction houses and major dealers moved from old masters and classicism to impressionism, fauves, surrealism, and expressionism. As examples during that period, two very early Picasso oils were auctioned for less than $5,000 each, and a major Van Gogh Arles period painting was sold for less than $100,000 at public auction in the early 1960s.

A frequent guest and active member of the Museum of Modern Art, Ann became a student of A.L. Chanin, a fine artist himself and a popular lecturer at MOMA. He inscribed a copy of his book *Art Guide/New York*, an encyclopedia of the state of mid-century art in New York, to her and Bert: "To my friends, the lovely Mrs. D'Armand and the skeptical, tolerant Mr. D'Armand — both of whom brighten my evening art sessions." While in New York, Bert arranged for the Museum of Modern Art to make a copy of Ann's 35mm nitrate print of *Detour*.

As the art scene in New York exploded, so did easy world travel. With New York as a base, and the introduction of fast-cruising, long-range jet planes, Ann and Bert were able to

Life in the '50s (left to right): Dr. Henry Ross, Ross's wife (and Ann's close friend) Glenda Farrell, Ann and Bert (1955).

make annual visits to countries across the globe. They attended bullfights in Spain, visited Bert's ancestral home in Poland, photographed nudes at St. Tropez, and collected art everywhere from Jamaica to Turkey.

Their annual holiday party in Havana, Cuba, served as their true Thanksgiving. Over the Christmas holidays during the 1950s, Ann and Bert would meet up with their old friends from both the Hollywood and Las Vegas years. Film people mixed with New Yorkers, the Vegas Kingpins flew in, rum flowed, and the tables were full. Being a child of the Depression, Ann never liked to gamble with her own money. Christmas in Cuba was always a treat because she'd roll the dice for others. Meyer Lansky loved to stake her in craps. He told her she was his prettiest and luckiest roller.

As they settled into married life, Bert thought Ann was becoming more Jewish, and he less so. She loved Jewish culture, feeling accepted and comfortable in Jewish society since her days at Fairfax High. She decided to convert to Judaism. In addition to her studies of art and gourmet cooking, Ann began attending schul. Bert, who was normally extremely supportive of Ann, did not encourage her conversion. He was of the generation that tried passionately to assimilate American culture and leave immigrant roots behind. He also told her he had absolutely no intention of attending temple with her.

The final showdown of faith in the D'Armand household came about when Mercedes Benz released the 230 SL Roadster in the early 1960s. Bert fell in love with the car, but Ann refused to let him buy one. She was still bitter about the Nazis and wouldn't own any German products. After several test drives, she was still unconvinced. Bert made his final stand. He pleaded with her, "Israel has forgiven the Germans, Ann, why can't we?" Ann finally gave in, and so began her own love of Mercedes Benz cars. The D'Armands placed an order and then traveled to Sindelfingen, Germany, to pick up a new Mercedes 230 SL. They drove it into Finland and from there into Russia. "Mr. Khrushchev was hot for some American dollars, so we thought we'd give the fat bastard a few." The Soviet concept of tourism was to fly in charters through Aeroflot, wall off groups of foreigners by isolating them in tourist hotels, show them the Kremlin in Moscow and the Hermitage in St. Petersburg, and Aeroflot them back home before indigestion set in. Not for the D'Armands. Bert spoke flawless Russian, and bought himself a new Polaroid camera to take instant pictures of the Russian people and give them away as gifts and social icebreakers as they drove from town to town.

The country wasn't set up for accommodating long-range drivers, so they were forced to sleep in large military barracks and tents by themselves. Though never questioned, they were consistently eyed with suspicion. "We weren't exactly hiding anything—we were driving in an open convertible and I was a blonde!" When they got to Moscow, a government car backed into the Mercedes, damaging the front grille. A small crowd began to gather. Within minutes security arrived and asked Bert to follow them with the car. They were led to a garage that did repairs for the KGB motor pool. The Mercedes was fixed on the spot. While they waited, Bert introduced the KGB to the joys of Polaroid photography.

Back in California, Ann's mother had resettled in Los Angeles and remarried. She ran a small gift boutique and jewelry counter in the lobby of the law offices of Loeb and Loeb, Bert's longtime attorneys. Louise visited New York annually, and often kept watch on Lass while Ann and Bert were overseas.

Ann kept her headshots up to date, and worked occasionally on local television and for national advertising clients. She did spots for Westinghouse, General Electric and Golden Books. Her image had gone from hard as nails femme fatale to sensitive, yet still hot, mother.

Ann's 1959 headshot photo while in New York.

In one inspirational religious film she made while in New York, *On the Right Side*, Ann plays the loving, understanding and enabling wife of a man with a gambling addiction. After receiving counseling from a priest, the family renews their bonds, and the reformed husband swears off gambling forever, much to the relief of his wife— Meyer Lansky's favorite crapshooter, Ann Savage!

During the 1960s, Bert began to do business with Julius Stulman, founder of the World Institute and scion to the Lumber Exchange Terminal on the East River in New York City. Stulman was a visionary global economist who pushed for nuclear disarmament and the rapid development of emerging nations. Stulman also was married to Janis Carter, a former actress who had come to work on the Columbia lot just as Ann was leaving. They were mutual friends of Jeff Donnell, and all met together frequently for tennis, society events and holidays.

Janis was creatively gifted in many

areas. She was a respected actress, a blonde beauty who was also an excellent writer and painter, had a beautiful singing voice, and possessed a natural gift for friendship. In Hollywood, Janis had been under contract to Howard Hughes and promoted to the press as "the girl with the bedroom eyes," and was rumored to have been Noah Dietrich's mistress throughout the 1940s. When Mrs. Dietrich heard the rumors, she named Miss Carter correspondent in the newspapers and sued for divorce. Around the same time, Janis quit movies for good and moved to New York, where she began working in live television and game shows like *Feather Your Nest*.

A frequent letter writer, Janis designed and watercolor-painted her own personal greeting cards. She was a devoted friend to Ann from the mid–1950s until her death in the mid–1990s. Their group often joined together for dinners with Burt and Ethel Aginsky, cultural anthropologists who had spent 25 years studying the Pomo Indians. The Aginskys considered the mythological Indian lore of the 19th century to be romantic nonsense, and Hollywood westerns to be commercial nonsense that masked the white man's lust for land and confiscation of native territories. This mix of the moneyed interests of foresting, living Hollywood mythology, and socially responsible academia made for lively debate over Ann's gourmet experiments, cooking recipes from her classes with Dione Lucas at Le Cordon Bleu.

By the mid–1960s, Ann began to long for the edge acting in features had given her. She enjoyed deep-sea fishing in Florida, but whenever she flew to a foreign country she knew she preferred flying to being on the water.

Bert was having increasing trouble with his heart, and wanted to leave New York and retire to Florida. Once they had moved, Ann missed the pace of the city and felt stifled in Miami. She began taking flying lessons. At first, Bert encouraged her, but when he saw that she had quickly developed an obsession, he objected. Ann wanted him to buy a plane. He said no. She was flying so often that he became actively discouraging. "Bert told me that small planes weren't safe. He said if I crashed and became disfigured, he'd put me away in a home, that he wouldn't be able to bear looking at me." This tactic enraged Ann, and, of course, increased her resolve to fly.

By 1968, Bert's heart and circulatory problems had become overwhelming. He had been misdiagnosed, and shuttled between Miami, New York, and Los Angeles to find proper medical care. Following surgery for an advanced aortic aneurysm, he was warned that he was still at risk. Ann had received so much conflicting information from the different doctors that she began to keep a diary of his illness. Being a no-nonsense pragmatist, Bert began to settle his accounts and move their household from Florida back to Los Angeles, using the Shoreham Tower apartment as a base. He created a will and planned his estate strategy. He drew closer to his long estranged son from his first marriage, visiting him several times in Las Vegas. After much consultation, Bert preferred the treatment he received in Florida and became an outpatient in Miami.

As an escape and refuge, Ann turned more and more to flying. Though Bert tried to rally and pretend he was feeling better than ever, they both knew that the odds were against him — if his aneurysm burst, it would be fatal. At the end of 1969, Bert suffered a severe attack and was rushed to the hospital. He was paralyzed and comatose, and he never recovered. After several days with no sign of improvement, Ann had to make the decision to terminate his life support. Bert had not wanted to be kept alive artificially. It was the most difficult decision she ever had to make. It was New Year's Eve, 1969.

Chapter 9

Flying Solo

Ann returned to Los Angeles, numb and alone, with nobody to turn to except her mother Louise. Los Angeles, like New York, had changed over the years; and by 1970, Hollywood and the strip, where she spent so much of her early life, had become overrun with street people. She didn't know where she fit anymore. "I had been so upset about Bert's condition for so long that I hadn't stopped to think much about the future." Initially, she withdrew. She hid out at the Shoreham apartment and refused to answer the phone or look at her mail. She couldn't face even her closest friends with the news. Glenda Farrell and Janis Carter tracked her down in Los Angeles and forced her out of her slump.

While Bert's estate was being settled, she took a position as a receptionist at Loeb and Loeb. Bert had used the firm since the 1930s, and she knew several of the attorneys. After some time, she began flying again, thought about returning to acting, and concentrated on rebuilding her personal life.

Flying led her to Hal Day. At first she was attracted to his plane, and then she warmed up to him. He was a quiet guy, an engineer at Rockwell working on the space program. He

Ann and her co-pilot pose with trophies after winning the 1975 Pacific Air Race (Women's Division).

was a serious flyer, and they copiloted very comfortably. After a few years Ann moved in with Hal, living with him near her mother in Hollywood.

Ann lived quietly during her middle years. She saw some of her old friends from movies and Las Vegas, like Babs Goldman and her twin sister Jimmie, and Gen and Harry Atoll, and she began regular rounds of tennis. For the holidays she and Hal often flew to Cabo San Lucas or La Paz in Mexico.

Though she performed her daily acting exercise in the morning, kept her SAG membership up to date, and followed new movies regularly, she kept her distance from the business. When *Detour* or one of her old films showed up on television, she'd watch it and save the TV listing, happy to know her movies were still shown. Otherwise she preferred to leave the past alone. She lived this way for a dozen years.

In 1983, UCLA staged a two-month retrospective of Edgar Ulmer's work. The opening night of the tribute featured a screening of *Detour*, to be followed by a discussion with (among others) Shirley Ulmer and Martin Goldsmith. In the *Los Angeles Times* that same day, Kevin Thomas praised both the film and Ann's performance, and concluded the article with: "As for Savage, who worked steadily in low-budget films throughout the '40s and early '50s, she reportedly now lives in the San Fernando Valley." At the time, Ann was still working for the Loeb and Loeb law office, and several of her co-workers who saw the article urged her to attend the screening. Ann entered the theater quietly, but during the discussion, when someone asked what had happened to Ann Savage, she announced, "I'm here!" She was invited to join the panel discussion and walked to the proscenium to a standing ovation. Ann later commented that she was especially thrilled to discover that 14 attorneys from her law office were also in attendance at that screening.

Though her rediscovery did not revive her film career, it put her at the center of a growing cult interest in *Detour*. She became close again with Shirley Ulmer. She was approached several times by producers who wanted to remake *Detour*. Among others, Wade Williams asked her to appear in his *Detour* remake in the early 1990s. She appeared on *Entertainment Tonight*, and seemed to enjoy playing against type, projecting her southern sweetness and offering no glimpses of the mighty Vera.

With her resurgence on the festival and revival circuit, and some television and newspaper coverage, she received and accepted offers to make brief appearances in the Paramount feature film *Fire with Fire* and the popular sitcom *Saved by the Bell*.

Shirley Ulmer and Ann, 1984.

Ann and Louise remained as close as ever, often sharing meals and attending movies together. Louise had been the only constant in her life, and when she passed away in the 1980s, Ann felt a loneliness she had never known.

In 1994 Ann left Hal Day and moved into her own apartment. She dumped her boyfriend when she was 73 year old, went out and bought some flashy cowboy boots, and took up country line dancing, becoming a popular regular at the Denim and Diamonds club. She said, "Life had gotten dull with Hal; he wanted to move to Arizona, and he just assumed I'd go along, without asking me. I was with him too damn long to be taken for granted!"

She found a beautiful apartment a half block up from the Sunset Strip, near Fairfax Avenue, and walked, or took the bus, to all her favorite haunts. She entertained her friends at Musso's and Canter's, and was a regular at Farmers Market. She was on a first-name basis there with the shopkeepers and food stand workers, and even started a weekly drive to help out a bag lady who spent her days in the food court. When Farmers Market expanded into the Grove Mall, she embraced the new additions, trying the restaurants out, and she made the plush, new, first-run movie theater a second home.

She played tennis every Sunday, weather permitting, at 8:30 in the morning, and would wander leisurely through the swap meet held in the parking lot of Fairfax High.

Hollywood and the Fairfax district were her neighborhoods. Separate from any associations with her career, she was at home there. Ann kept her 1970 Black Mercedes Benz 280 SL in immaculate condition. She drove the car fast, always with the top down. She called it the Black Beauty, and it never saw rain. She volunteered with local film societies and made public appearances regularly at the Egyptian theater, one of her favorite venues since the 1930s, and the site of her first premiere for *Klondike Kate* in 1943. The annual noir festival hosted by Eddie Muller at the Egyptian was a favorite of Ann's, and she'd always attend. This led to her appearance in Eddie's book *Dark City Dames: The Wicked Women of Film Noir*, and a run of festival and book signing live appearances.

Ann had expressed her desire to find a good part in a feature for many years. When Gloria Stuart was cast in *Titanic*, it challenged her professionally. She wanted to show what she could do, that she was still in touch with her acting spark. She was willing to meet, even audition, for any serious possibility. Her only requirement was that she be

Ann working on *My Winnipeg* (2006).

presented with a screenplay to read in advance of any meeting. Not only would this stipulation weed out the ones who just wanted to have lunch to meet her, but she could tell a good script in 5 seconds. She was only interested in an original project with an intelligent conception. This was her biggest lesson from *Detour*: if it's any good, it *has* to be in the script.

When Guy Maddin first appeared in Ann's life asking her to be in his film *My Winnipeg*, he didn't have a script. He sent articles about Winnipeg, an outline of the film, and some examples of his work, all of which she enjoyed. Ann caught Guy's spirit immediately. Among the DVDs she screened, she loved *Dracula: Pages from a Virgin's Diary* the most. Though a lifelong movie lover with very wide tastes, Ann had never liked the horror genre and always found the Dracula story repellant. Guy's telling of the tale was done is such an original way that it made a real impression on her. She also thought it was very sexy.

Ann and Guy Maddin celebrate the release of 2006's *Brand Upon the Brain!*

Guy was very entertaining on the phone, sincere in his respect for Ann's work, and very knowledgeable about movies, especially hers. When he sent some scenes and dialogue, and she read the argument with the daughter, she came onboard. The rest was preparation and practice.

While the film was being shot, Ann felt such love and support in Winnipeg that it was easy to put herself in Guy's hands and work the lines until he had what he wanted. They worked together very closely and comfortably. When she stumbled, Guy kept her energy up and the production moving forward. Then it was over as quickly as it had begun. Movies are like that, and she'd always known it. Intense collaboration, then you move on.

After the shoot Guy kept in touch with her, came to Los Angeles and shot some additional footage, and took her for lunch to Canter's deli. She adored him personally, and felt a deep sense of gratitude for the kindness, generosity and professionalism he'd shown her during *My Winnipeg*. She also enjoyed his work, and was delighted to be invited to a special screening of *Brand Upon the Brain!* at the Egyptian.

Later, after her health began to falter, she became more reclusive and stopped making public appearances. She stayed in the Fairfax district apartment until she needed to be attended by a skilled, registered nurse around the clock. During the last two months of her life, Ann was transferred to a well-equipped skilled care center so she could receive immediate professional attention, if needed. She had lived to see Barack Obama win as president, and *My*

Winnipeg named as one of the top ten movies of the year by *Time Magazine*. She was hopeful and looking forward to the future.

Ann passed away peacefully on Christmas day, 2008. For years she had enjoyed visiting the Hollywood Forever Cemetery, where she'd often make an afternoon of it and take a little picnic. She'd pay her respects to her friends: Edgar and Shirley Ulmer, Columbia boss Harry Cohn, and wardrobe designer Adrian. She'd stop and say hello to Moe Sedway and Ben Siegel — even though the deal didn't work out well in Vegas. She'd admire Marion Davies and say hi to Arthur Lake, who she worked with in *Blondie: Footlight Glamour*. She'd give a last sigh to Rudolph Valentino, then go and tell Bert she loved him and that she'd see him soon. She'd visit her mother Louise last and linger the longest, leave some flowers, then put her palm on the niche and say, "Thank you, Mother." Ann's services at Hollywood Forever were a true celebration of an extraordinary life, with shared remembrances from many friends and fans. After her urn had been anointed with Chanel No. 5 (her favorite perfume), she was reunited at last with her beloved Bert.

She'd no doubt be delighted to know that — per one of her final wishes — every year more of her old films are being reissued and rediscovered.

Her old friend and fan Johnny Grant, longtime honorary mayor of Hollywood, told her she was bigger in the new millennium than ever before, and that he thought she deserved a star on Hollywood's Walk of Fame; but Ann remained unconvinced, responding only:

"Honey, I don't want people walking on me!"

Part Two
Filmography

Major Film Roles

One Dangerous Night

(Columbia) Release Date: January 22, 1943

Screenplay: Donald Davis, based on a story by Max Nosseck and Arnold Phillips; "Lone Wolf" created by Louis Joseph Vance
Cinematography: L. W. O'Connell
Musical Director: M. W. Stoloff
Editor: Viola Lawrence
Art Directors: Lionel Banks and Robert Peterson
Set Decorator: George Montgomery
Producer: David Chatkin
Director: Michael Gordon
Cast: Warren William (Michael Lanyard/the Lone Wolf); Marguerite Chapman (Eve Andrews); Eric Blore (Jamison); Mona Barrie (Jane Merrick); Tala Birell (Sonia Budenny); Margaret Hayes (Patricia Blake); Ann Savage (Vivian); Thurston Hall (Inspector Crane); Warren Ashe (Sidney Shaw)

Synopsis

Michael Lanyard, aka reformed jewel thief "the Lone Wolf," and his butler Jamison are en route to a party one night when they come across a stranded woman next to her disabled car. They pick her up, find out her name is Eve Andrews, and agree to take her to her home.

Meanwhile, Cooper, a well-known criminal, is giving instructions to an assistant, Arthur; Arthur is to phone Cooper at 10 P.M. and tell him if "a certain party" has arrived at the airport. Arthur then meets two other men, and together they discuss how Cooper has been blackmailing wealthy patrons who lost money at his illegal casino; tonight, Cooper is expected to score a particularly valuable bracelet. The two men leave Arthur and head to Cooper's house, intending to steal the bracelet.

Lanyard and Jamison drop Eve Andrews off at Cooper's house, then Jamison reveals that he secretly stole Eve's handbag. Lanyard promptly turns the car around to return the handbag.

At Cooper's house, he's just admitted Eve, who is being blackmailed out of her bracelet, when two more women arrive — Sonia, who is to hand over a marquis diamond, and Jane, who is to pay a diamond clip. Suddenly the lights go out and a shot is heard. When the lights come back on, Cooper is dead. The three women flee just before Lanyard and Jamison arrive and discover the body; Jamison also finds the extorted jewelry, which he secretly pockets. When a motorcycle cop tickets Lanyard's illegally parked car, he also finds Lanyard and Jamison with the body and arrests them. Homicide detectives Dickens and Crane are called in to investigate, but Lanyard creates a diversion, and he and Jamison escape.

Lanyard and Jamison find Eve at the exclusive Park Hotel, where she's having her engagement party. They return Eve's bag, then Lanyard questions her about Cooper. Unfortunately for Lanyard, famed gossip columnist Sidney Shannon arrives, having just heard that Lanyard is wanted for murder. He and Lanyard strike a deal: Lanyard promises him plenty of juicy gossip if he gives Lanyard until midnight to find the real killer. Meanwhile, Jamison has followed Eve to a phone and discovered that she's called a club called the Balalaika. Lanyard, Jamison and Shannon head there and find Sonia with her husband. Jamison lures the husband away, giving Lanyard a chance to question Sonia. Outraged, she has him thrown out, but he's abruptly rescued by Vivian, an old flame; unfortunately for the Lone Wolf, Vivian is now working for the two thugs who still want Eve's bracelet. They capture Lanyard and leave him tied up with Vivian in a hotel room while they go to search Cooper's house. Lanyard manages to escape, and he meets up with Jamison and Shannon. Together they all return to Cooper's house. Just as they enter, Arthur calls to report that "a certain party" has arrived at the airport, and they immediately follow up on the clue. At the airport they find Patricia, a pretty young girl who is distraught when she learns of Cooper's death. They follow her to a hotel, where Arthur is trying to blackmail her. They

Sonia (Tala Birell, second from left) looks on as the Lone Wolf (Warren William, center) is escorted by Vivian (Ann Savage) in *One Dangerous Night* (1943).

burst in, and during the ensuing scuffle Arthur escapes and Patricia is injured.

Lanyard goes back to see Eve Andrews again, and finds her with Sonia and Jane; all three are now being blackmailed by Arthur. When Inspector Crane shows up, Lanyard just barely escapes and returns to the injured Patricia. Shannon joins them but turns strangely violent when Patricia confesses to loving Cooper. The Lone Wolf soon discovers the truth: Patricia is Shannon's wife, but was in love with Cooper, who was planning on running away with her until Shannon killed him. Just then the cops arrive, and when they find the missing jewels (which Jamison has planted) on Shannon, they immediately arrest him, clearing the Lone Wolf of all charges.

Commentary

Like *After Midnight with Boston Blackie* (Ann's second film), *One Dangerous Night* is a typical Columbia "programmer." In fact, the two films bear strangely similar plots: In both, a reformed jewel thief and his comic sidekick are falsely accused of a murder while caught in a hunt for stolen jewels; meanwhile, bumbling policemen and elegant night clubs contribute to the web of intrigue. Certainly the latter two elements were standard tropes of Columbia's serial films; whether other similarities were coincidental or the product of a film factory system, it's impossible to say.

One Dangerous Night is certainly the more successful of the two films, though, with less of the coincidences and contrivances that render the Boston Blackie entry downright embarrassing on occasion. *Night* is consistently amusing and enveloped in a sheen of faux sophistication, with the debonair Warren William as the Lone Wolf caught in the center of a ring of gorgeous—and slightly shady—blackmailed women. As with all the Lone Wolf films, the comic relief provided by Eric Blore as sidekick Jamison is often genuinely comic, and plays perfectly off William's gracefully aloof, deadpan persona.

If the film is consistently amusing, however, it becomes something more for the brief time that Ann Savage's Vivian enters the scene. This was Ann's first performance, and it's the kind of little acting gem that should have earned her an immediate starring role. She bursts onto the screen with great energy and charisma, but once she's alone with the bound Lone Wolf she transforms into an absolute dynamo of sexuality. As she runs her fingers through William's perfectly-combed hair and bends close over one shoulder while he offers her looks that are alternately fearful and tempted, for a few moments *One Dangerous Night* threatens to suggest an entire alternate Hollywood, one where overtly sexual bondage scenes were hidden in B-films, disguised from the cinematic watchdogs by a veneer of cheap thriller plot devices. William was a long-established top star for Columbia at the time, and for a young actress making her film debut to fondle him quite the way Ann does shows a fearless performer of tremendous potential. It's not hard to imagine Columbia chief Harry Cohn planning *Klondike Kate* for Ann after seeing her performance as Vivian.

Vivian (Ann Savage) accepts a gun, as a bound and nervous Michael Lanyard (Warren William) looks on.

The rest of *One Dangerous Night* is unremarkable, although nonetheless entertaining. That single debut performance, however, should be enough to warrant at least a minor rediscovery.

Behind the Scenses

"The Lone Wolf," a jewel thief-turned-private detective, first appeared in Louis Joseph Vance's 1914 novel *The Lone Wolf*. The character was featured in eight books and 24 films between 1917 and 1949, and also appeared in radio and television series.

Warren William played the character in nine films (more than any other actor), from 1939's *The Lone Wolf Spy Hunt* to 1943's *Passport to Suez*; *One Dangerous Night* was his second-to-last appearance as the character. William was a popular leading man in pre–Code Hollywood, typically appearing as a cunning rogue; later he portrayed several iconic mystery characters, including Perry Mason (in 1934's *The Case of the Howling Dog*) and Philo Vance (1934's *The Dragon Murder Case* and 1939's *The Gracie Allen Murder Case*). He also appeared as Dr. Lloyd in the classic horror film *The Wolf Man* (1941).

Eric Blore portrayed Jamison, the Lone Wolf's butler, in eleven of the films, starting with *The Lone Wolf Strikes* (1940) and ending with *The Lone Wolf in London* (1947). Blore made over 80 films during his career, including such classics as *Top Hat* (1935) and *Sullivan's Travels* (1941); he is also known as the voice of "Mr. Toad" in the 1949 Disney classic *The Adventures of Ichabod and Mr. Toad*. Blore was also Ann's friend and neighbor, and they appeared together in a popular 1943 tour for the USO.

Look for Lloyd Bridges as an airline gate attendant (Bridges has a larger role in the next Lone Wolf film, *Passport to Suez*).

Although Ann appears in both *One Dangerous Night* and the following Lone Wolf film, *Passport to Suez*, she plays different characters.

Thurston Hall, who plays "Inspector Crane," would work with Ann again in both the Blondie entry *Footlight Glamour* (1943) and the musical *Ever Since Venus* (1944).

The film's alternate title was *Lone Wolf Goes to a Party*.

After Midnight with Boston Blackie

(Columbia) Release Date: March 18, 1943
Screenplay: by Howard J. Green, based on a story by Aubrey Wisberg; Boston Blackie created by Jack Boyle
Cinematography: L. W. O'Connell
Musical Director: M. W. Stoloff
Editor: Richard Fantl
Art Director: Lionel Banks
Produced by: Sam White
Directed by: Lew Landers
Cast: Chester Morris (Boston Blackie); Richard Lane (Inspector Farraday); Ann Savage (Betty Barnaby); George E. Stone (the Runt); Lloyd Corrigan (Arthur Manleder)

Synopsis

Two thugs show up at the Flamingo Club to tell crime boss Joe Herschel that "Diamond" Ed Barnaby is getting out of prison tomorrow; Diamond Ed has three priceless diamonds hidden, and Herschel wants them.

The next day Ed is released and is met by his devoted daughter, Betty. She's got an apartment set up for him, but Ed knows he's being pursued and only wants to hang around long enough to give her the diamonds. He retrieves the jewels and rents a locker, unaware that he's being observed as he stashes the diamonds.

Onboard a train, ex-criminals Boston Blackie and the Runt receive a telegram from Betty, asking them to meet her. Two Inspectors, Matthews and Farraday, are also on the train and warn Blackie and Runt that they're just waiting for a reason to arrest them. Upon leaving the train, Blackie and Runt meet Betty, who tells them her father is now missing. Before they can search for Diamond Ed, Blackie and Runt have something else to take care of: Runt's wedding—to a stripper named Dixie Peach Blossom. With Matthews following, Blackie and Runt head to the home of Arthur

Manleder, a friend who is hosting the ceremony. Runt postpones his marriage long enough to accompany Blackie to Ed's locker. Ed, meanwhile, has been captured by Herschel's boys and tortured into revealing the location of the diamonds. When Ed is discovered phoning Matthews and Farraday, he's shot by Herschel.

The inspectors arrive at the locker just as Blackie opens it — and discovers that it's empty. Matthews and Farraday believe Blackie shot Ed, but Blackie and Runt escape before they're taken into custody. Blackie heads back to Manleder's apartment, where he finds everyone tied up and Betty missing; he soon receives a call telling him to arrive at the Flamingo Club with the diamonds in exchange for Betty. Blackie manages to pull three fake stones from Dixie's jewelry, and he arrives at the club just in time to see Herschel stashing the real diamonds — which Blackie promptly steals. He's caught soon thereafter by the thugs, but manages to escape and find Betty. They flee to the roof, and a wartime blackout assists them in eluding their pursuers.

The two thugs, meanwhile, realize that Herschel double-crossed them on the plan to share the diamonds, so they shoot him, then capture Blackie, who they believe has hidden the diamonds somewhere. Blackie uses Inspector Farraday's car to take the killers to his supposed hiding place; and, via the police radio, Matthews and Farraday hear both confessions and directions. When they realize they've been conned, the thugs fight Blackie, but he wins and finally turns them over to the police.

With the murders of Diamond Ed and Herschel finally solved, Blackie and Runt return to Arthur Manleder's to complete Runt's wedding — only to have Matthews and Farraday burst in to arrest Dixie for bigamy.

Commentary

After Midnight with Bloston Blackie is fairly typical of Columbia's series films — it sports an obviously low budget, a short running time, a convoluted plot and mostly solid performances throughout. The script is actually overly complex, and occasionally loses important plot points in favor of extended comic scenes; too much time is spent on the bumbling police inspectors, while the diamonds — the central device of the story — appear or disappear almost at random.

If the whole affair occasionally threatens to implode from the mix of confusion and sidetracking, it's held together by the off-key charm of Chester Morris as its eponymous hero. With his flattened nose and broad features, Morris is hardly the traditional handsome hero; nor does he have the debonair sophistication of Columbia's other reformed jewel thief, Warren William's "Lone Wolf." But Morris has an easygoing grin and affable manner that blend together into a unique screen charisma. His odd-couple interplay with George E. Stone's Runt is natural and entertaining.

After Midnight with Boston Blackie was Ann Savage's second film, and her character here is almost 180 degrees from her single appearance (in *One Dangerous Night*) as a conniving and seductive villainess — "Betty" is a sweet girl-next-door ingénue, and Ann turns in a lovely and earnest performance. When Blackie watches her walk out of one scene and mutters, "She's a swell kid," it's easy to understand his obvious affection for her.

The film does offer modern audiences an interesting glimpse into life during wartime: Maintenance men prepare offices for blackouts, train travel is still elegant, and a white man donning blackface (as Blackie does at one point) is meant to garner laughs, not winces. *After Midnight with Boston Blackie* never reaches the level of true camp (nor is it wildly offensive), but it offers mild amusement as a study in quaint history.

Behind the Scenes

"Boston Blackie" was a popular character who was created by author Jack Boyle in a number of early 20th-century short stories. The character appeared in a series of silent films (from 1918 to 1927), but didn't make it to the talkies until Columbia's 1941 *Meet Boston*

One-sheet poster for 1943's *After Midnight with Boston Blackie.*

Blackie. Columbia eventually produced 14 Boston Blackie films (ending the series in 1949 with *Boston Blackie's Chinese Venture*); *After Midnight with Boston Blackie* was the fifth film in the series. Like another popular Columbia character, "Lone Wolf" (Ann Savage appeared in two "Lone Wolf" films, *One Dangerous Night* and *Passport to Suez*), Boston Blackie is a reformed jewel thief now investigating crime. The films all feature Blackie's sidekick "the Runt" (played in all but the first and last films by George E. Stone), police Inspector Farraday (played throughout the series by Richard Lane), and Farraday's comic assistant Sgt. Matthews (played by several actors). Blackie was often assisted by Arthur Manleder (played in five of the films by Lloyd Corrigan) and Jumbo Madigan (either Cy Kendall or Joseph Crehan).

Columbia's press releases for this film indicate that they considered it to be Ann's first starring role, and one uncredited review from her scrapbook notes that she "turns in a pleasing performance."

Although Chester Morris was one of the first actors to be nominated for an Academy Award (for the 1929 film *Alibi*), he was best known for portraying Boston Blackie in the series of 14 Columbia films. Morris also played Boston Blackie in a 1944 radio series.

George E. Stone was a popular character actor who appeared in three films with Ann Savage (the other two were *Midnight Manhunt* and *Scared Stiff* [both 1945]).

Lew Landers was one of Hollywood's most prolific directors, with more than 160 films and television shows to his credit. He also directed Ann in *Two-Man Submarine* (1944).

Saddles and Sagebrush

(Columbia) Release Date: April 27, 1943

Screenplay and Story by: Ed Earl Repp
Cinematography by: Benjamin H. Kline
Editing by: William Claxton
Art Direction by: Lionel Banks
Set Decoration by: Frank Tuttle
Produced by: Leon Barsha
Directed by: William Berke
Cast: Russell Hayden (Lucky Randall); Dub Taylor (Cannonball); Ann Savage (Ann Parker); Bob Wills (Bob Merritt); the Texas Playboys (Musicians); William Wright (Krag Savin); Frank LaRue (Lafe Parker); Wheeler Oakman (Ace Barko); Edmund Cobb (Cutter); Jack Ingram (Trigger); Joe McGuinn (Blackie)

Synopsis

Lucky Randall is a crack shot who is surprised when he receives a job offer to work for local rancher Krag Savin for $100 a day; Lucky (and his sidekick Cannonball) are thrilled, and quickly agree. But what Lucky doesn't know is that Savin is hiring gunmen because he's taken over nearby Pinon City and is trying to drive out all the local settlers. Savin sends his main thug, Blackie, with a gang to burn down the Parker ranch, but old Lafe Parker and his spunky daughter Ann drive the mob off. Parker rides back into town to confront Savin, but Blackie shoots and injures him, then propositions Ann. Lucky, outraged, knocks down Blackie; then Lucky quits and announces he's going to work for the ranchers.

Lucky talks to the Parkers, then sends a wire to the state registrar to find out how much land Savin's already stolen. Savin's men find out about the wire and tell Savin.

The next day, Lucky's friends Bob Wills and the Texas Playboys show up in response to a telegram Lucky sent, arriving just in time to see Savin's men trying to stop the mail coach. Unfortunately, Savin's men steal the mail bags and escape before Bob and the Playboys can reach the coach. When Lucky finds out, he comes up with a plan to steal back the Parker cattle that Savin's already made off with. The Playboys agree to help, but instead of cattle they capture Blackie. They threaten to hang Blackie if he doesn't tell them about the coach robbery, but just as he starts to talk, Savin shows up and kills him. Bob and Lucky fight off Savin and his boys, and Ann shows up with the Playboys just as Lucky runs out of bullets. The Playboys shoot all of Savin's men, but Savin captures Ann and drives off in her buggy. Lucky rides after them and catches up just as

Lafe Parker (Frank LaRue, seated at left) looks on as his daughter Ann (Ann Savage) enjoys a moment with Lucky (Russell Hayden) in *Saddles and Sagebrush* (1943).

the buggy reaches a horse corral, where Lucky beats Savin in a fistfight.

Thanks to his courage, Lucky is named the first marshal of Pinon City.

COMMENTARY

Despite a plot that's about as new as a worn leather boot, *Saddles and Sagebrush* is wholly entertaining, thanks in no small part to the mix of action and the peppy country swing music provided by Bob Wills and the Texas Playboys. Veteran director William Berke keeps the pace snappy, and just enough comedy is provided by Dub Taylor's antics as Lucky's pal "Cannonball." *Saddles and Sagebrush* is the kind of lighthearted entertainment that made for an almost perfect second feature in a night's programming.

Part of the off-kilter charm of these westerns was their utter disregard for reality: The Playboys perform full songs while on horseback; no one's ever really hurt in a fight; perfectly-styled costumes and hair are never subjected to the cruel whims of dirt or (gasp) blood. *Saddles and Sagebrush* occasionally even wanders into the realm of pure absurdity, as when the captured bad guy Blackie is led off on horseback while the Playboys sing an upbeat song about the evils of cattle rustling and the payback entailed (meanwhile, Hayden rides right along, grinning wildly).

Russell Hayden ably displays why he was one of the top western stars at the time this picture was made — he's attractive, athletic, natural, and has a warmer presence than many of the other cowboy actors at the time. The film owes a considerable amount of its sheer likeability to his natural grace.

As befits the gleeful little-boys-playing-cowboys attitude of the movie, Ann Savage largely serves as the obligatory girl to be rescued, despite a promising opening when she hefts a rifle and pops off shots with dad. She's appealing throughout, though, and has a sweet rapport with Russell Hayden.

William Wright, as Savin, makes a fine bad guy; given his later chemistry with Ann Savage in *Dancing in Manhattan* (1944), it's unfortunate he has no real scenes with her here.

Saddles and Sagebrush also benefits from some picturesque location filming and overall solid production design.

Behind the Scenes

Bob Wills and his Texas Playboys were a popular group throughout the '30s, '40s and '50s, and were often credited with being the artists who popularized "Western Swing" (country music with jazz beats). Onstage, Wills was known for his fiddle playing and showmanship; the Playboys (basically his back-up band) changed numerous times over the years, but Wills always insisted they wear neat cowboy clothes while performing. Wills is now referred to as "the King of Western Swing" and is even cited as an influence on the development of early rock music. He and the Playboys perform four songs in *Saddles and Sagebrush*—"Hubbin' It," "Get Along My Pony," "Ki Yi Yippe Yea" and "Toodleumbo."

At the time of *Saddles and Sagebrush*, Russell Hayden was ranked one of the top ten cowboy stars. A natural athlete and horseman, he appeared in 27 Hopalong Cassidy films as "Lucky Jenkins," sidekick to star William Boyd. Hayden went on to be one of the developers of Pioneertown, a standing western set which appeared in many feature films and television series.

Dub Taylor — whose trademark became

(Left to right): Ann (Ann Savage), Lafe (Frank LaRue), and Lucky (Russell Hayden) greet Bob (Bob Wills), Cannonball (Dub Taylor), and the Texas Playboys in 1943's *Saddles and Sagebrush*.

his bowler hat — was one of the busiest character actors in film. Although he made his mark primarily in westerns, he would achieve his greatest success playing "Ivan Moss" in the 1967 classic *Bonnie and Clyde*.

Director William Berke, Russell Hayden, Dub Taylor, and Bob Wills and the Texas Playboys made 8 films together at Columbia: *The Lone Prairie* (1942), *A Tornado in the Saddle* (1942), *Riders of the Northwest Mounted* (1943), *Saddles and Sagebrush* (1943), *Silver City Raiders* (1943), *The Vigilantes Ride* (1943), *Wyoming Hurricane* (1944), and *The Last Horseman* (1944). All of the films except *A Tornado in the Saddle* featured a screenplay and/or story by either Fred Myton or Ed Earl Repp. Two of the films—*Saddles and Sagebrush* and *The Last Horseman*—feature Ann Savage as the female lead.

An uncredited review for this film in Ann's scrapbook noted that Ann "makes the typical western heroine stand out."

Saddles and Sagebrush has also been released under the title *The Pay-Off*, and was shot under the title *Outlaw Busters*.

Two Señoritas from Chicago

(Columbia) Release Date: June 10, 1943
 Screenplay by: Stanley Rubin and Maurice Tombragel; story by Steven Vas; additional dialogue by John P. Medbury
 Cinematography by: L. William O'Connell
 Edited by: Jerome Thoms
 Art Direction by: Lionel Banks
 Set Decoration by: William Kiernan
 Costume Design by: Travilla
 Musical Director: Morris Stoloff
 Dance Director: Nick Castle
 Produced by: Wallace MacDonald
 Directed by: Frank Woodruff
 Cast: Joan Davis (Daisy Baker); Jinx Falkenburg (Gloria); Ann Savage (Maria); Leslie Brooks (Lena Worth); Bob Haymes (Jeff Kenyon)

Synopsis

Daisy Baker is a would-be agent working in the trash department of a hotel in Chicago; her only two clients are Gloria and Maria, two of the hotel's maids. When Daisy finds a play in the trash one day, she submits it to a Broadway producer, Rupert Shannon, claiming to be the agent for the two Portuguese playwrights listed as the authors. When Shannon wants to put the play on Broadway, Daisy immediately cooks up a scheme with Gloria and Maria: They'll pass themselves off as relatives of the playwrights, and insist on playing the leads in the play as well. They perform a brief audition for Shannon, and he agrees to the deal. They also meet Jeff, Shannon's handsome young assistant, who is himself a talented composer and playwright working on a Broadway musical.

One day during rehearsals, two of Gloria and Maria's old friends show up and threaten blackmail unless Daisy can get them into the show as well. She has them audition for Shannon, and he agrees to hire them as background dancers.

The situation becomes even more complicated when the real Portuguese playwrights arrive in New York, having made a deal with Grohman, a rival producer, to run their show on Broadway. Daisy, Maria and Gloria all panic, and cook up a plan to perform so badly that Shannon will be forced to shut down the show. Unfortunately, their scheme backfires when Shannon merely decides to recast the leads.

As opening day approaches, the three ladies realize their only option is to confess to Shannon. When they do, he's furious and threatens to have them all arrested — until Daisy suggests he join forces with rival producer Grohman. But when Grohman finds out the two productions are the same, he has Shannon, Daisy, Maria and Gloria all arrested. Jeff bails Shannon out, and Gloria and Maria are released, but Daisy is left in lock-up.

Shannon prepares to close the show, but Maria and Gloria convince Jeff to put on *his* show in place of the Portuguese production.

Jeff's World War II–themed show debuts on opening night, just as Daisy manages to talk her way out of jail. The new production, which stars Jeff, Gloria and Maria, is an instant hit, and Daisy sets herself up as Jeff's agent — even while the police are arriving to escort her back to jail.

Maria (Ann Savage, at left) and Gloria (Jinx Falkenburg, right) confer with their agent, Daisy (Joan Davis, center), in *Two Señoritas from Chicago* (1943).

Commentary

With a lively and attractive cast (notably driven by the comic performance of Joan Davis), *Two Señoritas from Chicago* is a lighthearted '40s B musical comedy that is proof that surrealism had made an impact on Hollywood.

The film starts with an unusual premise, presenting three heroines who have committed a massive act of fraud and expecting the audience to approve of their scam. From there it moves on to become ever more outlandish: The Portuguese playwrights are presented as Spanish-accented buffoons who write tiki tunes; Daisy escapes a jail cell merely by throwing a hysterical fit; and, in the spectacularly ridiculous climax, a Broadway show is put together overnight.

Frank Woodruff's direction gets out of the way of the traffic in this romping pastiche. Shots are all framed wide, with lighting that doesn't give away the cheap sets. The three female leads do a creditable job of clowning, singing (or at least lip-synching), dancing, and looking attractive, and some of the slapstick physical humor is inspired. The musical numbers seem to have gotten the lion's share of the film's budget, and they do feature some extravagant costuming, if not exactly memorable songwriting.

Joan Davis is the dominant presence here, with Ann Savage and Jinx Falkenburg both serving as lovely backup to Davis's schtick.

Despite its shortcomings, *Two Señoritas from Chicago* still manages to be entertaining, thanks to the short (68-minute) running time and the energetic performances of the three female leads.

"Moon Dance" in *Two Señoritas from Chicago*: Maria (Ann Savage, second from left), Daisy (Joan Davis, center) and Gloria (Jinx Falkenburg, second from right).

Behind the Scenes

Although not a direct sequel, *Two Señoritas from Chicago* was a sort of follow-up to the 1941 Columbia film *Two Latins from Manhattan*, which also starred Joan Davis and Jinx Falkenburg.

Joan Davis was a popular comedienne who would eventually star in the classic television series *I Married Joan*. During the making of *Two Señoritas*, Joan schooled Ann in how to perform pratfalls (a skill Ann would put to use later in *Footlight Glamour* [1943]).

Co-star Jinx Falkenburg was one of the world's top models at the time she made *Two Señoritas from Chicago*.

This was the only film director Frank Woodruff made for Columbia. Woodruff, in fact, directed only ten features, most for RKO.

Early press releases for *Two Señoritas from Chicago* listed Edmund Lowe in the cast, although this was probably just Columbia's attempt to further build on a supposed romance between Ann and Lowe (a romance largely created by Columbia as a publicity gimmick, since the two were touring together promoting war bonds sales).

Passport to Suez

(Columbia) Release Date: August 19, 1943

Screenplay by: John Stone; story by Alden Nash
Cinematography by: L. W. O'Connell
Editing by: Mel Thorsen
Art Direction: Lionel Banks and Paul Murphy
Set Decoration by: Joseph Kish
Musical Director: M. W. Stoloff
Produced by: Wallace MacDonald

Directed by: André De Toth
Cast: Warren William (Michael Lanyard/the Lone Wolf); Ann Savage (Valerie King); Eric Blore (Llewellyn Jamison); Robert Stanford (Donald Jamison); Sheldon Leonard (Johnny Booth); Lloyd Bridges (Fritz); Gavin Muir (Karl)

Synopsis

Michael Lanyard ("Lone Wolf") and his faithful butler Jamison arrive in Alexandria, where Lanyard has been summoned by Sir Roger Wembley, head of Britain's local wartime intelligence. After checking in with his friend, nightclub owner and freelance seller of information Johnny Booth, Lanyard and Jamison are kidnapped and taken to see "Mr. X," a German who wants the Lone Wolf to steal for his government. With Jamison's life threatened, Lanyard agrees, and he and Jamison are released. After they're escorted out, Mr. X reveals to his assistant Fritz that Lanyard is really being used only as a diversion.

At the hotel, Jamison is pleasantly surprised to find that his son, Donald, an American Navy officer, and his fiancée, Valerie King, have arrived. Valerie claims to be working as a war correspondent, but Lanyard and Booth are both suspicious of her, especially when small squares of lace fall out of her purse.

Later that evening, one of Booth's informants, Cezanne, shows up with an important clue he's obtained: A secret message encoded on a piece of cloth reveals that the Axis forces are in Alexandria to attempt to steal the Allies' "S Plan," a chart which shows the layout of mines in the Suez Canal. Later, as Cezanne leaves Booth's nightclub, he's followed and murdered by another operative, Rembrandt.

In the hotel that night, Valerie has a secret meeting with Mr. X, and reveals that she's actually working for him. Her assignment was to seduce Donald so that she could learn the layout of the local U.S. Admiralty office and break in to steal the S Plan. Meanwhile, Booth remembers that he's seen Valerie before, with a French officer. He and Lanyard realize Valerie is a spy.

Lanyard hires another informant, Whistler, to follow Valerie. Whistler returns with information that her contact is in a laundry, and a stolen message details Valerie's mission to steal the S Plan and then escape on a sub.

Before they can act, Mr. X reappears and tells Lanyard that his mission is to steal a specific Navy file tonight; they've taken Jamison, and if Lanyard refuses, Jamison will be killed. Lanyard steals the file, and Jamison is returned to him, but they're both captured by Sir Roger's men. Sir Roger tells them that the S Plan has been stolen from the Admiralty, and Lanyard realizes he was used as a diversion. Sir Roger tries to arrest him, but Lanyard escapes in a car with Jamison.

After abandoning the car in a back alley of Alexandria, Lanyard and Jamison stumble across Donald, just returning to consciousness after being knocked out. They find the laundry that Whistler mentioned following Valerie to, and discover that it's the secret headquarters of Mr. X. They break in and find out the S Plan chart has been destroyed and transferred to the crystal in Valerie's watch. When Valerie calls, they trick her into revealing her location. However, before they can reach her, Rembrandt appears, kills Valerie, and takes the watch.

Lanyard, Donald, Jamison and Booth reach Valerie's hotel, and they find clues that lead them to realize she was murdered by Rembrandt, who has been spotted escaping in a car with Mr. X. Booth comes up with a way for Lanyard to stop the Germans before they can reach their submarine: He has access to an old biplane equipped with guns. Lanyard takes the plane, tracks down the getaway car in the countryside, and manages to shoot it off the road.

With the Germans foiled and the watch containing the S Plan retrieved, Jamison and Lanyard are looking forward to returning home — until Sir Roger summons them for a new adventure.

Commentary

Passport to Suez is an efficient little thriller that owes as much to *Casablanca* as it does to any of the previous entries in the "Lone Wolf" series. Like Michael Curtiz's 1942 classic, *Pass-*

One-sheet poster for *Passport to Suez* (1943).

The deceitful Valerie (Ann Savage) confronts Karl (Gavin Muir) in *Passport to Suez*.

port to Suez* is a spy thriller set against an exotic Mediterranean background; however, where the leads in one are enacting a doomed romance, the stars of the other are caught in a more platonic web. At the heart of *Suez* is the playful and devoted relationship between Michael Lanyard (the Lone Wolf) and his butler Jamison. Lanyard repeatedly risks both reputation and life in the rescue of his friend; and, in fact, even the introduction of the tempting spy Valerie King fails to interest Lanyard much beyond her involvement in the mystery he must pursue to keep Jamison safe.

That the mystery is frequently convoluted and other times convenient doesn't help. A bewildering array of characters come and go throughout the story; one character turns up dead before he's even been introduced. A trio of stool pigeons (Cezanne, Rembrandt, Whistler) inexplicably bear the names of famed artists, and start knocking each other off. Arranged meetings never happen; secret passages are set up and never used; informants crash through ceilings for no apparent reason; and important clues are stumbled upon without real effort being put into their discovery. Perhaps strangest of all — in terms of the film's screenplay, that is— is the use of the protagonist, who never demonstrates the skills that have earned him the status of a legendary thief (his one robbery consists almost entirely of casually plucking a file from a cabinet).

However, the pleasures of a B-film like *Passport to Suez* are seldom to be found in the screenplay, but rather in the execution. Andre De Toth's direction is frequently moody and suspenseful. Working with Columbia veteran cameraman L. W. O'Connell, he creates frames full of shadows and high contrast, employing more moving camera than is usual in lesser-budgeted films of the period, and also making evocative use of tight close-ups. De Toth's pacing is uneven — he spends too much time on dialogue exchanges with the strange informants Cezanne and Whistler — but he handles the action scenes with verve. Despite the obvious monetary limitations, he makes the film's climax — as Lanyard, flying an old biplane, attempts to shoot the villains' fleeing vehicle off the road — exciting both visually and narratively.

De Toth's work is largely matched by the solid cast. Although Warren William is obviously no longer a spry Lone Wolf here, he brings his usual bearing and elegance to the performance; and his natural aloofness is balanced by the comic relief of Eric Blore's Jamison. Ann Savage, as the not-so-innocent Valerie, makes for a smart, edgy villainess; she lets us feel the tension as the trap closes in around her, even while she struggles to retain some control. It's a pity that her scenes with Lanyard are limited to brief dialogue exchanges; her best moments are with her boss, Karl, when he confronts her in her hotel room. Her sudden transformation from ambitious but sweet fiancée to experienced professional seductress is superb and genuinely surprising.

The film is also aided by an effective production design (which suggests the Mediterranean locale with a few simple touches, like ornaments and archways) and an effective use of music.

All in all, *Passport to Suez* is a tidy and enjoyable suspense picture which displays the best attributes of the 1940s studio B pictures.

BEHIND THE SCENES

Passport to Suez was the first American film directed by Andre De Toth, who would go on to direct the 3-D horror classic *House of Wax* (1953) and receive an Academy Award nomination for writing the 1950 Western *The Gunfighter*. De Toth had started making films in his native Hungary in 1939, and after trav-

Valerie (Ann Savage) and the Lone Wolf (Warren William) in *Passport to Suez*.

eling through Europe he fled the continent in 1940 and came to America, where he found a fan in Columbia's Harry Cohn. Cohn had seen and liked one of De Toth's pictures, and Columbia hired De Toth, but he made only two movies for them (the second was a well-regarded 1944 Nazi war drama called *None Shall Escape*).

De Toth had no love for *Passport to Suez*; he thought the script "stank" and called the finished film "Goddamned shit." He was given a seven-day shooting schedule, but by the third day he was already three days behind schedule. When Cohn called him into the office, De Toth requested that the line "to the best of my ability" be removed from his contract. Cohn refused, and De Toth delivered the film seven days late. Actor Sheldon Leonard later recalled that De Toth's camera was in "constant motion, anticipating a technique that did not become general until decades later." De Toth also used a crane during the shoot, something virtually unheard-of in 1940s B-filmmaking.

Passport to Suez was one of two films screened at a 2009 American Cinematheque tribute to Ann's life and career (the other film was Guy Maddin's *My Winnipeg*).

Alternate titles for the film were *A Night of Adventure*, *The Clock Strikes Twelve*, and *The Clock Struck Twelve*.

Blondie: Footlight Glamour

(Columbia) Release Date: September 30, 1943

Screenplay by: Karen DeWolf and Connie Lee, based on the comic strip characters created by Chic Young
Cinematography by: Philip Tannura
Film Editing by: Richard Fantl
Art Direction by: Lionel Banks and Edward C. Jewell
Set Decoration by: Robert Priestley
Music Supervisor: M. W. Stoloff
Produced and Directed by: Frank Strayer
Cast: Penny Singleton (Blondie Bumstead); Arthur Lake (Dagwood Bumstead); Larry Simms (Alexander Bumstead); Ann Savage (Vickie Wheeler); Jonathan Hale (J. C. Dithers); Irving Bacon (Mr. Crum); Marjorie Ann Mutchie (Cookie Bumstead); Danny Mummert (Alvin Fuddle); Thurston Hall (Randy Wheeler); Daisy (herself)

Synopsis

Dagwood Bumstead's boss, Mr. Dithers, is upset when he finds out that plans for a new defense plant have been scuttled; he's built 50 homes near the location of the proposed plant, and now he can't sell them. He sees an alternative, though, when his old friend Randy Wheeler shows up to tell Dithers that he's concerned about his daughter, Vickie, who wants to act and is now engaged to a money-grubbing director. Dithers knows that Wheeler builds tool plants, so he comes up with a deal: He'll get the Bumsteads to babysit Vickie if Wheeler will consider building a plant near Dithers' houses. Wheeler tentatively agrees, and Dithers immediately makes plans for a trip to the plant location; he also makes arrangements for Dagwood to pick up Vickie at the train station.

Dagwood arrives at the station, mistakenly expecting a small girl, but soon discovers that Vickie is a grown-up — and a very attractive one. Dagwood's wife Blondie at first blows her stack when she sees the lovely woman who'll be staying in her home for several weeks, but Vickie soon wins her over with a proposal to cast Blondie in a play. Vickie has written "Mad Moonlight," and convinced Mr. Dithers' wife to finance and appear in the play; she also puts Dagwood in the play, and brings in her boyfriend Jerry Grant to direct.

As he's completing the business trip with Wheeler, Dithers finds out about the play, and, recognizing that the deal could be called off if Wheeler finds out his daughter is acting again, he struggles with increasingly elaborate ruses to distract and delay Wheeler.

Opening night of "Mad Moonlight" arrives, and everything that can go wrong does: Cues are missed, lines are forgotten, and Dagwood falls through a trapdoor at the end of the first scene.

Meanwhile, Wheeler finds out about the play, and as he races to the theater he tells Dithers their deal is off.

The players attempt to carry on with the

play, but finally Vickie is so humiliated onstage that she walks off and agrees to marry Jerry if they can leave immediately. Blondie and Dagwood go after them—just as Wheeler and Dithers arrive at the theater and wind up onstage before the howling audience.

Dagwood and Blondie reach home just as Vickie is packing, but she overhears Jerry telling Dagwood that he's only marrying her for her money, and she calls off the wedding. Dithers and Wheeler show up, and Vickie tells her delighted father that she's giving up acting forever—and that the tool plant deal is back on.

COMMENTARY

The "Blondie" series was a lucrative one for Columbia, and this entry makes it easy to see why. Despite considerable mugging and over-the-top slapstick, *Footlight Glamour* is often genuinely funny and always entertaining.

This was the 13th entry in the series; so by this time actors Penny Singleton and Arthur Lake, as Blondie and Dagwood, were firmly in command of their characters—she is chipper and collected in the face of any catastrophe, he is bumbling and frantic by comparison. However, the film is almost stolen by four-year-old Marjorie Ann Mutchie, who possesses astonishing comic timing for a toddler. She gets the film's best line (and delivers it exquisitely) when she eyes Vickie as Dagwood first shows up with her and asks Blondie, "Is she daddy's bonus?"

Ann Savage is a delight as well, more than holding her own against both the more experienced adults and the unnaturally gifted child. She perfectly captures the theatricality of a

Ann Savage and scene-stealer Marjorie Ann Mutchie in a staged photo from *Blondie: Footlight Glamour.*

stage actress who's not nearly as talented as the actress playing her; when she strides boldly onstage during the play, completely unaware that the Bumsteads' dog is seated on her gown's train, her gestures and resulting expression are the punchline to the film's funniest visual gag.

Also noteworthy is the production design of Lionel Banks—both the sets and costumes capture the exaggerated simplicity of a comic strip, and are capable of producing a few smiles on their own.

Although some of the humor is certainly dated (see, for example, a lengthy opening sequence regarding wartime food rationing), *Blondie: Footlight Glamour* still contains enough chuckles to make it worth a viewing—not to mention a terrific comic performance from Ann Savage.

BEHIND THE SCENES

Created by Murat Bernard "Chic" Young, the *Blondie* comic strip first saw print on September 8, 1930, and has been running ever since; *Blondie* still appears in over 2,000 newspapers. The strip, which centers on the four members of the Bumstead family (and their dog Daisy), has spawned films, radio and television series, and even the "Dagwood" sandwich.

Columbia produced 28 films in the "Blondie" series, beginning with *Blondie* in 1938 and concluding with 1950's *Beware of Blondie*. All starred Penny Singleton as Blondie and Arthur Lake as Dagwood.

Director Frank Strayer directed all previous films in the series, but *Footlight Glamour* marked the end of his "Blondie" involvement. He directed nine more features and one television show before leaving the industry in 1951.

Actor Thurston Hall also appeared with Ann in *One Dangerous Night* (1943) and *Ever Since Venus* (1944).

Writers Karen DeWolf and Connie Lee worked on many of the "Blondie" films; Lee also wrote additional dialogue for *Ever Since Venus*.

Ann's hair was dyed red for *Footlight Glamour*, since they didn't want her natural blonde to conflict with Penny Singleton's. It was (appropriately) re-dyed for her next film, *Dangerous Blondes* (1943).

Footlight Glamour was double-billed with the Columbia wartime drama *Destroyer* (somewhat ironically, since *Destroyer* originally listed Ann in the cast, although she does not appear in the film).

Dangerous Blondes

(Columbia) Release Date: September 23, 1943

Screenplay by: Richard Flournoy and Jack Henley; based on a story by Kelley Roos
Cinematography by: Philip Tannura
Film Editing by: Jerome Thoms
Art Direction by: Lionel Banks and Walter Holscher
Set Decoration by: Joseph Kish
Musical Director: M. W. Stoloff
Produced by: Samuel Bischoff
Directed by: Leigh Jason
Cast: Allyn Joslyn (Barry Craig); Evelyn Keyes (Jane Craig); Edmund Lowe (Ralph McCormick); John Hubbard (Kirk Fenley); Anita Louise (Julie Taylor); Frank Craven (Inspector Clinton); Michael Duane (Harry Duerr); Ann Savage (Erika McCormick); William Demarest (Detective Gatling): Hobart Cavanaugh (Pop); Frank Sully (Detective Henderson); Robert Stanford (Jim Snyder); Lynn Merrick (May Ralston)

SYNOPSIS

Barry Craig is a crime fiction writer who believes he can outsmart real detectives—which he can, thanks largely to the help of his talented wife Jane. He gets his chance one night when Jane's friend Julie Taylor suddenly appears, begging the Craigs to help her—she believes the photography studio where she works is being stalked by a murderer. The Craigs arrive at the studio and meet the sophisticated owner, Ralph McCormick, and his assistants, shady Harry Durer and sunny Kirk Fenley. The McCormick studio is in the midst of photographing celebrated socialite Isabelle Fleming; but, unfortunately, Mrs. Fleming is murdered during the session. As the suspects wait for Inspector Clinton and the police to arrive, the Craigs begin interviewing them and soon discover some suspicious facts: McCormick's wife is set to inherit the Fleming fortune; a woman who left the session in tears was the first wife of Isabelle's late husband; and Julie is in love with McCormick.

The police soon arrive and call in two more suspects: Erika McCormick, Ralph's glamorous wife; and Roland X. Smith, Isabelle's nervous chauffeur. Not long after Inspector Clinton begins interrogations, the first Mrs. Fleming is found dead in her home from an overdose of pills. Clinton promptly declares the case a murder/suicide and closes it.

The Craigs aren't convinced, however, and continue their investigation. They break into the McCormick studio after hours, but their attempt at uncovering more clues is thwarted when they have to flee a night watchman. Barry confronts Inspector Clinton with his theory and, after he leaves Clinton, confesses to Detective Gatling that he knows the first Mrs. Fleming was not the murderer.

On his way out of the police station, Barry is accosted by the press and tells them he believes the real murderer is still at large. The next day Barry's statements make headlines, but his glee is diminished when he's threatened by two thugs who order him to stay away from the press.

Goaded by the headlines, Roland X. Smith comes to see the Craigs and tells them that Lee Kenyon, a model who was present during the photo session, recently came to the Fleming house and was paid $10,000. The Craigs go to talk to Kenyon, who tells them that Mrs. Fleming offered him $10,000 to stay away from Erika, who is in love with a man who is not her husband — but it's not him. Kenyon tells them that Harry Durer is a childhood friend of Erika's, and he's probably Erika's secret lover.

That night at home, the Craigs receive a call from Erika McCormick, who says she can name the killer; but before she can finish, the line goes dead. The Craigs arrive at the McCormick home only to discover that Erika is now the latest victim of the killer, and Ralph has been taken into custody.

The next day the Craigs receive a letter from Julie asking them to drop the case. They realize that a phone call mentioned in the letter gives McCormick an alibi. They interview McCormick in jail, and he reveals that Erika had just asked for a divorce.

Suspecting Durer, the Craigs return to the studio and attempt to trick him into confessing — but the one who ends up confessing is Kirk Fenley, who was actually the one having an affair with Erika. He pulls a gun on Barry but doesn't know Inspector Clinton is hiding nearby with the police. Fenley is gunned down, and Barry Craig is now terrified of gunshots — a phobia which Clinton gleefully exploits by smashing a vase behind Barry as he walks out.

Edmund Lowe and Ann Savage play husband and wife in 1943's *Dangerous Blondes*.

Commentary

Although it would be easy to dismiss *Dangerous Blondes* as Columbia's attempt at a low-budget cash-in on MGM's very successful series of *Thin Man* movies, that would be a disservice to a film that is, in its own right, a clever and well-crafted comic whodunit. If Allyn Joslyn and Evelyn Keyes can't quite match the sparkling wit and chemistry of William Powell and Myrna Loy, they come close enough to lift *Dangerous Blondes* above similar B-movie fare of the time. Add to that Keyes' own considerable sex appeal and a fine supporting cast, and *Blondes* deserves its own small space in movie history.

Dangerous Blondes does suffer from some of the same script problems that frequently plagued the 1940s B mysteries—subplots that go nowhere (just who are those two thugs who threaten our heroes twice?), the final revelation of a murderer who has barely been a suspect before—but for the most part the film overcomes those problems with a fast pace, snappy direction and skilled performers. If Joslyn is occasionally slightly stiff on his own, his interplay with Keyes is sweet, funny and sometimes even genuinely sexy. The film's low budget occasionally shows at the seams (the sets have that slightly cobbled-together-from-other-sets look), but the supporting cast is worth the price of admission (or rental) alone: In addition to Ann Savage, there's Edmund Lowe, William Demarest, Frank Sully, John Abbott, and—most amazing of all—Dwight Frye (playing one of those inexplicable thugs).

Ann Savage exudes decadent glamour in her small part as Lowe's estranged wife, and it's not hard to see why the plot centers in part on her love affairs. But *Dangerous Blondes* re-

Ralph McCormick (Edmund Lowe, second from left) comforts his wife Erika (Ann Savage) in *Dangerous Blondes*.

ally belongs to Evelyn Keyes, and it's a pleasure to see another of Hollywood's underrated actresses shine in a delightful little comic mystery.

BEHIND THE SCENES

Although Evelyn Keyes and Ann Savage would later be accorded similar status as two of the leading film noir actresses, *Dangerous Blondes* is the only movie they ever made together. Keyes is the female star of *Dangerous Blondes*, and in her autobiography, *Scarlett O'Hara's Younger Sister*, she mentions that she liked *Dangerous Blondes* (which she refers to as a "good comedy"). Evidently, so did Columbia, since Keyes and her *Blondes* co-star Allyn Joslyn were re-teamed in a similar film a year later, *Strange Affair* (they also appeared together in 1947's *Thrill of Brazil*).

Ann would appear with Edmund Lowe again 8 years later in the television series *Front Page Detective*.

Character actor Frank Sully (who appears here as Detective Henderson) made four films with Ann, all in 1943: *One Dangerous Night, The More the Merrier, Two Señoritas from Chicago* and *Dangerous Blondes*. Sully appeared in over 150 films and dozens of television shows. His last movie was 1968's *Funny Girl*, in which he had a small uncredited role as a bartender.

Dangerous Blondes marks the final film appearance of character actor Dwight Frye, who appeared in both the classic 1931 horror films *Dracula* (as Renfield) and *Frankenstein* (as Fritz, the hunchbacked assistant). Frye plays one of the two thugs who accosts the Craigs, and has no lines. He died from a heart attack not long after finishing *Dangerous Blondes*. He was 44.

Alternate titles for *Dangerous Blondes* were *Reckless Lady, Restless Lady*, and *The Case of the Dangerous Blondes*.

Klondike Kate

(Columbia) Release Date: December 16, 1943

Screenplay by: Houston Branch and M. Coates Webster; based on the story "The Life of Kate Rockwell Matson" by William A. Pierce

Director of Photography: John Stumar
Musical Director: M. W. Stoloff
Choreographer: Mary Carroll
Film Editor: Mel Thorsen
Art Director: Lionel Banks
Set Decorator: Louis Diage
Produced by: Irving Briskin
Directed by: William Castle
Cast: Ann Savage (Kathleen O'Day); Tom Neal (Jefferson Braddock); Glenda Farrell (Molly); Constance Worth (Lita); Sheldon Leonard (Sometime Smith); Lester Allen (Duster Dan); George Cleveland (Judge Horace Crawford)

SYNOPSIS

When a trainload of dance hall girls arrives in the Yukon gold rush town of Totem Pole in 1897, the entire male population turns out to greet them, including Jefferson Braddock, proprietor of the Great Northern Lights Hotel and Dance Hall. The girls, led by Molly, expect to be met by Jeff's rival Sometime Smith; but when Braddock offers to double their pay, they're happy to be "hijacked" by the handsome young man.

One woman steps off the train and is dismayed when she's immediately manhandled by a desperate miner. After she fights the man off, Braddock approaches her, kisses her, and receives a slap — which he takes with a grin. As they prepare to leave the train depot, Molly tells Jeff that the young lady isn't one of her girls, but is, in fact, "a good kid."

The young lady finds the town's lone attorney, Judge Horace Crawford, and introduces herself as Kathleen O'Day. She tells the judge that her father Michael bought property in the area and left Kate the deed before he passed on. The property turns out to be the Great Northern Lights itself, now owned by Jefferson Braddock. When Kate exclaims that her father's partner, Tom Wilkins, was supposed to be in charge of the hotel, Crawford tells her that Wilkins was "strung up" a while back.

Crawford takes Kate to the Great Northern Lights, where Molly and her girls are already entertaining the miners with vaudeville and dance. Braddock claims to have purchased the property from Wilkins, and Kate demands a trial. Judge Crawford, who is obviously working with Braddock, sets a trial for the following day. Meanwhile, Braddock, who is attracted to Kate, woos her with dinner and his easy control over the rough-and-tumble business of the dance hall and casino.

Their dinner is interrupted by the arrival of Sometime Smith, who is angry over the way Jeff hijacked his girls. When Sometime pulls a gun on him, Jeff manages to wrestle the sidearm away and orders Sometime out.

Returning his attention to Kate, Jeff offers her a room in the hotel, with the obvious intention of seducing her. But she manages to outmaneuver him, and the frustrated Jeff winds up sharing a room with his sidekick Duster.

The next day the trial is held in the saloon, and Kate soon realizes it's a complete farce — the witness stand is a chair set atop a table, Crawford handpicks the jury, and Jeff buys all of the jurors drinks. Furious, Kate takes Braddock's gun and turns it on Crawford, demanding the return of a retainer fee she's already paid; then she finds Molly and vows to get even with Jeff.

The next day Kate visits Jeff in an enticing black gown and asks for a singing job. He agrees to give her a shot, and that night she performs to great acclaim. Jeff immediately offers her a dinner and a full job, even though his former girlfriend and lead performer, Lita, tries to warn Kate off, telling her that Jeff is not "the marrying kind." Kate is not deterred.

Later on, Kate and Braddock go for a walk, and Kate flirts with Braddock outrageously. But when he leans in for a kiss, she feigns sudden fatigue and retires to Molly's room, where the two women share a laugh over Kate's scheming.

The next day Sometime Smith shows up in the dance hall and talks to Lita, who has now been reduced to working as a cashier. Later she visits Sometime, who tells her he wants to take over the Great Northern Lights. He offers Lita a partnership if she'll plant a crooked deck of cards at the casino. She agrees.

That night Sometime appears at the casino and challenges Jeff to a card game, offering $10,000 in gold against the Great Northern Lights. Jeff accepts, even when Sometime suggests that Lita pick the card deck. As Kate watches, the two men each prepare to draw a high card. After Jeff loses the second draw, he realizes the deck is rigged; but it's too late — Sometime now claims ownership of the Great Northern Lights. Jeff challenges him to a gunfight, but is stopped when Kate makes a passionate speech in favor of law, suggesting that any winner of a gunfight should be subjected to hanging. Later on, Jeff tells Kate that he's angry, but he softens when she tells him she didn't want to see him killed, and kisses him.

Lita visits Sometime and says she's leaving because she's afraid that Jeff knows she was behind the marked deck. She demands $10,000 from Sometime, who tries to kill her, but she shoots him first.

When Sometime is found dead, a lynch mob forms and comes for Jeff. Kate and Judge Crawford manage to talk the mob down while Duster rustles up an equally large gang ready to defend Jeff. The two sides engage in a climactic brawl, and the hotel catches fire during the fight, burning to the ground.

As Jeff and Kate stand over the ruins later on, Kate receives a letter from Juno certifying her as the legal owner of the Great Northern Lights. She and Jeff decide to get a new place together, and they embrace.

COMMENTARY

Klondike Kate was William Castle's second film as a director, and was made fifteen years before Castle would find success as the horror schlockmeister behind the gimmicky hits *House on Haunted Hill* (1959), *The Tingler* (1959) and *13 Ghosts* (1960). *Klondike Kate*, bereft of gimmicks, shows Castle as a workmanlike director who could stretch a budget to offer up a reasonable recreation of a vanished period, but who possessed little sense of style or control of his material.

The biggest problem with the film is that the promise offered up by the title — that the story will revolve around a spunky, pioneering female lead — is revealed to be a cheat in the third act, which focuses on the male protagonist's effort to hang on to his dance hall,

Showdown in *Klondike Kate*: villain Sometime Smith (Sheldon Leonard, ironically in white hat) takes the casino from Jefferson Braddock (Tom Neal, with gun) while Kate looks on (Ann Savage, right).

reducing the eponymous Kate to little more than a minor supporting character.

That's particularly a pity because Ann Savage as Kate is very good in the first two-thirds of the film. When she first arrives in Totem Pole, she seems slightly naïve and perplexed; but by the time she's realized that Braddock and the Judge are intent on rooking her out of her property, she's transformed into an outraged woman determined to win back what's rightfully hers. The script throughout sets up a playful battle of the sexes between Kate and Jeff, but offers little payoff. In one scene, for example, Kate asks Jeff to teach her the card game faro, and we expect to see Kate try to scam her opponent in a game — but that scenario goes instead to the male antagonist, the curiously named Sometime Smith. During the climactic brawl, there's not so much as a shot of Kate smacking a bottle over a head or two; she simply vanishes, creating a black hole that sucks the film into oblivion.

Savage also occasionally seems to play against the material here, although that works to her advantage, making the film more interesting than it would have been had she played it all straight. In one scene, for example, in which Jeff Braddock's former girlfriend Lita tells Kate that he's not interested in marriage, Kate answers that he might be with the right woman. The scene as written seemed to be a lovelorn confession, but Savage plays it with a knowing smile that suggests she's willing to marry the enemy if it will return her property to her. Likewise, when she asks him to teach her faro, there's no question that her motives are anything but friendly.

This was the first pairing of Ann Savage and her *Detour* co-star Tom Neal, and Neal is slightly uneven playing a role that, in a bigger-

Legendary wrestler and B-movie actor Tor Johnson (right) gives Ann a hand up on the set of *Klondike Kate*.

budgeted film, would have gone to Clark Gable. Where Gable could offer up a knowing grin with considerable natural aplomb, Neal occasionally looks more like a lecher than a lead. Still, he does have considerable charisma with Ann, and represents a solid male presence playing opposite her.

The recreation of the Yukon mining town and late 19th-century vaudeville is quite good overall, although again Castle occasionally seems to be asleep at the wheel. The musical production numbers lapse in and out of authenticity, for instance (Kate's solo song is particularly egregious, a wildly anachronistic 1940s ballad complete with full orchestration, while the onscreen musical accompaniment consists entirely of one pianist). And at one point every girl in the chorus line is inexplicably revealed to be holding a live poodle. The strangest scene in the film is one in which Kate and Jeff go for a midnight walk—along narrow wooden planks perched precariously over what seem to be open sewers filled with scum-laden water. Castle and his screenwriters seem to like this curious and inappropriate bit so much that they even have our hapless couple enact the same walk *twice*.

As a director, Castle was clearly better suited to films employing "Emergo" and "Percepto."

Behind the Scenes

Although the name "Klondike Kate" was popularly applied to nearly any woman whose name was Kathleen and who found herself in the Yukon during the Gold Rush, there was one definitive Klondike Kate who dubbed herself "Queen of the Yukon" and who was involved with the making of the film. She was Kathleen "Kitty" Rockwell Matson, a red-haired beauty who was a popular performer in Dawson City, Canada, for several years during the Gold Rush. She was born in 1876 in Junction City, Kansas; but after her parents divorced, Kate and her mother moved to Spokane, Washington, where Kate's mother soon married a well-to-do local attorney named Frank Bettis. Kate was surrounded by luxury for most of her childhood, and when she matured into a lovely and flirtatious teen, she was packed off to private boarding schools. After her mother and Bettis broke up, the youthful free spirit was placed briefly in a convent in Valparaiso, Chile, where she learned to sneak out at night and soon collected seven diamond engagement rings. When her mother learned of Kitty's latest entanglements, she sent for her impulsive daughter, and Kitty soon found herself in Manhattan. With her mother unable to make a decent living for the both of them, Kitty took a job as a chorus girl and fell in love with the stage. Promised a job in Spokane, she jumped at the chance to return to her childhood town; but upon arriving, she discovered that she'd actually been contracted as a dance-hall girl and was expected to sell drinks to her customers as well.

When the Klondike Gold Rush hit in 1896, Kitty saw the opportunity to mine her own kind of gold, and she found a place in the Savoy Theatrical Company in Dawson, where she soon discovered she could earn $500 a night — often in gold nuggets thrown onstage during her performances (she probably also engaged in some form of prostitution). Around the turn of the century she met Alexander Pantages, a handsome Greek immigrant and new arrival in Dawson, and fell in love instantly. They became business partners and eventually lived together; Kate always claimed that Pantages promised to marry her, but he left her when the Gold Rush ended. Kate sued him for breach of promise to marry, claiming he'd used her money to open his theater in Seattle, and they eventually settled out of court. Pantages went on to become the mogul behind the Pantages theater circuit (the Pantages theater in Hollywood, which operates to this day, was the last venue built for Alexander Pantages).

By 1943 Kate was living in Bend, Oregon, making public appearances at pageants, parades, and grand openings, and taking in boarders. When Columbia announced a motion picture based on her life, Kate came to Hollywood, where she spoke with *Klondike Kate*'s screenwriters and served as technical advisor. She enchanted columnist Louella Parsons and radio personality Bob Burns, and taught Ann Savage, Jinx Falkenburg and Evelyn Keyes to "roll their own." However, she argued with the producers over the depiction of the girls in the film (she thought their costumes were too revealing, and was disappointed that Ann never wore lit candles in her hair!), and returned to Oregon, disillusioned. When the film was released she told one reporter that it was "entirely fictional."

However, a hand-written letter from Kitty to Ann indicates that Kitty was happy with Ann's performance:

> Ann dear child, Keep your rose colored glasses always and Happiness to the girl I hoped would play this part. Faithfully, "Aunt Kate" Kate Rockwell Matson.

Kitty Rockwell's real life was, in many respects, considerably more interesting than the Klondike Kate portrayed on the screen; but, as Kate herself noted, "I've done so much living they couldn't possibly get it all on the screen in an hour's show."

Kate was also a character in another film shot in 1943 (although it wasn't released until 1946), the Bing Crosby-Bob Hope vehicle *Road to Utopia*. In that movie Kate was portrayed by Hillary Brooke.

Bruce Bennett was originally cast opposite Ann in *Klondike Kate* but was replaced by Tom Neal — partly because Neal had delivered a well-reviewed performance in Columbia's wartime drama *Behind the Rising Sun* (1943).

William Castle also directed Ann's Columbia screen test (in which she was paired with western star Tom Keene).

Klondike Kate premiered at the famed Egyptian Theater in Hollywood as the bottom half of a double bill with the Frank Sinatra-starrer *Higher and Higher*. Ann proudly attended the world premiere at the Egyptian.

What a Woman!

(Columbia) Release Date: December 28, 1943

Screenplay by: Therese Lewis and Barry Trivers; based on a story by Erik Charell

Cinematography by: Joseph Walker

Film Editing by: Al Clark

Art Direction by: Lionel Banks and Van Nest Polglase

Set Decoration by: William Kiernan

Original Music by: John Leipold

Musical Director: M. W. Stoloff

Produced and Directed by: Irving Cummings

Cast: Rosalind Russell (Carol Ainsley); Brian Aherne (Henry Pepper); Willard Parker (Professor Michael Cobb); Alan Dinehart (Pat O'Shea); Edward Fielding (Sen. Howard Ainsley); Ann Savage (Miss Drake); Norma Varden (Miss Timmons); Douglas Wood (Dean Alfred B. Shaeffer); Grady Sutton (Mr. Clark); Lilyan Irene (Minna); Frank Dawson (Ben); Hobart Cavanaugh (Mailman)

Synopsis

The editors of *Knickerbocker* magazine want an interview with Anthony Street, the elusive author of the current runaway best-

The real Klondike Kate (Kate Rockwell Matson, right) and her cinematic counterpart Ann Savage on the set of ***Klondike Kate***.

seller *The Whirlwind*; however, everyone knows that "Anthony Street" is a pseudonym, and no one can find the real writer. Given the difficulty of tracking down the author, the *Knickerbocker* editors approach their star reporter, Henry Pepper, with an alternative: He can instead interview Street's agent, Carol Ainsley. Although Pepper expresses disdain for working with women, he takes the assignment.

He finds Ainsley at her office, where she's holding frantic meetings with her staff about finding a leading man for the film version of *Whirlwind*. As Pepper listens in, Carol looks at a bio of "Anthony Street" again and realizes he sounds exactly like the character from *Whirlwind*. She immediately makes arrangements to track down the author, and Pepper — sensing a great story — follows.

Carol travels to bucolic Buxton, Pennsylvania, where she soon learns that "Anthony Street" is actually university professor Michael Cobb. When Carol spots Cobb, she's initially thrilled, because he does indeed match the physical description of the character perfectly; but when she talks to him about taking the role, he turns her down flat. Pepper continues to tag along, following Carol as she heads to the university, where she manages to play both Cobb and the college's dean until Cobb agrees to come to New York with her.

Upon arriving in New York, Cobb is surprised to find out that he'll be staying in Carol's apartment. She immediately puts him through a battery of photographic sessions, costume fittings and exercises, and finally sets him up with an actress, Miss Drake, to film a screen test. Unfortunately, the test is a disaster, and Carol immediately tries to show Cobb the proper way to play a love scene (as Pepper

Carol Ainsley (Rosalind Russell) introduces actress Jane Hughes (Ann Savage) to "the Whirlwind" (Willard Parker) in ***What a Woman!*** (1943).

watches). Her intentions backfire, however, when Cobb falls in love with her.

They re-shoot the screen test, and this time Cobb is fantastic. Arrangements are made to ship Cobb out to Hollywood. Pepper, meanwhile, also reveals his attraction to Carol, but when she fails to return it, he tells her the interview is done. Upset by Pepper's dismissal, Carol assigns her assistant to accompany Cobb to Hollywood while she makes a trip to visit her elderly father for his birthday. However, Cobb surprises her by showing up at her father's mansion, where he promptly proposes to Carol. A few minutes later her assistants—who have all been alerted by Cobb—arrive, as does Pepper, who has been invited to serve as best man. Carol is initially too stunned by Cobb's proposal to reject him, especially since he's already informed the press; however, after Pepper suggests that the marriage is just one more business function for Carol, she loudly informs the entire household that she won't be marrying Cobb. She returns to Pepper, and he happily takes her in his arms.

COMMENT

Columbia may have thought it had a surefire hit on its hands by casting Oscar nominees Rosalind Russell and Brian Aherne in a romantic comedy, but, unfortunately, *What a Woman!* is more misfire than surefire. A romantic comedy requires real sizzle between its leads, and the triangle of Russell/Aherne/Willard Parker simply can't deliver so much as a suggestion of a spark. The script puts its characters through unbelievable transformations and is never quite as witty as it wants to be.

Russell works hard to carry the film, and it's to her credit that it has any movement at all; she's lively and energetic, and is perfectly fine portraying a successful businesswoman. However, she's not matched by Aherne, who is simply too arch and casual in his portrayal of ace reporter Henry Pepper; he literally plays scenes with his feet up and apparently half-asleep. Worst of the leads, though, is Willard Parker, who does have the inherent masculinity his character requires, but is wooden and dull. Of course the script requires his character to transform from quiet, sensitive professor Michael Cobb to showy, loud Anthony Street without so much as a connecting scene; it's doubtful that even a Cary Grant could have pulled this character off.

Irving Cummings' direction is frequently strange, with some shots as poorly chosen as the cast (there are even a few obvious jump cuts in the film, especially at the beginning). The central conceit of *What a Woman!* is amusing—an agent trying to turn an unassuming writer into his vital leading man—but the dialogue rarely, if ever, approaches true wit. The script also flirts with pop psychology (Pepper attempts to analyze Carol throughout their relationship), but the outcome of the analysis—that Carol needs to give up business and find love instead—is likely to feel dated and more than slightly sexist to modern audiences.

Ann Savage provides the film's one genuine laugh, and it comes almost in spite of the material. Playing the young actress brought in to rehearse with the inexperienced (in more ways than one) professor, the frank sexual appraisal she offers on first seeing Cobb suggests what the film *could* have been—funny and sexy. In other words, *What a Woman!* could have been a real romantic comedy instead of a largely misfired dud.

BEHIND THE SCENES

Rosalind Russell had been nominated for an Academy Award (for *My Sister Eileen*) one year earlier; she was later nominated for *Sister Kenny* (1947), *Mourning Becomes Electra* (1948), and *Auntie Mame* (1959). Brian Aherne was nominated for his work in *Juarez* (1939).

Director/producer Cummings started his career as an actor in the silent film era, and by the mid–1920s was working steadily as a director. He directed 80 films; *What a Woman!* was one of his last (he made three more afterward).

According to Ann, Rosalind Russell and Harry Cohn had such a bitter feud that Cohn was barred from his own set. Russell had threatened to walk off the Columbia lot if Cohn walked on her stage. Such working conditions do not help a romantic comedy play lighter than air.

Alternate titles for the film were *Ten Percent Woman* (in the beginning of the film, agents are referred to as "ten-percenters") and *The Beautiful Cheat*.

Two-Man Submarine

(Columbia) Release Date: March 16, 1944

Screenplay by: Griffin Jay and Leslie T. White; based on a story by Bob Williams
Cinematography by: James Van Trees
Film Editing by: Jerome Thoms
Art Direction by: Lionel Banks and Cary Odell
Set Decoration by: George Montgomery
Musical Director: M. W. Stoloff
Produced by: Jack Fier
Directed by: Lew Landers
Cast: Tom Neal (Jerry Evans); Ann Savage (Pat Benson); J. Carrol Naish (Dr. Augustus Hadley); Robert B. Williams (Walt Hedges); Abner Biberman (Gabe Fabian); George Lynn (Norman Fosmer); J. Alex Havier (Fuzzytop)

Synopsis

On an isolated island in the Pacific, a small group of Americans have set up a secret lab to make penicillin, using a mold that grows in the island's caves. The group is led by Jerry Evans, who is looking forward to the arrival of his replacement soon. But Jerry receives a shock when that replacement turns out to be an attractive blonde named Pat Benson. After parachuting onto the island, Pat is introduced to the rest of the team: Walt Hedges is in charge of the preparation of the penicillin; Gabe Fabian is the local overseer who supervises the island's small contingent of natives; and Doc Hadley is the drunken, misanthropic medical man who oversees their health.

That night Walt reveals that three bottles of penicillin are missing from their stores; the Axis powers don't have the formula for penicillin, and part of the team's mission is to keep the formula and the drug safe. When Walt hears a strange noise in the jungle later, he goes to investigate and finds a two-man Japanese submarine anchored just offshore. The following morning Walt is found stabbed to death. The tension among the team escalates when Jerry chases off someone trying to steal the penicillin formula. He burns the formula but tells the team he's committed it to memory.

Fabian gets a few moments alone with Pat and attempts to blackmail her with a cigarette he found near the formula. She plays along, agreeing to join him for dinner later.

Just then a shipwreck survivor, Fosmer, washes ashore. Doc tries to treat him, but he seems to be delirious and incapable of answering questions.

That night Pat overhears the natives report to Fabian that men are landing on the is-

Tom Neal and Ann Savage in *Two-Man Submarine* (1944), their second film together.

land. She goes to warn Jerry, and they discover the two-man submarine anchored just offshore, with a man in the jungle signaling to it. Jerry fights and kills the man in the jungle, then discovers Fabian helping two Japanese soldiers. Jerry and Pat capture Fabian and the Japanese — until Fosmer arrives, having miraculously recovered. He captures Jerry and Pat, and introduces himself as Captain Von Spanger of the German Navy.

Von Spanger proceeds to torture Jerry in an attempt to gain the penicillin formula, but both Pat and Doc Hadley offer up fake formulas to halt the torture. Finally, Jerry escapes into the jungle with a grenade.

The Japanese fleet is about to arrive at the island, and Jerry discovers that they plan on refueling from an underwater tank hidden in a cove. He swims out to the tank and rigs the grenade to explode when the tank is opened. Onshore he encounters Doc, who tells him Von Spanger has taken Pat hostage aboard the submarine. Desperate to save her before the Germans attempt to refuel, Doc and Jerry swim out to the submarine and fight the Germans until they can free Pat. Jerry and Pat leap from the sub to swim ashore while Doc stays behind, sacrificing himself so they can escape. Doc is shot by the Germans just before they attempt to refuel and blow themselves to pieces.

Later on, American forces arrive and congratulate Pat and Jerry on uncovering the Axis plot. Jerry and Pat will remain stationed on the island, but ask the American naval commander to marry them before he leaves.

COMMENTARY

Two-Man Submarine is a minor thriller that's typical of the B pictures churned out during the war years. The short running time (62 minutes) is both a blessing and a curse, since too many plot threads are left wafting in the tropical breeze. What starts off as a Japanese two-man sub anchored just off the unnamed island becomes, by the picture's end, a fully-crewed German U-boat; while protecting the formula for penicillin production essentially vanishes during the climax, as the story suddenly becomes about fuel tanks hidden in the island's cove. At one point Jerry fights and kills a man we've never seen (and who is never mentioned again). And when Fabian attempts to blackmail Pat, she goes along with him — even though she's later revealed to be completely innocent.

As usual for the films of this period, ethnicities are confused (both Germans and Australians have flat American accents) or treated with condescension (the island natives are given names like "Fuzzytop" and reduced to little more than grinning and head-bobbing). The central conceit behind the film — that of an isolated group working in secret to produce penicillin — is promising, but *Two-Man Submarine* can't seem to keep its focus in its headlong rush to the next action scene.

Fortunately, the picture has a capable leading man of action in Tom Neal, who gets to show off more of his physical skills here than in movies like *Detour* or *Klondike Kate*. Neal, in real life a former college boxer whose physique nearly rivaled that of Errol Flynn's, performs virtually the entire last quarter of the movie shirtless, as he swings from rooftops, pummels the bad guys and dives into lagoons. He's an attractive and virile presence; and if nothing else, *Two-Man Submarine* provides a glimpse into the action star that Neal could have been (had he appeared in films with better scripts and not derailed his career with his notorious off-screen displays of temper).

Unfortunately, Ann Savage doesn't get the same opportunities Neal does in *Two-Man Submarine*. Her character is largely reduced to a damsel-in-distress who looks pretty while standing on the sidelines watching the men do all the work. Her performance veers from looking mildly bored to slightly over-the-top displays of emotion, as she struggles to inject some life into her underwritten character. Coming just two films after her lively starring turn in *Klondike Kate*, this cardboard cutout of a role must have been disappointing to Ann.

Two-Man Submarine benefits from the inclusion of J. Carrol Naish in the role of the curmudgeonly Doc Hadley. Naish, a two-time

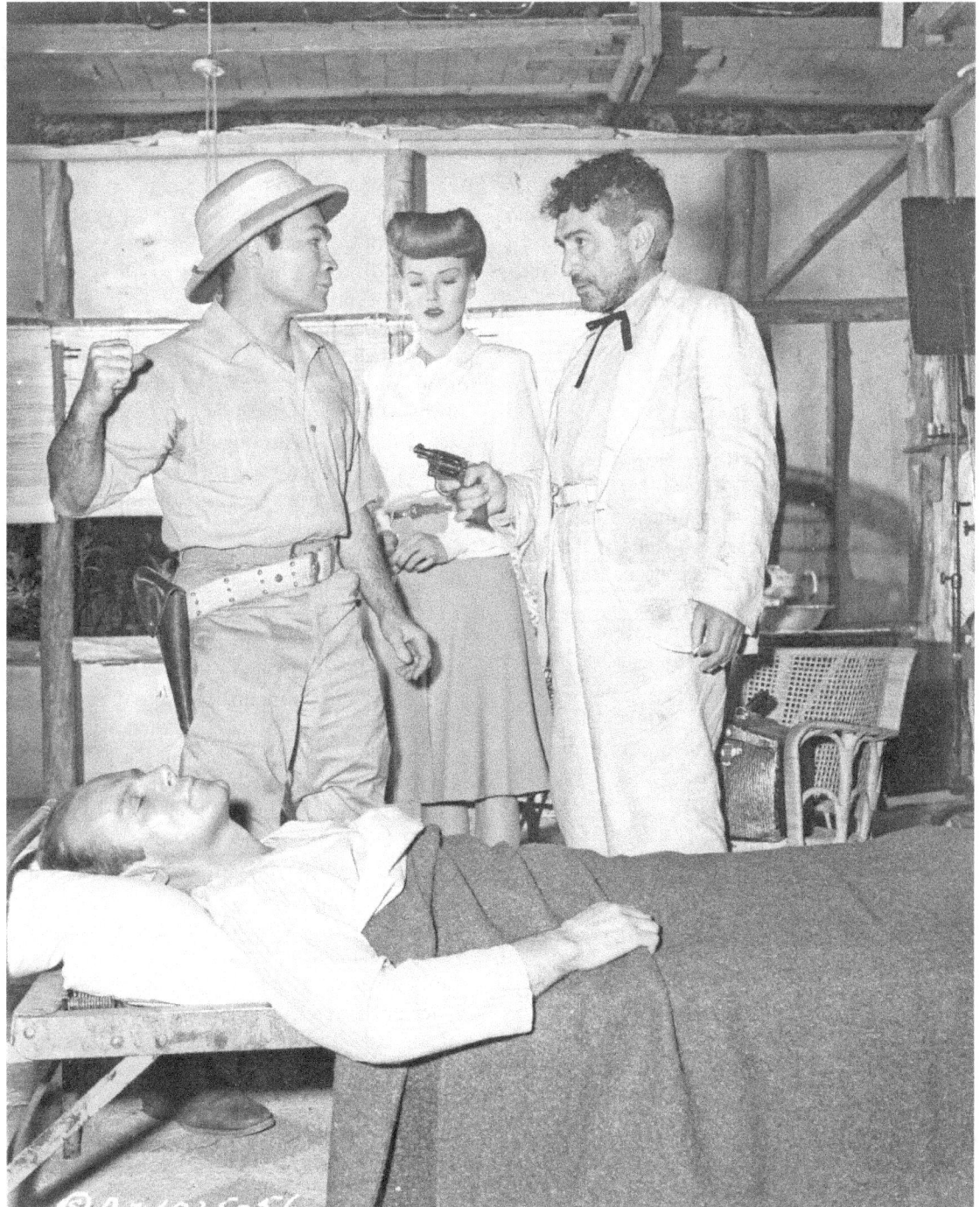

Dr. Hadley (J. Carrol Naish, right) confronts Fabian (Abner Biberman) as Pat (Ann Savage) looks on in *Two-Man Submarine*.

Academy Award nominee who is now also fondly remembered for his work in such horror films as *House of Frankenstein* and *The Monster Maker* (both 1944), is sympathetic and believable as the doctor who drinks too much, prefers the company of animals, and finally sacrifices himself for a young couple.

One element of *Two-Man Submarine* that has earned it a small place of notoriety with modern film buffs is the entire cast's persistent mispronunciation of "penicillin" (they place the accent on the second syllable). Although the drug was originally discovered in 1928, it wasn't used to successfully treat a human patient until 1942, and wasn't mass-produced until 1944. When *Two-Man Submarine* was originally released in early 1944, penicillin was still new enough to cause some confusion in the correct pronunciation of the name.

Behind the Scenes

Two-Man Submarine was the second film Ann would make with veteran director Lew Landers (the other was *After Midnight with Boston Blackie* [1943]). Landers directed well over a hundred films and dozens of early television shows before directing his last feature (*Terrified*) in 1963.

In one interview, Ann noted: "I had to make three retakes during the picture, because I had been taught to pronounce penicillin incorrectly."

The Last Horseman

(Columbia) Release Date: June 22, 1944

Screenplay and Story by: Ed Earl Repp
Cinematography by: George Meehan
Film Editing by: Jerome Thoms
Art Direction by: Lionel Banks
Set Decoration by: Robert Priestley
Produced by: Leon Barsha
Directed by: William Berke
Cast: Russell Hayden (Lucky Rawlins); Dub Taylor (Cannonball); Bob Wills and the Texas Playboys (Bob and the Bar W crew); Ann Savage (Judy Ware)

Synopsis

Lucky Rawlins, his sidekick Cannonball, and Bob and the rest of the Bar W crew are just returning from a cattle drive carrying a $12,000 check for the sale of the steers; the money will help save their boss and his ranch from foreclosure. But when Lucky is tricked into riding off alone, he's robbed of the check, and his boss, Williams, is forced to sign the check. Lucky chases after the bad guys and catches one of them, Slade.

The other two villains make it to town, where they turn the check over to their boss, Watson, who is also the town banker. Watson can now foreclose on the Bar W ranch and sell it to the railroad company; Watson's the only one who knows the railroads will soon be building a station in the town.

In the morning, Lucky hands Slade over to the town sheriff and goes to the bank to find out who cashed the stolen check. Watson, of course, lies and tells Lucky that a stranger cashed the check. Although Lucky is dating the bank's pretty teller, Judy, she's loyal to her employer and won't reveal any more.

When Watson tells Lucky and Mr. Williams that he'll be foreclosing on Wednesday, an elderly bank employee, Saunders, overhears and offers to make a loan to Williams. Lucky decides to round up enough cattle to provide collateral.

Lucky and Cannonball head to the saloon, where Lucky recognizes the other men who robbed him. A bar brawl ensues, and Lucky and Cannonball are knocked out.

Watson, meanwhile, comes up with a plan: Tonight during the town dance his men will break Slade out of jail, while Watson will take care of Saunders.

That night at the dance, Bob Wills and the Texas Playboys perform and are joined by Cannonball on xylophone. As Lucky and Judy dance unawares, Watson steals Williams' pistol and uses it to gun down Saunders. Meanwhile, the rest of the Watson gang successfully help Slade escape from jail.

Although the sheriff arrests Williams for Saunders' murder, he agrees to release the rancher into the custody of Lucky, so he can help round up the cattle they need to sell quickly to buy off the foreclosure.

Lucky finds a buyer for the beef, but when one of Watson's men poses as a state cattle inspector and claims the cattle are infected, the buyer backs out. To retaliate, Lucky goes into town and spreads the word that the real inspector is coming in via stagecoach the next day. When the villains show up to ambush the

Pat (Ann Savage) and Jerry (Tom Neal) continue to mispronounce "penicillin" in *Two-Man Submarine*.

stagecoach, they're unprepared for the counter-attack launched by Lucky and the Bar W hands. They shoot down all but two of Watson's men, who ride back into town and warn the boss to flee. Lucky arrives just in time to stop Watson, and they fight atop the roofs of the town's buildings. Lucky finally knocks Watson out and finds the money that will replace the stolen check.

A short time later the railroad makes a

deal with Williams for a station in town where cattle will be loaded. With no more lengthy cattle drives before him, Lucky looks forward to settling down with Judy.

Commentary

The title *The Last Horseman* may have been an inside joke, because this film marked the end of the cycle of "Lucky" films that Russell Hayden made at Columbia with director William Berke and co-stars Dub Taylor and Bob Wills and the Texas Playboys. By this time the series was definitely showing its age. With essentially the same plot as the earlier *Saddles and Sagebrush* (1943) but even cheaper production values (at one point Cannonball is carrying anachronistic Flintlock pistols, and many of the costumes look distinctly mid–20th century), *The Last Horseman* sometimes feels like a tired horse ready to head out to pasture.

What *The Last Horseman* does have going for it is a whopping six songs performed by Bob Wills and the Texas Playboys. As always, the songs are upbeat and lend parts of the film a wonderful rhythm.

There are several well-staged fights (especially the climactic one between Lucky and Watson), but the stagecoach ambush feels truncated and holds too long on the comedic device of Cannonball in drag as a stagecoach passenger — a device that wears out its welcome pretty quickly. Hayden is still amiable and accomplished, but poor Ann Savage only appears in a few scenes and plays a woman apparently incapable of figuring out that her banker boss is also the town villain.

Despite the considerable enjoyment offered up by the Playboys, *The Last Horseman* is at best a mildly entertaining western, at worst a pale imitation of the earlier and superior *Saddles and Sagebrush*.

Behind the Scenes

The six songs performed by Bob Wills and the Texas Playboys are "O.K. Oklahoma," "The Idaho Plains," "Trouble on the Range," "Ridin' on Down," "Dreamy-Eyed Waltz" and "Camptown Races."

Dub Taylor was a real xylophone player (a skill he acquired as a vaudeville performer), which is why he plays that instrument in the town dance scene.

The Last Horseman's alternate title was *Suicide Range*.

Ever Since Venus

(Columbia) Release Date: September 14, 1944

Screenplay and Original Story by: McElbert Moore and Arthur Dreifuss, with additional dialogue by Connie Lee and Victor McLeod
  Director of Photography: Benjamin Kline
  Musical Director: Mario Silva
  Choreography: Jack Boyle
  Film Editor: Otto Meyer
  Art Director: Lionel Banks and Cary Odell
  Set Decorator: Ross Dowd
  Costume Design: Travilla
  Produced by: Sigmund Neufeld
  Directed by: Arthur Dreifuss
  Cast: Ina Ray Hutton (Herself); Hugh Herbert (P. G. Grimble); Ann Savage (Janet Wilson); Ross Hunter (Bradley Miller); Billy Gilbert (Tiny Lewis); Glenda Farrell (Babs Cartwright); Alan Mowbray (J. Webster Hackett); Marjorie Gateson (Maud Hackett); Thurston Hall (Edgar Pomeroy); Fritz Feld (Pierre)

Synopsis

Cosmetics mogul J. Webster Hackett and his wife are in the audience during a club performance by Ina Ray Hutton and her orchestra. Hackett is quite taken with the lovely bandleader and sends her a personal invitation to perform at his upcoming beauty supplies show. Ina accepts.

Backstage, Ina encounters a frantic songwriter named Tiny Lewis. Tiny gives her a song, which Ina passes off to her arranger, Babs. Babs promises to respond to Tiny in 24 hours.

Tiny returns home and runs into his new neighbor, a lovely young lady named Janet. In his apartment Tiny encounters his two roommates, the handsome young Brad and eccentric artist Pierre, finishing up the creation of a new lipstick they've named "Rosebud." Excited about the product's possibilities, Brad runs off to a drugstore and tries to sell "Rosebud." When both the store owner and a customer act disinterested, Brad impulsively turns to a woman and begins to apply the lipstick. He completes the demonstration by kissing the woman, who happens to be his new neighbor Janet. After she slaps him and runs out, he follows her home, where he tries to apologize by buying her flowers. She finally forgives him, and, after meeting his roommates, tells them she runs a beauty department. She suggests they try to sell "Rosebud" at the upcoming beauty show, and even offers to help them obtain entrance to the show. Janet and Brad also begin a romance.

Brad, Tiny and Pierre go to see Hackett about getting a booth at the beauty show, and he tells them they need a thousand dollars. Unfortunately, they have no money — until Ina Ray selects Tiny's song to perform at the beauty show and awards him one thousand dollars.

They buy their appearance at the show, but are disappointed to arrive and discover that they've been assigned to booth #13, which is so far away from the central floor that it doesn't even appear on the show's map. At first there's no interest in "Rosebud"; however, their fortunes begin to change when Janet chats up Mr. Grimble, a manufacturing tycoon, and Tiny sings with Mr. Pomeroy, the number one buyer of cosmetics. Before long Pomeroy has promised to place his orders this year with Brad's company, and he cancels his standing order with Hackett.

Hackett, furious, cons Pierre into selling

Ever Since Venus (1944): Brad (Ross Hunter), Janet (Ann Savage) and Michel (Fritz Feld) try to sell "Rosebud."

"Rosebud" to his company for $5,000. When Brad, Tiny and Janet find out, they think it's over — until Tiny talks to Babs, who likes Tiny and thinks she can get the contract back. That night she arranges a meeting with the lecherous Hackett and uses her feminine wiles to escape his clutches — with the contract.

The climax of the beauty show arrives, and after a spectacular Ina Ray Hutton number about the history of beauty, "Rosebud" is announced as this year's grand prize winner. When Hackett tries to throw the award out by claiming that the rules state the winning product must have a manufacturer, Grimble steps forward with a deal to be the lipstick's official manufacturer.

The two new couples — Brad and Janet, and Tiny and Babs — celebrate their victory.

Commentary

Ever Since Venus is a delightful lower-budget musical comedy, and demonstrates how a B film could equal any of the A pictures in entertainment value (if not art). Although *Venus* lacks the presence of any of the era's major musical stars, it has a solid center in real-life bandleader Ina Ray Hutton, who provides both visual glamour and several original toe-tapping songs (including "Glamour for Sale" and the opening number, "The Wedding of the Samba and the Boogie"). The cast is a splendid olio of Columbia contract players, and shows off the comedic talents of Hugh Herbert, Billy Gilbert, Fritz Feld and Glenda Farrell to excellent advantage. The simple plot serves the music and comedy well, staying fo-

Janet (Ann Savage) charms Mr. Grimble (Hugh Herbert) in *Ever Since Venus*.

cused on the tried-and-true story of young entrepreneurs struggling against class barriers to achieve success. As Brad and Janet, the young couple at the center of all the frisky events, Ross Hunter and Ann Savage are sweet and likeable without becoming maudlin; they make an attractive pair and do well (lip-synching) in their own musical numbers. Ann's Janet, in fact, is the embodiment of sensible girl-next-door; she's charming without being naïve, hard-working without being hard. It's difficult to believe that, within a year of this performance, she would be terrifying men everywhere as Vera in *Detour* and as the elegant, sensual murderess in *Apology for Murder*.

What *Venus* does have in common with something like *Apology for Murder*, however, is an interesting subtext of feminine empowerment. Aside from Janet's no-nonsense business sense and Ina Ray's confidence in leading an orchestra full of men, there's also Glenda Farrell's Babs, a laconic musical arranger who's not afraid to vamp the wealthy womanizer when necessary but would rather be with the impoverished and overweight (but talented) Tiny. With the exception of the typically handsome young male lead Ross Hunter, the men in *Venus* are all idiosyncratic and impractical, and seem to fail when women aren't around to guide them (in fact, when Janet is awarded nothing more than a job as secretary in Brad's new company at the film's conclusion, we strongly suspect that she'll actually be the one running things). If *Venus* marked one of Ann Savage's only performances in the typical ingénue role, at least the film itself offers something beyond the usual boy-meets-girl scenario.

The film also integrates comedy, music, drama and even some light fantasy well. Humorous bits involving Fritz Feld's manic artist Pierre painting Billy Gilbert's Tiny in various strange outfits are kept short and fun, and there's even a nod to screwball comedies in the frantic pace of the scene wherein Babs essentially seduces J. Webster Hackett to snag the contract he scammed out of Pierre. Although the film avoids out-and-out fantasy, it does offer up some whimsical historical recreations in the grand finale when Ina Ray sings a number ("Glamour for Sale") that leads us through a history of beauty, including cavewomen, Cleopatra, and Napoleon's Josephine.

Although obviously made on a small budget, *Venus* shines in all the technical areas as well, with simple but effective photography, sets and costumes.

Behind the Scenes

Ever Since Venus was not actually produced by Columbia, but was one of four productions that Columbia acquired from Darmour, Inc. in 1944.

Ever Since Venus is chiefly known now as the only major film appearance of Ina Ray Hutton, the Big Band era's only female bandleader (dubbed the "Blonde Bombshell of Rhythm"). Hutton was also an attractive vocalist and tap-dancer who led an all-female band, the Melodears, from 1934 to 1939; her all-male orchestra was disbanded in 1946. Later she founded a new all-female band, which she led from 1951 to 1956.

Ever Since Venus boasts an interesting cast. Ross Hunter's acting career was brief, but he went on to become an Academy Award–nominated producer whose films included *Imitation of Life* (1959), *Pillow Talk* (1959), *Flower Drum Song* (1961) and *Airport* (1970). Hugh Herbert's trademark nervous mannerisms were credited as the inspiration for the cartoon character Daffy Duck. Billy Gilbert appeared in hundreds of films spread over five decades, from 1929's *The Woman from Hell* to 1962's *Five Weeks in a Balloon*. Alan Mowbray had been involved with the founding of the Screen Actors Guild in 1933 (he had provided funding for the Guild's start). Glenda Farrell had also appeared with Ann in *Klondike Kate*, and they were friends off-screen. And Fritz Feld delighted generations of moviegoers and television fans with his distinctive "pop-pop," made by clapping his hand to his mouth.

Producer Sigmund Neufeld was also involved with PRC, and produced their *Double Indemnity* knock-off *Apology for Murder*, with Ann in the femme fatale lead.

The Unwritten Code

(Columbia) Release Date: October 26, 1944

Screenplay by: Charles Kenyon and Leslie T. White; story by Charles Kenyon and Robert Wilmot
Cinematography by: Burnett Guffey
Film Editing by: Gene Havlick
Art Direction by: Perry Smith
Set Decoration by: Joseph Kish
Musical Director: Mischa Bakaleinikoff
Directed by: Herman Rotsten
Cast: Ann Savage (Mary Lee Norris); Tom Neal (Sgt. Terry Hunter); Roland Varno (Cpl. Karl Richter); Howard Freeman (Mr. Norris); Mary Currier (Mrs. Norris); Bobby Larson (Willie Norris); Teddy Infuhu (Dutchy Schultz)

Synopsis

Somewhere at sea, an English ship carrying German prisoners is torpedoed. Two of the Nazi prisoners survive and find an English interpreter who has also survived. One of the Germans, Karl Richter, takes the interpreter's dog tags and passes himself off as Ronald Cheever to the Allied rescuers.

Richter winds up at a U.S. military hospital located near the Midland POW camp. Nurse's aide Mary Lee Norris is caring for Richter, who is now believed to be Cheever, a British officer. Richter flirts with Mary Lee, but she's devoted to her boyfriend, Sgt. Terry Hunter, who works as a guard at the nearby camp.

While Richter is recovering, a high-ranking Nazi officer, Luedtke, arrives at the camp. He asks some of the other prisoners about Richter and is told he drowned.

When Richter is released from the hospital, he moves into Mary Lee's boarding house. Almost immediately he acts in a suspicious manner—he's upset over a newspaper headline about the bombing of Berlin, and he tries to pull Mary Lee into an unwanted embrace. He's also very interested in the POWs, who work during the day at a farm about a mile away. That prompts him to visit the local hardware store, where he purchases maps and arranges to buy a number of guns.

"Cheever" gets orders to return to England, and he realizes his time is short. His partner at sea, Krause, escapes from the camp and meets up with Richter, who tells him the plan will be put into motion the following night.

Two neighborhood boys, Willie and Dutchy, have grown suspicious of Richter and begin following him. Terry, meanwhile, is also suspicious, so he calls the British Consul and asks for more information on Cheever.

That night Richter and Krause break into the hardware store, steal all the guns and return to the boarding house, where they hide both Krause and the weapons in a nearby barn. Unfortunately for the Germans' plan, Willie and Dutchy spot Krause hiding in the barn, and Dutchy runs to get Terry while Willie keeps an eye on Krause. Richter overhears Dutchy's report to Terry, however, and he races to reach the barn before Terry.

Terry and Mary Lee arrive at the barn only to find Krause holding Willie hostage. Richter arrives and shoots Krause in a desperate attempt to maintain his identity as Cheever. The ruse works, and Richter is released.

A short time later Richter attempts to escape with the guns, but Terry is waiting and captures him. Terry reveals that the British Consul supplied a photo of Cheever. Richter's plan to free the Germans is foiled, and Terry is happily united with Mary Lee.

Commentary

Like the earlier *Two-Man Submarine*, *The Unwritten Code* pairs Tom Neal and Ann Savage in a wartime thriller about secret plots in an isolated location.

The film explores a fascinating (and now largely forgotten) aspect of wartime America: prisoner-of-war camps housing mostly Nazi inmates. And *The Unwritten Code* begins promisingly, with a German officer assuming the identity of an Englishman and finding himself in an idyllic American backwater burg located near one of these camps. It would have been easy to forgive *The Unwritten Code* some of its larger blunders—like making the dis-

In this posed still from 1944's *The Unwritten Code*, Richter (Roland Varno) has apparently been captured by Sgt. Hunter (Tom Neal) and Mary Lee (Ann Savage).

guised German so obviously evil that even two pre-pubescent kids can figure him out, or setting up a past rivalry between Richter and another German, Luedtke, then never exploring that — had it not been for the larger error of not being able to decide whether it's an adult thriller or a boys' adventure story. At the halfway point the film suddenly focuses on the two youngsters, Willie and Dutchy, taking it upon themselves to unmask "Cheever," and the transition is jarring.

The Unwritten Code also fails because it never makes its villain's plot clear — if he successfully breaks his fellow Germans out of the prison camp, just where are they planning to go? Although we're never told where the "Midland" camp is located, it seems to be deep in the American heartland, making it unlikely that a large number of escaped prisoners would easily find their way back to Germany. Because the script never makes Richter's final destination clear, it never builds much suspense.

It's also a shame that *The Unwritten Code* relegates its heroine to little more than window dressing. Ann Savage is solid, despite a script that essentially asks her character to overlook an attempted rape on the part of Richter.

Tom Neal is fine as the heroic Sgt. Hunter, but again the script undercuts him, basically assigning him the role of cleaning up where the kids leave off. As the villain, Roland Varno is aristocratic but on the hammy side, making his bad guy intentions somewhat obvious.

There is one amusing in-joke buried in *The Unwritten Code*: Ann's character — who

Mary Lee Norris (Ann Savage) listens to jokes about being a pin-up model in *The Unwritten Code*.

works in a military hospital as a nurse's aide — is jokingly referred to as a "favorite pinup." Off-screen, Ann was indeed one of the most successful wartime pinups, and her appearances in publications like *Esquire* and *Yank* magazines undoubtedly graced hundreds of tents and soldiers' barracks.

Behind the Scenes

The most interesting aspect of *The Unwritten Code* is its use of a German prisoner-of-war camp on American soil. Although most Americans are aware of such Japanese camps as Manzanar, few know that over 400,000 prisoners from the European conflict were also held in the U.S. in hundreds of camps spread across the country. *The Unwritten Code* authentically shows the prisoners engaged in manual labor, for which they were paid a small wage (they could use the money to purchase supplies, such as cigarettes). But where *The Unwritten Code* is not accurate is in suggesting that the prisoners were anxious to escape. In fact, many prisoners from the camps chose to stay in America after the conclusion of the war.

The Unwritten Code is the only film Herman Rotsten ever directed, although he did work on a few other pictures (including Edgar G. Ulmer's *Strange Illusion* [1945]) as a dialogue director.

This was the final film that Ann Savage and Tom Neal would make together at Columbia (they'd previously appeared in *Klondike Kate* and *Two-Man Submarine*). Of course, a year later they would be onscreen together again in PRC's *Detour*.

Look for a small appearance by a young Blake Edwards (who would later become a major director, with the *Pink Panther* movies and many others to his credit) as "Swede."

The Unwritten Code was shot under the title *A Nazi in the U.S.A.*

Dancing in Manhattan

(Columbia) Release Date: December 14, 1944

Screenplay and Original Story by: Erna Lazarus
Director of Photography: L.W. O'Connell
Musical Director: Morris Stoloff
Film Editor: Richard Fantl
Art Director: George Brooks
Set Decorator: George Montgomery
Produced by: Wallace MacDonald
Directed by: Henry Levin
Cast: Fred Brady (Eddie Martin); Jeff Donnell (Julie Connors); William Wright (Steve Crawford); Ann Savage (Valerie Crawford); Cy Kendall (Inspector Kirby); Howard Freeman (George Hartley)

Synopsis

A wealthy businessman, Mr. Hartley, is being blackmailed. He's set up a sting with Inspector Kirby involving passing five thousand dollars in marked bills to the blackmailers, a sophisticated pair of grifters named Steve and Valerie Crawford. However, when the transfer is made at the glitzy Silver Palms nightclub, Valerie thwarts Inspector Kirby by hiding the money in a salad bowl. As the Crawfords are escorted from the club, the remains of the salad are thrown out in the trash.

The next morning a trashman, Eddie Martin, finds the bills. Although Eddie's conscience tries to tell him to notify the authorities, Eddie dreams of marrying his girlfriend Julie in style, so he decides to keep the money. Unfortunately for Eddie, both Inspector Kirby and the Crawfords are anxious to get the money, too, and they get Eddie's name from a Silver Palms employee.

Eddie goes on a spending spree, buying Julie an expensive gown and promising her an evening at the Silver Palms. At first Julie wonders if Eddie has robbed a bank for this money, but he finally convinces her that he won it in a lottery.

Eddie and Julie arrive at the Silver Palms for their big date — with both Inspector Kirby and the Crawfords hot on Eddie's tail. Playing the part of a big spender, Eddie hands out huge tips, but his generosity turns against him when a hatcheck girl figures out the bills are marked. The Crawfords move in next, converging on Eddie and convincing him that they have an insider tip on a hot stock. Eddie is about to hand over the last of the money to the Crawfords when Valerie overhears the hatcheck girl talking about the marked bills. She takes Steve out of the restaurant, but he tells her he can remove the markings from the bills, so they continue with the stock scam.

Eddie agrees to accompany them to their office where the transaction will supposedly take twenty minutes; he plans on returning to the Silver Palms to dance with Julie when he's done. At the office, Eddie and Steve Crawford get into a fistfight that ends only when Inspector Kirby arrives and catches Steve with the money.

When Eddie reappears at the Silver Palms, he finds Mr. Hartley, the wealthy blackmail victim, waiting for him with a reward check for five thousand dollars — but, more importantly, Eddie and Julie finally get to dance at the Silver Palms, which literally turns into heaven for them.

Commentary

The paper-thin *Dancing in Manhattan* has a title implying a sparkling Astaire-Rogers style musical; but instead, *Dancing in Manhattan* is an attempt at blending the comedy and crime genres. With barely enough plot to fill half its short running time, the film is bloated with long comic routines, such as one involving a rich drunk who stumbles into Eddie and Julie's date and refuses to leave. The casting doesn't help matters. In the lead role of Eddie, former radio personality Fred Brady (he's referred to in the film's trailer as "Radio's Inimitable Comedian") lacks any charisma or charm; and especially odd is Cy Kendall, an actor who would look perfectly at home playing a mafia don but

Grifters Steve and Valerie Crawford (William Wright and Ann Savage) try to get past Mrs. Bundy (Dorothy Vaughan, center) in *Dancing in Manhattan* (1944).

here is cast as the intrepid and stalwart Inspector Kirby. Poor Jeff Donnell, in the role of Julie, comes across as simply childish, since the script frequently requires her to pout or burst into tears for no good reason (the fact that her expensive evening dress causes her to bear an uncanny resemblance to a Disney animated heroine doesn't help).

Dancing in Manhattan comes to life only when it focuses on the glamorous and larcenous Crawfords. Both William Wright and Ann Savage are terrific in these roles, and they have an attractive and amusing chemistry. Especially good is the moment when Valerie pretends to mistake Eddie for someone else and literally hurls herself at him, planting a kiss on him that suggests the stunned look on Brady's face has nothing to do with the art of acting. As with *Apology for Murder*, Ann displays a hearty sexuality lurking just beneath the polished and poised surface.

The film's direction occasionally segues into bizarre out-and-out fantasy. When Eddie finds the money in the restaurant rubbish, he engages in an argument with a disembodied voice (the fact that the voice sounds nothing like his doesn't help to establish that this is his conscience talking); while at the film's end, Eddie and Julie literally dance out of the nightclub and into the stratosphere. Like the movie's intrusive and prolonged comedy sequences, these brief stabs at fantasy do nothing to enliven the proceedings. The director, Henry Levin, would have a long career as a studio journeyman, making a few well-regarded fantasy films in the '50s (including *Journey to the*

Center of the Earth), but here he seems unsure about the rules of genre and how to make a picture that's consistent in tone throughout.

BEHIND THE SCENES

Actor Cy Kendall — here cast against type as the police inspector — did indeed usually play thugs (see, for example, *After Midnight with Boston Blackie* [1943], in which he stars opposite Ann as Joe Herschel, a sleazy nightclub owner who kills in pursuit of a fortune in diamonds).

Jeff Donnell had a lengthy career as a supporting actress, including an appearance as "Aunt May" in a 1977 television version of *The Amazing Spider-Man*, and an eight-year run as "Stella Fields" on the popular soap opera *General Hospital*. Off-screen, she was a lifelong friend of Ann's.

Dancing in Manhattan was shot under the title *Tonight We Dance*. It was the last of the 16 films Ann Savage made during her tenure at Columbia.

Scared Stiff

(Pine-Thomas Productions/Paramount) Release Date: June 22, 1945

Screenplay by: Geoffrey Homes and Maxwell Shane
Cinematography by: Fred Jackman, Jr.
Music by: Alexander Laszlo
Film Editing by: Henry Adams
Art Direction by: F. Paul Sylos
Set Decoration by: Roy Berk
Directed by: Frank McDonald
Cast: Jack Haley (Larry Elliot); Ann Savage (Sally Warren); Barton MacLane (George "Deacon" Markham); Veda Ann Borg (Flo Rosson); Roger Pryor (Richardson); George E. Stone (Mink); Robert Emmett Keane (Professor Wis-

Jack Haley and Ann Savage in a lobby card from *Scared Stiff* (1945).

ner); Lucien Littlefield (Charles Waldeck/Preston Waldeck); Paul Hurst (Sheriff); Arthur Aylesworth (Emerson Cooke); Elly Malyon (Mrs. Cooke); Buddy Swan (Oliver Waldeck)

Synopsis

Larry Elliot is an expert chess player who is currently working as a reporter — a job he's not very good at. After he completely misses the news about the notorious "Deacon" Markham escaping from prison, his editor gives him one last chance: cover a beauty pageant in a remote town called Grape City. At the bus terminal, Larry meets an eccentric professor and an obnoxious pre-adolescent genius; he's also distracted by Sally Warren, a pretty young antiques dealer, and finally winds up on the wrong bus.

When the bus reaches its destination — a remote inn — the passenger next to Larry is found murdered. Although the other passengers insist that Larry wait until the authorities arrive, Larry is desperate to complete his assignment and so tries to steal a car; unfortunately, someone has tampered with all the available vehicles, stranding Larry, Sally, and the other passengers. Larry overhears the boy genius talking about a headless corpse that was just discovered, and a few minutes later Larry finds a head in his hatbox. Sally arrives in Larry's room and shows him her own secret — a number of incredibly rare chess pieces, which she claims were given by Kubla Khan to Marco Polo. Sally, however, only has the white pieces, which she's just purchased from Preston, one of the two twin brothers who own the inn; the other twin, Charles, has the black pieces and won't sell them. Charles strikes a strange deal, though: If Larry will play him in a chess match, he'll sell the pieces. Larry agrees, and while he plays Charles, Sally hides the valuable white pieces in Larry's room.

After the chess game, Larry accompanies Charles to a safe to get the black chessmen, and they encounter a mysterious figure who knocks them both out and escapes with the chessmen.

The sheriff and his men arrive, and say they're looking for "Deacon" Markham. Sally and Larry then learn the truth about the priceless chess pieces: They actually belonged to Markham, which is why he's on his way here. With the arrival of the law, Larry panics about the head in the hatbox, but when the police capture him he discovers the head was nothing but a cabbage. He returns to his room only to find Markham there, demanding the return of his chessmen. When Sally enters, Markham hides in the room; but Sally hides as well when a detective enters and tells Larry that the man who was murdered on the bus was also connected to the chess pieces. Suddenly there's a flurry of activity, and Markham escapes.

The next day Sally and Larry both search the inn for the chess pieces, and both are captured. Larry, who's knocked out, comes to in the wine cellar, where Markham and his sidekick Mink are hiding out. He manages to trick Markham and his stooge into falling into a giant wine vat, but then he runs into the real killer — the eccentric professor. Larry subdues him just as the police show up.

Later, the (drunken) bad guys are collected by the police, and Larry is not only a hero, he's got the story he needs to keep his job.

Commentary

Scared Stiff may not be particularly scary, but "stiff" is an appropriate description of its pace and attempts at generating laughs. The comedy here is almost always unfunny, frequently embarrassingly so; and the mystery is poorly developed and needlessly confusing, with too many characters heading in too many different directions. Some comic scenes are interminable (especially one in which Larry sneaks through a garage at night, inadvertently setting off car horns), repeating the same dud joke over and over; others, such as a climactic one in which Larry beats the pre-teen savant, are just mean-spirited.

Unfortunately, the lackluster plot isn't helped by the strange performance of leading man Jack Haley, who mugs his way through his part with little conviction or attention to detail. Ann Savage is capable and glamorous as the wily antiques dealer Sally, but any possibility of romance fizzles because of Haley's apparent lack of real attraction to her. Even the production values are lacking here, with some shots in the wine cellar simply too dark to clearly make out.

The only interesting element of *Scared Stiff* might be an odd subtext that would lend itself well to modern queer film theory: The movie is packed with scenes that bring Larry's sexuality into question, whether it's a sleeping man's hand falling into his lap on the bus or a deputy who offers, somewhat suggestively, to "tuck him in" at night (and then there's Haley's seeming disinterest in Ann Savage). While it's tempting to review *Scared Stiff* as an early example of gay cinema, the jokes are neither daring nor offensive enough to really earn it a place in any film history. *Scared Stiff*, in the final analysis, is simply forgettable.

Behind the Scenes

Director Frank McDonald was a former railroad worker and stage actor who worked as a scriptwriter and dialogue director before going on to direct over a hundred B films. Apparently McDonald was never quite comfortable with his chosen career—actress Evelyn Keyes once noted, "I've never seen anyone as terrified of directing as Frank McDonald."

"Geoffrey Homes" is a pseudonym for screenwriter Daniel Mainwaring, who went on to write the classic films *Out of the Past* (1947, based on his own novel) and *Invasion of the Body Snatchers* (1956).

Star Jack Haley is, of course, best remembered for his performance as "the Tin Man" in 1939's *The Wizard of Oz*.

George E. Stone is probably most well-known for his portrayal of sidekick "the Runt" in twelve Boston Blackie films, including *After*

Scared Stiff: Sally (Ann Savage) and Larry (Jack Haley) engage in hijinx.

Midnight with Boston Blackie (1943), which starred Ann Savage.

Scared Stiff was re-released under the title *Treasure of Fear*.

Midnight Manhunt

(Pine-Thomas Productions/Paramount) Release Date: July 27, 1945

Screenplay by: David Lang
Original Music by: Alexander Laszlo
Cinematography by: Fred Jackman, Jr.
Film Editing by: Henry Adams
Art Direction by: F. Paul Sylos
Set Decoration by: Roy Berk
Directed by: William C. Thomas
Cast: William Gargan (Pete Willis); Ann Savage (Sue Gallagher); Leo Gorcey (Clutch); George Zucco (Jelke); Paul Hurst (Murphy); Don Beddoe (Detective Lt. Max Hurley); Charles Halton (Henry Miggs); George E. Stone (Joe Wells)

Synopsis

It's night in a downtown setting as a mysterious man creeps into the Empress Hotel, enters a room, guns down a victim and escapes with a box full of diamonds. A few minutes later, a beat cop, Murphy, runs into the Last Gangster Wax Museum to report having just found the dead body of notorious gangster Joe Wells. Sue Gallagher, a down-on-her-luck reporter who lives just above the museum, enters, overhears Murphy, and tells the museum owners, Miggs and Clutch, that she could make her career with a story like this. She almost gets her chance when the body goes missing, only to turn up again just outside her apartment. She hides the body by posing it in the wax museum, then sets about writing the story.

Meanwhile, her ex-boyfriend, Pete Willis, himself a reporter, shows up with police detective Lt. Hurley. Hurley leaves when he finds out there's no body, and Willis questions Sue, but she's still angry at him about their breakup.

In the museum, Miggs finds Wells' corpse, and lets Clutch talk him into moving the body elsewhere so suspicion won't fall on them. As they load the body into a car, the killer arrives, having trailed blood from the Empress Hotel to the museum. He confronts Sue, tells her he wants the body, and knocks her out.

When the manager of the hotel calls the police, Willis puts the clues together and realizes Sue had the body. He arrives at the museum in time to confront the killer, and arranges a meeting in one hour to turn over the body. When Hurley arrives a short time later, he arrests Sue for body stealing.

After Sue is taken away, Clutch returns to the museum and tells Willis that he and Miggs dumped the body in a freight car; unfortunately, Miggs was arrested for trespassing in the train yard and is now in police custody.

At the jail, Sue is bailed out just in time to meet the incoming Miggs, who tells her about the freight car. Outside she runs into the killer, who is on his way to meet up with Willis, but he changes his destination when Sue tells him about the encounter with Miggs.

Willis and Clutch arrive at the freight car first and carry the body off. Not long after, Sue and the killer arrive, followed by the police. Sue manages to escape the killer's clutches and runs off, meeting Willis at his home. The killer arrives and tells them his name is Jelke, and that he's been tracking Joe Wells for some time. He refuses to tell them why he needs the body, and Willis agrees to take him to a taxi where the body is waiting. They reach the taxi, pile in with the corpse, and head for a ferry. Once aboard, Jelke reveals his real interest in the body: He's been hired to recover the diamonds, but he instead intends to tell his employers that he couldn't find Wells and keep the diamonds for himself. He tries to shoot Willis and Sue, but Sue knocks him out with a ship's pulley. Willis also reveals that the "body" in the taxi was actually Clutch, who was supposed to protect them but slept through the confrontation.

Back at the police station, Sue, Willis and Clutch turn over Jelke; then Willis reveals the real location of the body: the trunk of Lt. Hurley's car. With the case wrapped up, Willis prepares to call in the big story — and offers Sue a shared byline and a kiss.

Half-sheet movie poster for *Midnight Manhunt* (1945).

COMMENTARY

Midnight Manhunt is an average B mystery, with a capable cast but direction that feels strangely stagebound and editing that occasionally lingers too long on comic bits.

The first half of the film in particular feels like Act One of a play—virtually all of the action takes place in the wax museum and is shot from the same angles. The art direction is barely passable—the wax museum is limned with perhaps four or five mannequins and a few obvious prop heads—and does nothing to break the film out of its theatrical sensibility. Prologued comic bits are given to Leo Gorcey (who is undeniably funny in some of them), further slowing down the pacing. An improbable script (exactly *why* most of the characters seem positively obsessed with hiding a corpse is never really answered) doesn't help this cardboard production.

Fortunately, a solid cast does. William Gargan makes a wry and likable leading man, and his repartee with Ann provides some real sparks (it's also interesting to see the young Savage—all of 24 here—cast opposite an obviously older leading man). Ann Savage has a sarcastic, spunky sex appeal as the jaded reporter, and it's no wonder that even the erudite, sinister (and always reliable) George Zucco seems swayed by her charms.

Midnight Manhunt is perhaps most interesting viewed as a transitional film for Ann Savage. It was her second picture after leaving Columbia, and offers her the sort of leading part she was given too rarely during her tenure as a studio contract player. She seems more assured here than in *Scared Stiff*, her first independent outing, and displays both glamour and real style in her performance. If it seems as if she's warming up in *Midnight Manhunt*, consider that she followed this film immediately with *Detour* and *Apology for Murder*, two of the finest performances of her career. If *Midnight Manhunt* isn't quite in the same category with those, it can only be the fault of the film itself, not an actress freed from studio constraints and finding herself on camera at last.

BEHIND THE SCENES

Director William Thomas was (with William Pine) one half of the successful Pine-Thomas Productions; the two producers were nicknamed "the Dollar Bills" because their films were cheaply made and always turned a profit. (Ann appeared in two other Pine-Thomas pictures, *Scared Stiff* [1945] and *Jungle Flight* [1947]). *Midnight Manhunt* was Thomas's first film as director.

Midnight Manhunt marks one of the few appearances by Leo Gorcey that wasn't in a series film. Gorcey would follow *Midnight Manhunt* with his final appearance as one of the East Side Kids, and a year later he would make his debut as one of the Bowery Boys.

The pressbook for *Midnight Manhunt* describes Ann as a "pretty red-headed green-eyed gal," and adds:

> A devotee of sophisticated comedy, Ann is an ardent fan of Tallulah Bankhead and Jean Arthur. Her worst fault is saying the wrong thing at the wrong time. She listens to the New York Philharmonic, but also likes jazz and Bing Crosby. Ann is now under contract to Producers William Pine and William Thomas.

The film's working title was *One Exciting Night*.

Pete (William Gargan), Sue (Ann Savage), and Jelke (George Zucco) go for a ride near the climax of *Midnight Manhunt*.

Apology for Murder

(PRC) Release Date: September 27, 1945

Screenplay and Original Story by: Fred Myton
Production Manager: Bert Sternbach
Director of Photography: Jack Greenhalgh, A.S.C.
Special Effects: Ray Mercer
Musical Director: Leo Erdody
Film Editor: Holbrook N. Todd
Art Director: Edward C. Jewell
Set Dresser: Elias H. Reif
Produced by: Sigmund Neufeld
Directed by: Sam Newfield
Cast: Ann Savage (Toni Kirkland); Hugh Beaumont (Kenny Blake); Russell Hicks (Harvey Kirkland); Charles D. Brown (Ward McKee); Pierre Watkin (Craig Jordan); Sarah Padden (Maggie); Norman Willis (Allen Webb); Eva Novak (Maid); Budd Buster (Jed, the Caretaker); George Sherwood (Lt. Edwards); Wheaton Chambers (Minister)

Synopsis

The wealthy Kirklands are arguing about money when brash reporter Kenny Blake bursts into their home. Blake's heard about an impending financial deal and demands an interview from Mr. Kirkland. When Kirkland turns Blake down and orders him out, Blake spots Kirkland's seductive wife Toni and is immediately smitten. Before Blake leaves, he and Toni flirt, revealing a mutual attraction.

Blake returns to the offices of the *Daily Tribune*, where he has to tell his boss, Ward McKee, that he couldn't get an interview with Harvey Kirkland. McKee, who has an obvious affection for Blake, nevertheless chews him out for drinking too much. Blake retorts with a comment about his "starvation wages."

When Blake leaves work that night, Toni is waiting for him in her car. She drives to an isolated area, and they embrace. Later they share drinks at her home, and Blake is upset to realize she's Kirkland's wife, not daughter. She appears to be distraught as she tells him that Harvey won't give her a dime if she files for divorce, and Blake allows her to seduce him again. Later, she tells him she wishes her husband would suffer a fatal accident and suggests that one could be arranged. Blake is horrified and leaves; after he does, Toni throws her empty glass after him.

Blake, however, can't stop thinking about Toni, and when she appears at his apartment a few nights later he embraces her again and agrees to help her do whatever is necessary to escape her miserable marriage. A few days later Toni tells him that she believes Harvey will file for divorce first and try to smear her name, so she'll receive nothing.

Blake receives a phone call from Toni shortly thereafter; she tells him that Harvey is going up to their mountain cabin for one night, then will be returning to file the divorce papers. Left with no alternative, Blake agrees to meet up with Toni and murder Harvey that night.

At the rustic mountain lodge, Harvey and his lifelong friend Craig Jordan are arguing about a business venture when they're overheard by the lodge caretaker. After the caretaker leaves to get some provisions, Harvey and Craig laugh off the argument and make plans to go fishing.

Their plans are interrupted, however, when Harvey gets a call from Toni; she claims she was coming to the cabin when her car failed, and she asks Harvey to come get her. He agrees, and leaves Craig Jordan to fish alone.

Toni and Blake hide Blake's car, then wait for Harvey to drive down the narrow, twisting mountain road. There's a moment of tension when the caretaker's car passes them first and stalls in front of them; however, the caretaker manages to get the old crate going again and is gone by the time Harvey arrives. Toni is waiting for Harvey, seated by the roadside and claiming a twisted ankle. As Harvey kneels to help her with a shoe, Blake appears and hits him twice with a heavy wrench. He then places Harvey's body back in his car, and together he and Toni push the car over the side of the steep road.

The following day Blake is assigned to cover Kirkland's death. He arrives at the mountain lodge only to find the homicide division there, investigating the obvious murder (the car's ignition was off, it wasn't in gear, and the corpse had bled too much). The caretaker

In this lobby card from 1945's *Apology for Murder*, Toni Kirkland (Ann Savage) sets up her husband Harvey (Russell Hicks).

tells the police that he saw Jordan and Harvey arguing, and — as a relieved Toni and a guilty Blake look on — Jordan is arrested for Harvey's murder.

While Blake wrestles with a guilty conscience, Toni discovers that Harvey's will has left everything to charity. Against Blake's wishes, she decides to challenge the will in court.

Meanwhile, Blake's boss, McKee, begins to suspect that Jordan — who is now on Death Row — may not be the real murderer. He visits Blake one night to discuss his theory and just barely misses seeing a personalized handbag that Toni has left on Blake's couch. Blake begins to grow increasingly nervous.

McKee, believing that Toni and an unknown man were actually Harvey's murderers, pays a visit to her one night and narrowly misses discovering Blake there. A day later a woman in a ranch house near the Kirklands' mountain lodge says she saw a strange man driving the road the day Harvey died, and Blake fears that she'll recognize him. Although he barely dodges a meeting with the witness, Blake is shocked when the lodge caretaker shows up in the newspaper office and tells them that he discovered tire tracks and two sets of footprints near the place where Harvey's car went off the road.

McKee pays another visit to Blake that night and tells him that he's got a private detective trailing Toni. So far the detective has found out that she has a history as a golddigger, that she's hired an attorney named Allen Webb to represent her in court when she challenges Harvey's will, and that she's dating the attorney. Devastated by this news, Blake stakes out Toni's house and sees her kissing Webb. He breaks in and hears Toni offering the same promises to Webb that she once made to him. Furious, Blake slugs Webb and turns on Toni. Toni, however, pulls out a gun and warns Blake that she'll get away with a self-defense plea. He disregards the warning and advances anyway, and she does shoot him. She sets the gun down to check on Webb, who is recovering from Blake's blow; they both look up to see that Blake is standing now and has the gun. He shoots Webb first, then turns the gun on Toni, who tries to buy her way out with tears and pleading. "Even if they tried you for life, you'd find some fool on the jury who wouldn't convict you," Blake says just before he kills her and staggers out.

Blake makes his way back to the newspaper office and, knowing that he's mortally wounded, immediately begins typing out a confession. McKee, meanwhile, discovers that Toni and Webb are both dead. When he finds Blake's lighter at the scene, he returns to the newspaper office, arriving just in time to watch Blake die.

COMMENTARY

Although *Apology for Murder* is frequently regarded as one of the more obvious examples of out-and-out copying on the part of the 1940s independent studios, the film actually has many pleasures to offer beyond its obvious debt to *Double Indemnity*.

Released in 1944, *Double Indemnity* not only marked Billy Wilder's third film as director, but also featured a screenplay by Wilder and Raymond Chandler, based on James M. Cain's classic thriller. The film was a financial and critical success for Paramount (it garnered seven Academy Award nominations, including Best Picture), and some film scholars have even argued that it provided the basis for all later entries in the *film noir* cycle. In his seminal 1978 essay "*Film Noir*: A Modest Proposal," James Damico argues that *film noir* can be identified not only by its chiaroscuro lighting and frame composition, but by a story structure that he describes thusly:

> Either he is fated to do so or by chance, or because he has been hired for a job specifically associated with her, a man whose experience of life has left him sanguine and often bitter meets a not-innocent woman of similar outlook to whom he is sexually and fatally attracted. Through this attraction, either because the woman induces him to it or because it is the natural result of their relationship, the man comes to cheat, attempt to murder, or actually murder a second man to whom the woman is unhappily or unwillingly attached (generally he is her husband or lover), an act which often leads to the woman's betrayal of the protagonist, but which in any event brings about the sometimes metaphoric, but usually literal destruction of the woman, the man to whom she is attached, and frequently the protagonist himself.

Certainly that's an accurate description of both *Double Indemnity* and *Apology for Murder*.

But where *Indemnity* has all the gloss and sheen that would be expected from a studio production — including three major stars in Fred MacMurray, Barbara Stanwyck and Edward G. Robinson — *Apology* cannot fall back on high production values to sustain its 68-minute running time. What it does offer, however, is an overt and earthy sexuality that's largely missing from its glossy big-budget cousin.

In *Double Indemnity*, MacMurray plays Walter Neff, an insurance salesman who enters into an affair with Phyllis Dietrichson (Stanwyck), a stifled but anklet-wearing matron. Beyond the affair, Walter and Phyllis also engage in a pact to murder her husband in such a way that the "double indemnity" clause of his insurance will pay off to their advantage. Neff, whose boss Keyes (Robinson) frequently touts the jaded thirtysomething as his best salesman, is convinced that years of figuring insurance scams will give him the edge in pulling off one of his own. Close-ups of MacMurray as he plots the murder — and becomes increasingly excited — imply that Neff is more interested in the gamesmanship aspect of the murder than his lust for Phyllis. The film also spends a considerable amount of time on Neff's relationship with father figure Keyes;

Wilder himself described *Double Indemnity* as "a love story between the two men." Add to that Stanwyck's performance — her aloofness suggests the impossibility of any form of genuine sexual interaction — and *Indemnity* can occasionally become a chilly and intellectual exercise.

Apology for Murder, on the other hand, dispenses with *Indemnity*'s lengthy dialogue passages, complicated set-up and Neff/Keyes interaction and goes right for the throat (or perhaps some other body part). Compare the introduction of Phyllis to *Murder*'s version of her, Toni: Phyllis is shot from a low angle as she stands stiffly on a second-floor landing, clad only in a towel (and the unfortunate blond wig she wears throughout the film). The shot is a classic set-up for a femme fatale, suggesting both power and sexuality. Toni, on the other hand, is discovered arguing about money with her husband while seen only as a pair of shapely legs, the rest of her hidden by the angle and an overstuffed chair; all we can see is one leg crossed over the other, swinging with insouciant disregard. When newspaperman Blake bursts into the office and Toni finally deigns to offer him a look, that kicking gam is followed by a half-lidded, welcoming smile. A moment later she walks past Blake, offering him an even more provocative look as she exits. Ann Savage plays these moments with an exhilarating combination of bravado and seduction, and there's never a question that Blake has fallen for *her*, not the temptation to murder.

In fact, the most interesting difference between *Double Indemnity* and *Apology for Murder* is how clearly the latter's female protagonist is delineated as the aggressor and the superior force. In the beginning of Wilder's film, Stanwyck's character only hints at the notion of murder; it's Walter Neff who first bluntly articulates it. But in *Murder*, Toni states her intention to Blake right up front, pondering murder via a faked accident; when Blake walks out on her, she furiously hurls a glass after him. Although the actual murder scene replicates *Indemnity*'s shots (as her husband is killed off-screen, the femme fatale is filmed in impassive close-up), the position of the men is more interesting in *Murder*, with the doomed husband literally kneeling before his wife, while a gesture from her tells the murderer to act. Men are, quite literally, at Toni's feet.

And with good reason: Savage's Toni takes a sexualized performance as far as it could go in Hayes Code-Hollywood. She doesn't just sit on a couch, she *sprawls* on it, commanding the scene with a cocktail in one hand and legs crossed towards the hapless male. In *Indemnity*, we're told that Phyllis was the first Mrs. Dietrichson's nurse; but a background check on Toni reveals the more obvious truth, that she's "a golddigger." When Toni hooks up with sleazy attorney Allen Webb, there's little question that she's sleeping with him; he even offers to take her to an isolated

Femme fatale personified: Ann Savage in *Apology for Murder*.

"roadhouse," and receives a coy smile in return. The script also eschews *Indemnity*'s more polite dialogue about how Neff and Phyllis need to be "on the same trolley car"; instead, when Toni suspects that Blake's resolve might be failing, she exclaims, "Are you turning out to be a jellyfish? ... I counted on the help of a man." A few beats later, she adds, "You'd better let me do the thinking for you." In both her open presentation of her sexuality and her take-charge attitude, Savage's Toni is both far more progressive and far more interesting than most of the feminine leads of the period's other films. Her surface elegance belies a character formed in back alleys and cheap rooms, a woman who has mastered seduction and control.

The rest of the cast performs adequately. Hugh Beaumont, who would later become the quintessence of American fatherliness as Ward Cleaver in the television series *Leave It to Beaver*, trades in MacMurray's hard-bitten cynicism for down-on-his-luck pathos (which is not always successful). But he has a solid chemistry with Savage and is particularly good in the scene where his boss reveals Toni's affair with the attorney — his slumping shoulders and strained expression convey Blake's descent well.

Apology for Murder most obviously fails when set against the production values of *Double Indemnity*, but does offer an enlightening look at how 1940s B-movie companies like PRC worked alongside the likes of Paramount. In 1938 the initial anti-trust suit had been filed against the major Hollywood studios, and had paved the way for low-budget companies like PRC; however, by the first half of the following decade the studios still owned most of the theaters, with companies like Monogram, Republic and PRC owning only a few less-lucrative show places. These companies typically

Blake (Hugh Beaumont) and Toni (Ann Savage) plot in this lobby card from ***Apology for Murder.***

made films with budgets of less than $100,000, shooting schedules of six days, and sets borrowed from other more lavish productions (during World War II, the independents took another financial hit when the government rationed raw film stock). *Apology*'s director, Sam Newfield, made an astonishing thirteen films the year he made *Apology for Murder*; most of the other movies were westerns or adventure pictures with titles like *Border Badmen* and *White Pongo* (interestingly, he did make several films with Hugh Beaumont). Obviously Newfield had little emotional investment in *Murder*; offering up something on the level of *Indemnity*'s huge sets or vivid location shooting was out of the question. However, Newfield, working with cinematographer Jack Greenhalgh and the PRC art department, managed to give *Apology for Murder* a decent enough look — the Kirklands' wealthy mansion is believable, for example — although their limitations occasionally show to embarrassing effect, as when Harvey's fatal car crash is played entirely off-screen. Music is also a problem; where *Indemnity* boasted a stunning score by Miklos Rozsa, *Apology* staggers along on music cues likely lifted from a stock library and not always fitting for the scenes they accompany. More successful is the wardrobe, particularly Ann Savage's outfits, which use broad-shouldered padded jackets and tailored slacks to emphasize her sex appeal and, later, masculine authority (and more credit to Savage, who chose her own outfits for the film).

In his essay "Out of What Past? Notes on the B *film noir*," Paul Kerr notes that "the paucity of 'production values' (sets, stars and so forth) may even have encouraged low budget production units to compensate with complicated plots and convoluted atmosphere." Although this is plainly not the case with *Apology for Murder*—which, if anything, considerably simplifies the plot it so liberally borrows from — the script nonetheless contains both suspense and wit, with jokes that may be racier than anything offered by the studios at the time. "If you intend to run out of gas, I'll tell you when," Blake says to Toni when she picks him up after work. In *Murder*'s script, double entendres are followed by translucent actions: After Toni pulls the car over, she and Blake almost immediately wind up in a clinch, and in the next scene they've returned to her home and are consuming what can only be described as post-coital cocktails. The script is fast-paced and undeniably enjoyable, with appropriate tension and snappy dialogue laced throughout. *Murder*'s script (and, amusingly enough, "original story") are credited to Fred Myton, although *Detour*'s director Edgar Ulmer also claimed to have been involved with a draft.

Even though we've seen *Apology for Murder*'s story executed before and with more finesse, the film nonetheless deserves recognition for both the sheer entertainment value it offers and, especially, for Savage's superb portrayal of Toni. In Savage's gifted hands, what could have been yet another riff on the glacial and fatal beauty instead becomes a look at woman as fearless and gleeful sexual predator, a performance that—by suggesting a woman who is both capable and sexually liberated — is decades ahead of its time.

BEHIND THE SCENES

Apology for Murder was the first release of three films Ann made for Producers Releasing Corporation (PRC); the others were *Detour*, which she shot earlier, and *Lady Chaser*, made a year later.

PRC's promotional materials came up with some spectacular descriptions of Ann's characters— the trailer for *Apology* calls her "An Irresistable She-Devil" (and in the trailer for *Lady Chaser* she's "A Daring Adventuress").

Director Sam Newfield began his career in the late silent era and made hundreds of movies, mainly westerns; he also made several horror films with George Zucco, including *The Mad Monster* (1942) and *The Flying Serpent* (1946). He later directed Ann in *Lady Chaser* (1946) and *Jungle Flight* (1947). His brother, Sigmund Neufeld, was one of PRC's production executives and also one of their producers. Newfield also directed pictures for PRC under the aliases "Peter Stewart" and "Sherman Scott."

Director Newfield, screenwriter Fred Myton, and star Hugh Beaumont all worked (a year later) on a PRC version of Brett Halliday's *Murder Is My Business*.

Hugh Beaumont, who, of course, would go on to find fame as "Ward Cleaver" in the television series *Leave It to Beaver*, would later star with Ann in *Pier 23* (1951).

Apology for Murder was actually shot under the working title *Single Indemnity*. During one interview, Edgar G. Ulmer (director of *Detour*, and one of PRC's most popular directors) took credit for *Apology*'s script:

> At the beginning of the season, Fromkess [Leon Fromkess, head of PRC] would sit down with me and Neufeld and we would invent forty-eight titles. We didn't have stories yet — they had to be written to fit the cockeyed titles.... When *Double Indemnity* came out and was a huge success, I wrote a picture for Neufeld which we called *Single Indemnity*. We were able to write that junk in about two weeks.... Paramount made us take the title off.

Ulmer goes on to incorrectly cite the film's final title, confusing it with the 1948 thriller *Blonde Ice*, which was produced by Fromkess's right-hand man at PRC, Martin Mooney.

One television distributor listed the title as *Murder with Apology*.

Detour

(PRC) Release Date: November 30, 1945

Screenplay by: Martin Goldsmith (based on his novel)
Original Music by: Erdody
Cinematography by: Benjamin H. Kline
Film Editing by: George McGuire
Art Direction by: Edward C. Jewell
Set Decoration by: Glenn P. Thompson
Costume Design by: Mona Barry
Produced by: Leon Fromkess
Directed by: Edgar G. Ulmer
Cast: Tom Neal (Al Roberts); Ann Savage (Vera); Claudia Drake (Sue Harvey); Edmund MacDonald (Charles Haskell, Jr.); Tim Ryan (Diner Proprietor); Esther Howard (Holly); Pat Gleason (Joe)

Synopsis

A disheveled man in a rumpled suit hitches a ride and gets dropped in Reno, where he steps into a diner for coffee. He's Al Roberts, and he's unshaven and surly. When asked where he's heading, he answers only, "East." He almost gets into a fight with a trucker who plays the song "I Can't Believe You're in Love with Me," but finally goes back to his coffee. The song takes Al back...

In the dingy little Break o' Dawn club in New York, Al is the piano player, happily leading a small orchestra in "I Can't Believe You're in Love with Me" as his girlfriend Sue performs the vocals. After the club closes, Al plays Chopin's Fantasie Impromptu while Sue stands by admiringly, but when she suggests that he should be playing Carnegie Hall, he's bitter about his lack of success as a pianist. They leave the club to walk home, and when Al tries to talk about their marriage Sue gives him bad news: She's leaving to pursue stardom in Hollywood. Al is so hurt and angry that he can barely kiss her good night.

Some time later Al is playing solo at the Break o' Dawn, turning a Brahms piece into boogie-woogie. When a customer tips him ten dollars, Al excitedly phones Sue in Hollywood and tells her he's decided to join her.

Al begins hitchhiking his way across the country. Somewhere in Arizona he's picked up by a man named Charles Haskell Jr. Haskell keeps popping pills and he sports deep scratches on the back of his hand that he received from a woman (who he then tossed out of the car). Haskell, who tells Al he's a bookie, also reveals a long scar on his arm that he earned "dueling" as a kid; he put the other boy's eye out, ran away from home, and hasn't been back since.

They stop at a restaurant, where Haskell buys Al dinner. Haskell wants to make L.A. by Wednesday so he can bet on a horse at Santa Anita. He tells Al he got cleaned out by one race in Miami — he lost "38 grand." They leave the restaurant and Al starts driving; as Haskell sleeps, Al imagines his future with Sue after she's become a star, singing "I Can't Believe

You're in Love with Me" with a big band and wearing a designer dress.

Al's dream is interrupted when it starts to rain. He pulls the car over to raise the convertible's top, but when he opens the passenger door, Haskell tumbles out and his head hits a rock. Al realizes instantly that Haskell is dead, and that he would likely be considered a murder suspect. He drags the corpse off the road and down into a gully, where he takes Haskell's wallet and switches clothes with him — Al will now be assuming Haskell's identity. As Al returns to the car, a motorcycle cop appears and tells Al to move the car, then takes off.

Al starts driving again, and as day breaks he reaches the state line, where's he's anxious about passing through a checkpoint. The border guards ask routine questions. Al assures them he is Charles Haskell Jr., and he's waved on through.

Exhausted, Al stops at a cheap motel to sleep. He suffers nightmares about the trip and Haskell's death, and wakes with a start when the maid knocks on his door. Al cleans up, then makes plans: He'll ditch the car somewhere near L.A. He goes through Haskell's stuff and finds he's carrying $768. Al also finds a letter indicating that Haskell intended to try to rook his old man by claiming to be a Bible salesman.

Al continues on. He pulls up at a gas station near Desert Center, where he sees a woman hitching, and he offers her a ride. Her name is Vera, and she "looked as if she'd just been thrown off the crumbiest freight train in the world." She tells Al she's heading to L.A., then falls asleep as he drives. Al is just starting to feel sorry for her when she wakes up, turns a glare on him, and asks, "Where did you leave his body?" She knows the car and she knew Haskell, and Al realizes she's the "animal" who gave Haskell the scratches on his hand. Rueing his bad luck in picking up this one woman, Al muses: "That's life ... whichever way you turn, fate sticks out a foot to trip you." Vera clearly believes that Al murdered Haskell, and when Al offers her Haskell's $768 she's not satisfied, because Haskell told her he was going to bet $3,000 on the horse at Santa Anita. She also mocks his plan to ditch the car, telling him that it would be safer to sell the car, since a deserted car "always rates an investigation."

They reach L.A., where Vera rents an apartment as Mrs. Charles Haskell so they'll have a legitimate address when they sell the car. Vera, clearly in complete control of Al, takes the bedroom and assigns him the Murphy bed. She also begins to flirt with him: When she purrs "I'm first in the bathtub," she offers him a seductive smirk.

After her bath, Vera relaxes with cigarettes and alcohol while Al paces nervously, irritated by a neighbor playing a saxophone. Vera tells him to cheer up, since she hasn't turned him in, and Al joins her in getting "tight." The talk turns to death, and Vera is plainly uncomfortable; she also begins to cough. When she finally decides to turn in, she massages Al's shoulders suggestively, but he's plainly not interested. Vera tells him she's got the keys to the apartment, then she angrily heads into the bedroom.

Al decides to try calling Sue, but as soon as he hears her voice he begins to fear discovery by Vera and hangs up.

In the morning, Vera dresses in a sexy black outfit and they head off to sell the car. She wants $2,000 for it, but the deal finally closes at $1,850. Al goes into the dealer's office to sign over the papers, but almost runs into a snag when he can't name his insurance company. Suddenly Vera bursts into the office and says they're not selling the car. Perplexed, Al follows her out and they head for a drive-in, where Vera explains by showing him a newspaper article: Charles Haskell Sr. is close to death, and his son and heir is being sought. Vera wants Al to pose as Haskell Jr., but Al says he won't do it. "You sap!" Vera snarls, then suggests they could split the dough fifty-fifty.

They return to the apartment. As they play cards that night, Al realizes it's a "death watch" — they're really waiting for Haskell to die. Vera reveals that she's dying ("I'm on my way out"), and their argument escalates. Very drunk now, Vera tries to call the police, and they tussle over the phone, during which Al twists her arm slightly. Furious at this minor

Detour (1945): Al (Tom Neal) and Vera (Ann Savage) arrive in Hollywood.

injury, Very finally rushes into the bedroom with the phone, locking the door behind her. Desperate to prevent her from calling the cops, Al tries to pull the phone cord from under the locked door. He finally busts down the door to find Vera dead, strangled by the phone cord. Shocked, Al looks around the room at all the surrounding evidence — their empty liquor bottles, packages from a store where they shopped, her purse — and he realizes his only chance is to run. He's literally staggering as he leaves the apartment.

Al, back in the Reno diner, finishes his recollection by noting that he can't return now to either New York or Los Angeles, nor can he ever see Sue again. He leaves the diner, noting that "someday a car will stop to pick me up that I never thumbed ... yes, fate — or some mysterious force — can put the finger on you or me for no good reason at all." As Al strides forlornly down a dark road, a police car pulls over and Al is arrested.

Commentary

Exactly 32 minutes into *Detour*, the luckless protagonist Al Roberts — who is driving a stolen car and wearing a dead man's clothes — pulls into a gas station "outside of Desert Center" and spots a young female hitchhiker. As soon as Vera starts striding towards Al's car — her eyes shadowed, hair tangled, the hint of a sneer on her lips — we know that both Al's life and the film's plot have just taken a serious left

Al (Tom Neal) and Vera (Ann Savage) discuss Murphy beds in ***Detour***.

turn into something new and terrifying. Sure enough, within three minutes Vera fires off one of cinema's most ferocious glares at the squirming Al, and *Detour* moves from efficient and stylish "B" noir to classic status, all with the introduction — at the film's halfway point, yet — of one character.

From 35 minutes on, Ann Savage owns *Detour*.

Of course, Vera is not solely her creation. Savage herself has always been quick to acknowledge not just Edgar Ulmer's direction of her, but also author Martin Goldsmith's contribution. In the original novel of *Detour*, Vera likewise makes her entrance at the halfway mark, and within a page of picking her up Al is telling us, "Her mouth and eyes were enough to give a man the jitters." Goldsmith retains much of Al's narration straight out of the book (the "freight train" line), but, fortunately, jettisons a subplot involving Al's girlfriend Sue working in L.A. as a waitress and involved with a suicidal young actor. In the novel, Vera is compelling enough a creation that readers are tempted to skip the sections she's not in.

However, in the hands of a lesser director Vera could have been just one more film noir femme fatale, a sleek and elegant creature with an icy veneer and a cool beauty. Ulmer, however, understood that Vera needed to be as truly revolting as Goldsmith had described her; she's every woman you've ever passed on a rundown street corner and tried to avoid, the one making the scene at the restaurant, or who you spot in the liquor aisle of the store and think, "That one's trouble." Ulmer knew she had to be genuinely repellant, and that he'd need a skilled and fearless performer to pull her off.

He got much more than that in Ann Savage.

In some respects, casting Ann must have been risky. Yes, she was exactly the same age as Vera (24), and with the right makeup could certainly fit the description of Vera possessing "a beauty that's almost homely because it's so damned real." But her career prior to *Detour* had mostly involved playing Columbia studio ingénues, girls-next-door and can-do career women. Only a few performances — the deceitful fiancée of *Passport to Suez*, the seductress who likes her men bound in *One Dangerous Night*— hinted at anything more, and in both of those films she's still beautiful, elegant and composed. No, she'd never done a role like Vera before.

But then again, neither had any other actress in Hollywood. Vera was almost entirely unique for the time, a nightmarish harpy presented without a shred of glamour or sympathy. After *Detour* was released, Ann's work was compared to that of Bette Davis in *Of Human Bondage* (1934) and some of the films of Susan Hayward; but it's difficult — if not impossible — to imagine either of those actresses willing to allow themselves to look as genuinely unattractive as Ann Savage did in *Detour*. Decades later, actresses like Charlize Theron would make films like *Monster* and win Academy Awards for inhabiting similarly ugly characters, but in 1945 it simply wasn't done.

And, of course, it's not just a matter of outward physical appearance. Ann spits out her lines with such venom that she's literally hoarse through much of the film. Every gesture — Vera doesn't take off her shoes at the end of a day, she rips them from her feet and *hurls* them across the room — resonates with a fury that few actresses would have been willing to portray. It would be easy to simply dismiss Vera as a "castrating bitch," a description that dovetails neatly into certain critical (i.e., Freudian) readings of the film. But Vera's rage is so deeply rooted in the character that she transcends such specious categorization. "Force of nature" is perhaps the most appropriate description of her.

Which is why her introduction half-an-hour into *Detour* is so energizing. Up until then, *Detour* is a decent little thriller, one that encompasses both the movement of a road picture and the nihilism of true *film noir*. Tom Neal — once groomed to be Columbia's own B-movie version of Clark Gable — portrays Al with an intriguing combination of surliness and anxiety; he also looks obviously worn, with his stubble and sweat. He's the classic lit-

Al (Tom Neal) and Vera (Ann Savage) get tight in *Detour*.

tle guy who's never had a shot, with an extra patina of depression. He performs Goldsmith's staccato narration well, spitting out lines with nervous speed.

But, of course, *Detour*'s first half is most famous for Ulmer's direction, which incorporates elements of German expressionism and sometimes simply dispenses with reality altogether, as when the lighting in the diner goes dim until it narrows to a single spot on Al's face. Ulmer is justifiably famous for some of *Detour*'s strange shots—like the one in the diner that abruptly pulls back to frame a giant coffee cup in the foreground. The shots aren't simply showy, but rather paint a picture of a bleak world where even ordinary objects can take on ominous proportions.

Yet, as stylish as *Detour*'s first half is, it's not extraordinary. No, it takes the introduction of Vera to raise the film to that level.

In the second half of *Detour*, Ulmer abandons much of the first half-hour's showy direction to (wisely) focus on the actors. Much of the last half of the film takes place in a small apartment, lending even more claustrophobia to Al's predicament and letting the camera linger on the two actors. It's at this point that Vera gets to show more of her dark colors, as she becomes alternately domineering, seductive, vicious, and pouty, all while Al frets and paces. Erdody's score is particularly interesting in this second half, as it plays against Vera's more obvious qualities. In *Strains of Utopia*, Caryl Flinn notes that "the leitmotiv is in fact quite pleasant, a short, romantic melody that harmonically interacts with other musical ac-

Detour: Al (Tom Neal) listens with growing dread as Vera (Ann Savage) calls the police.

tivity," and suggests that this makes it "difficult to consider Vera as purely 'evil.'"

One of the most intriguing aspects of *Detour*, at least from the point of view of the modern Hollywood screenplay, is that this is truly a two-act film. There's no third act in which Al attempts to pull off the con job on Charles Haskell Sr., nor do Al and Vera confront authority and offer a final fight. *Detour* never gives into storytelling conventions; no chase or battle with police could be as involving as watching Al and Vera's relationship deteriorate into drinking bouts, arguments and finally death. Nor, of course, are we offered any shred of hope. Vera is never redeemed, and Al will always lose.

Some reviewers have questioned Al's motives in staying in that apartment; in one famous essay, Andrew Britton even suggests that Al has obviously made up the entire story to cover his murder of Haskell. However, it's a tribute to the power of Ann's performance that *Detour* never feels illogical or irritating. On some subconscious level we might recognize that Al finds her as horribly compelling as we do, and so we allow the film to deny Al the obvious exit.

In the novel, Al finally gives in and strangles Vera, although he persists in calling it "accidental" (with the ridiculous rationale of "Somehow, as we struggled for the [phone], her throat got in the way"). *Detour*—filmed at the height of the power of the Hayes Code — couldn't get away with an onscreen killing, and so Ulmer and Goldsmith improvised by creating Vera's famous death scene in which she's strangled by the phone cord. Ultimately, this ending serves both the story's theme of fate and Tom Neal's sad-sack performance more than a murder would have, but there's no doubt that audiences would have been heartily cheering Al on had he deliberately killed Vera.

Vera's death also provides Ulmer with a chance to demonstrate his directorial virtuosity in a final, famous shot: As Al realizes he's accidentally strangled Vera, the camera moves from him to Vera's dead face, to the phone, to her hair brush, to an empty bottle of liquor, to her shoes, to empty boxes, to her coat, to the phone outlet, to the cord, and finally back to Roberts, all while moving in and out of focus. Not only is the shot a bit of technical ingenuity, it also serves to establish all of Al's ties to Vera (the evidence that will damn him in a court of law), and it leads back to the framing device of the diner, where we now fully understand why Al is brooding and desperate.

When Al finally leaves the diner and is picked up by a Highway Patrol car in the final shot, we the audience are offered more than simply the dubious pleasure of watching justice in action; rather, we also experience some relief in knowing that Al's fated free fall has finally hit bottom.

At least he's free forever of Vera. Fortunately for us, though, Vera — and Ann Savage's performance — lives on, now justifiably recognized as one of the screen's great villainesses and most human of monsters.

Behind the Scenes

Since its original release in 1945, *Detour* has become possibly the most famous and most critically examined B-film of all time. Andrew Sarris has called *Detour* the "most despairing and most claustrophobic of all B pictures." Myron Meisel noted that "*Detour* is an exercise in sustained perversity," and commented on its "mad poetic tragedy." In the *Los Angeles Times*, Kevin Thomas called *Detour* "One of the most relentlessly intense psychological thrillers anyone has ever filmed." Roger Ebert includes an essay on *Detour* in his "Great Films" series, and says, "It lives on, haunting and creepy, an embodiment of the guilty soul of film noir. No one who has seen it has easily forgotten it." In 1992, *Detour* was selected for inclusion in the National Film Registry, which was created by Congress in 1988 to preserve "culturally, historically, or aesthetically significant films." *Detour* remains the only B film selected for inclusion.

And it only took 40 years for *Detour* to receive these accolades.

Detour's history, especially after its initial release, is one of the great rediscovery stories of cinema. *Detour* began life in 1939, with Martin M. Goldsmith's original novel (first published in hardback by Macauley and Company). The book was reasonably well received (one reviewer compared it favorably to the work of *Double Indemnity*'s author James M. Cain), and Goldsmith started to receive nibbles from Hollywood. He finally optioned his novel to B-studio PRC (Producers Releasing Corporation) for $15,000 and the understanding that he would also write the screenplay adaptation. It was extraordinary enough at the time to allow a book's original author to also pen the screenplay adaptation that *Detour*'s pressbook includes an article titled "Novelist Does Own Screenplay." The article goes on to state that Goldsmith had no experience with screenwriting and spent a week "read[ing] every good script he could get hold of" (Goldsmith's inexperience as a screenwriter is borne out by a close examination of the script, which features some slightly inconsistent use of standard screenplay lingo and format). Goldsmith's first draft included some of the novel's secondary plot, in which Al's girlfriend Sue becomes involved with a young actor in Hollywood. It's unclear at exactly what point that material was lost; the strange editing of Al's phone conversations with Sue suggests that the material may have been cut relatively late (although there's no indication that any of it was ever actually shot). Ulmer and the film's associate producer, Martin Mooney (the latter was probably the man responsible for bringing the *Detour* property to PRC in the first place), were both frequently employed to doctor PRC's scripts, and Ulmer has taken credit for some of the most

In this scene from *Detour*, shot in the parking lot of PRC, Al (Tom Neal, in car) and Vera (Ann Savage) try to sell Haskell's car.

memorable scenes of *Detour*'s script, including the notorious death-by-phone-cord ending for Vera (Goldsmith, however, has likewise claimed this finale as his).

In the old model of distribution, audiences were offered two pictures for the price of one ticket — an "A" picture, with bigger budgets and stars, and a "B" picture, with smaller budgets and lesser-known actors. The studios took such a significant chunk of the box office for the A pictures that, with their overhead, producing the B pictures was usually not economically feasible. Consequently, B studios arose to fill the need for the bottom halves of the double features. PRC was one of the main Hollywood B studios (ranking perhaps slightly below Republic and Monogram). They churned out dozens of low-budget "programmers" every year, mainly westerns and thrillers, and 5-day shooting schedules were not unusual.

PRC was founded in 1938 as Progressive Pictures Corporation; by 1945 it had undergone both a name change and corporate restructuring, now operating as a subsidiary of Pathe Industries, Inc. Leon Fromkess was president and head of production, Sigmund Neufeld (who produced many of PRC's pictures) was listed as a production affiliate, and Edgar Ulmer was one of the company's most popular directors. Ulmer, born in Austria in 1904, learned his craft in the German film industry of the 1920s and '30s, working (usually as a set designer and illustrator) with legendary directors like F. W. Murnau and G. W. Pabst; his peers included Fritz Lang, Billy Wilder and Fred Zinnemann. His first major film as a director was 1934's Universal horror film *The Black Cat*. Although the film was an artistic success, Ulmer ran afoul of Universal's owners (by marrying the film's script supervisor, Shirley, who was then engaged to a Laemmle nephew). Ulmer went on to work mainly for independents, making Yiddish films, westerns (under a pseudonym), and even a musical for black audiences, *Moon Over Harlem* (1939). In 1943 Ulmer joined PRC, working in a variety of capacities — script doctor, director, producer. Although Ulmer was given both miniscule budgets and small paychecks (*Detour*'s budget shows Ulmer's salary as $750), he claimed that he stayed with PRC for three years because they gave him artistic freedom. He made nearly all of PRC's most highly regarded films, including *Bluebeard* (1944), *Strange Illusion* (1945) and *Club Havana* (1945). (Ulmer first met Ann on the set of the latter film, when that picture's star, Tom Neal, brought Ann by to suggest her for the role of Vera.) Ulmer went on to make several more critically praised films — including 1955's *The Naked Dawn* — before passing away in 1972. Ulmer is now recognized as "a man of qualities ... [who] provided one of the links between German Expressionism, with its exaggerated lighting, camera angles and dramaturgy, and the American film noir, which added jazz and guilt" (Roger Ebert). Peter Bogdanovich has said, "Nobody ever made good films faster or for less money than Edgar Ulmer" (a comment Ulmer would undoubtedly have agreed with — his tombstone bears the words "Talent Obliges," which was one of his favorite phrases). Andrew Sarris went even further in his praise of Ulmer: "He is no longer one of the private jokes shared by auteur critics, but one of the minor glories of the cinema."

Near the end of his life, Ulmer said he thought the original novel was "a very bad book" and claimed to have rewritten the script. "I was always in love with the idea," Ulmer told

Edgar G. Ulmer, director of *Detour*.

Peter Bogdanovich, "and with the main character — a boy who plays piano in Greenwich Village and really wants to be a decent pianist ... and then, the idea to get involved on that long road of Fate — where he's an absolute loser — fascinated me." When asked to name his favorite films he made, Ulmer cited *Detour*, *The Black Cat* and *The Naked Dawn*.

One of the odder stories surrounding *Detour*'s transition to screen involves actor John Garfield, who reportedly urged Warner Brothers to acquire the property for him (with Ida Lupino playing Vera, and Ann Sheridan as Sue). Warner offered PRC's president (and *Detour*'s credited producer) Leon Fromkess $25,000 for the rights, but Fromkess declined. (*Detour*'s pressbook lists a higher figure, claiming that "a Hollywood agent offered PRC $70,000 for the completed script.")

Fromkess was quite taken with Ann when they first met, and he immediately offered her a five-year contract. Ann, who had just left her Columbia and Pine-Thomas contracts behind, was in no hurry to be tied to another long-term contract, so she turned the offer down. However, Fromkess agreed to hire her on a two-picture basis. After *Detour* and *Apology*, he hired her for one last film with PRC in 1946, *Lady Chaser*. (Not long after that picture, PRC was renamed Eagle-Lion Studios, and in 1951 Eagle-Lion was completely absorbed into United Artists.)

Ann was apparently the only actress Ulmer ever seriously considered for Vera. Ulmer's widow, Shirley (who was also *Detour*'s script supervisor), said, "My husband saw in Ann a sort of hunger in her eyes and such a lack of conceit and egocentricity that he felt she could play the beaten-up, beaten-down Vera better than any of the other actresses, who would have resorted to makeup and artifice." In *Detour*'s pressbook, Ann is (amusingly) quoted as saying, "I've played screen meanies in my career, but this new role is the meanest of the lot!"

Tom Neal was an easy hire as well, since he was under contract to PRC and had just completed *Club Havana* with Ulmer.

Playing a singer in *Detour* came easily to Claudia Drake, who grew up in Southern California as a child of vaudeville. With her sister Ella (then 8 years old), 5-year-old Claudia toured the vaudeville circuit as the La Marr Sisters; the great Bill Robinson called them the greatest child performers of the day. She was later spotted singing in a casino by Busby Berkeley, who signed her to a contract at Warner Brothers. Drake went on to become Bill Boyd's leading lady in the Hopalong Cassidy westerns.

Music was also a key factor in *Detour* (as it is in a number of Ulmer's films). Although the script called for the song "Sophisticated

Shot through the apartment set's window, Vera (Ann Savage) and Al (Tom Neal) play cards in this rare production still from ***Detour*** (note lamp stand to left).

Lady," the rights to that Duke Ellington classic were simply out of PRC's reach, but "I Can't Believe You're in Love with Me," ten years past its prime when *Detour* was made, was affordable. Caryl Flinn has suggested that this song was ultimately a better choice for the film, since it implies Al's obsession with the past. Al also plays Chopin's Fantasie Impromptu in C Minor in the Break o' Dawn club, and the score later incorporates parts of the piece, which had become the popular song "I'm Always Chasing Rainbows" (a particularly ironic title to find its way into *Detour*).

Detour was released to theaters in the U.S. on November 30, 1945. Another of the contemporary myths surrounding *Detour* has it that the film went virtually unnoticed. In his book *More Than Night*, James Naremore says, "As far as I can determine, its only U.S. review was in *Variety*, which said that it was 'okay as a supporting dualer.'" However, *Detour* did indeed receive more American newspaper reviews than just *Variety*; a November 21, 1946, ad in the *Hollywood Reporter* promoting Ann Savage (and listing General Artists Corp. as her "exclusive management") includes blurbs from *The Evening Bulletin, Providence*, the *Hollywood Reporter*, and *The Hawaii Times, Honolulu*. The *Evening Bulletin* review called her performance "nothing short of astounding"; the *Hollywood Reporter* said Ann gave "a most outstanding performance"; and *The Hawaii Times* noted that she "dominates the show with splendid acting." (Both *The Hawaii Times* and *The Evening Bulletin* compare Ann's work to that of Bette Davis in *Of Human Bondage*, as did the review in the *Los Angeles Times*.) The trade ad, incidentally, is accompanied by a glorious photo of blonde and beautiful Ann, obviously in an attempt to prove that Vera was a masterful performance.

Detour also received a bigger than usual push from PRC. To begin with, the film's budget included enough money to option both the original book and the song "I Can't Believe You're in Love with Me" (it was virtually unheard of for a "Poverty Row" production to spend precious dollars optioning music). The film's pressbook is also far more involved than usual, featuring original line art portraits of the actors and a large array of promotional materials. There's little doubt that PRC thought it had something special in *Detour*.

Reflecting back on her career, Ann later suspected that her work in *Detour* might actually have hurt her career at the time, an observation that could very well have been the sad truth. In a 1988 newspaper interview she said:

> I was very disappointed that I never got the recognition I should have gotten from that performance. I just couldn't seem to adjust to the fact that no one seemed to want to give me a crack at better roles. It was one of the things that really had to do with my dropping out. I was actually hurt by it.

Her performance as Vera was certainly the highlight of her career, but it was also a one-of-a-kind role, a portrait of feminine rage and empowerment that was played for neither glamour nor camp. It was almost as if Ann had transgressed against Hollywood's rigid standards of what was expected from its actresses, and as a result she had now sacrificed her career.

The real critical recognition of *Detour*, however, was still decades away. When the French began to explore cinema history and the auteur theory in the '50s, *Detour* started to receive some attention. Throughout the 1960s and 1970s the film played frequently on television, garnering a whole new audience; in fact, a survey of its ratings in newspapers and *TV Guide* shows the film progressing from two stars to three stars to finally, in the 1980s, the full four-star "classic" categorization. Andrew Sarris praised the film in his influential 1968 *The American Cinema*, and it was officially accorded "cult" status when Danny Peary included it in his 1981 volume *Cult Movies* (in which he refers to Vera as "the most despicable female in movie history").

After her now-legendary appearance at UCLA in 1983, Ann began to find herself in demand again. The Ulmer retrospective toured the country, and *Detour*, in particular, found a new generation of fans. Ann was invited to attend screenings of the film; she was the subject of interviews and newspaper articles; and, in 1985, she was the star of her own tribute, as the Vagabond Theatre in Los Angeles ran a two-day screening of *Detour* and *The Last Crooked Mile*. More recently, *Time Magazine*'s Richard Corliss chose Vera as one of his "Top 10 Greatest Villains."

Detour's rediscovery also owed something to the increased interest in *film noir*. By the 1990s *film noir* was the subject of dozens of books, and *Detour* was one of the prime examples of the genre. In his 1992 study of *film noir*, Andrew Spicer referred to *Detour*'s "existentialist gloom" and "highly expressive visual register," and noted, "Its grim, 'un–American' fatalism was characteristic of the emerging cycle of *film noir* that ... used the exigencies of wartime production to develop into an oppositional mode of film-making which challenged mainstream practices." Spicer also singled out *Detour*'s provocative poster (which features a staged photo of Al and Vera lounging against a lamp post) as an example of how the B-*film noirs* used sex and mystery on their posters to market to the same audience that was buying hard-boiled crime paperbacks. In his 1998 book *More Than Night: Film Noir in Its Contexts*, James Naremore talks about the film's meager budget:

> *Detour* is so far down on the economic and cultural scale of things that it virtually escapes commodification, and it can be viewed as a kind of subversive or vanguard art.... Vera ... makes every femme fatale in the period look genteel by comparison.... She taps into a raw nerve of greed and exploitation that lies at the core of the film.

Detour has also been reviewed in terms of feminist critique, Weimar cinema, Marxist theory, "film gris," "film asphalte," the theory of the unreliable narrator, and as a critique of Holly-

Staged publicity photo of Ann Savage and Tom Neal from ***Detour***.

wood. In 2008, *Detour* received its own book-length study (as part of the BFI Film Classics series) by Noah Isenberg.

Detour's history didn't end with academic criticism and film fan idolatry, either. In 1992, video distributor Wade Williams directed a remake of the film (set in 1942), starring Tom Neal Jr. as Al and Lea Lavish as Vera. Williams had approached Ann about playing a part in the movie (the newly-added character of Haskell's mother), but she declined (the part eventually went to another 1940s actress, Susanna Foster). Later in life, Ann turned down any part that seemed to trade on her Vera performance, not wishing to be identified solely with that role.

Ulmer had also considered a *Detour* remake. In 1969 Ulmer wrote a screenplay called *The Loser*, which was essentially a retelling of *Detour* set in the hippie milieu of the late '60s. In his notes for "King of the B's: A Retrospective of the Films of Edgar G. Ulmer," Bill Krohn notes that "During his last years he was working on a remake of *Detour* based on research in Haight-Ashbury."

The Spider

(20th Century-Fox) Release Date: December 1945

Screenplay by: W. Scott Darling and Jo Eisinger; based on the play by Lowell Brentano and Fulton Oursler, with additional dialogue by Irving Cummings Jr.
Original Music by: David Buttolph
Cinematography by: Glen MacWilliams
Film Editing by: Norman Colbert
Art Direction by: Richard Irvine and Lyle Wheeler
Set Decoration by: Harold Cramp and Thomas Little
Produced by: Ben Silvey
Directed by: Robert Webb
Cast: Richard Conte (Chris Conlon); Faye Marlowe (Delilah "Lila" Neilsen, alias Judith Smith); Kurt Kreuger (Ernest, alias Garonne); John Harvey (Burns); Martin Kosleck (Mikail Barak); Mantan Moreland (Henry); Walter Sande (Det. Lt. Walter Castle); Cara Williams (Wanda Vann); Charles Tannen (Det. Tonti); Margaret Brayton (Jean); Ann Savage (Florence Cain); Henry Seymour (Ed); Jean Del Val (Henri Dutrelle)

Synopsis

In New Orleans, a woman named Judith Smith meets up with private investigator Chris Conlon; she tells Chris that she hired his partner, Florence Cain, to find her missing sister. When Chris goes to his apartment to talk to Florence about the case, they joke for a few moments—until Florence is strangled in another room.

Certain that the police will try to pin Florence's murder on him, Chris seeks the help of his assistant Henry and they move the body to Florence's apartment. When Chris tries to report back to Judith Smith, she's disappeared, and he soon realizes she gave him a fake name.

The next day the New Orleans police question Chris about the murder, but they don't have enough evidence to keep him. When Chris returns to his office he finds a man named Barak waiting for him, asking for the evidence that Florence claimed to have had. Barak tries to pull a gun on Chris, but after Henry knocks Barak out, he also vanishes.

Chris attends the performance of famed mentalist Garonne and realizes that his assistant, Lila, is "Judith Smith." He confronts her after the show and tells her that Florence has been murdered. The mysterious Barak also appears and is revealed to be Garonne's manager.

Chris breaks into Flo's apartment and finds some hidden clippings about "the Great Garonne" and a woman who was murdered a few years ago. The victim, who was strangled in a nearby hotel, was never identified, and the killer was never found. Chris realizes the slain woman was Lila's sister.

At the Hotel Bourbon, Chris speaks to the manager, Dutrelle, and is shown the register from that night; the name signed by the killer was "Eric Campbell." The manager says he could recognize the strangler again, so Chris buys him a ticket to Garonne's show; but Dutrelle is murdered before he can attend. This time Chris is arrested by the police.

Chris arranges a meeting with Lila and tells her he knows who killed her sister. He asks Lila to trick Garonne into signing the name "Eric Campbell," and then he escapes. Lila succeeds with Garonne, and when Chris compares the two signatures he finds they match perfectly. Garonne catches up to Lila and Chris and pulls a gun on them, but just then the police arrive and Chris is exonerated.

COMMENTARY

As a vehicle for lead actor Richard Conte, *The Spider* is modestly successful; but as an overall film, its script shows all the classic signs of a Hollywood broth spoiled by too many cooks.

The Spider opens with a voice-over supplied by "Judith Smith," offering a few notes about New Orleans, but that's both the last of the narration and nearly the last of the locale (which is defined by, and used for, little more than the neon sign for the "Creole Bar"). As watchable as Conte is in the lead, his New York/Italian-American accent and look is out of place in New Orleans, and he's saddled with an over-the-top sidekick in the form of Mantan Moreland's "Henry," an eye-popping African American cliché that was surely unfunny (if not offensive) even in 1945.

The direction and cinematography are suitably shadowy and moody, but ultimately can't save a screenplay that doesn't even offer an explanation for its own title.

What could have been the film's most compelling element — a gritty, urban male/female detective pair who may or may not be romantically involved — is sadly dispensed with mere moments after it's introduced, when Ann Savage's Florence Cain is strangled (while inexplicably cowering in silence). Savage and Conte plainly make a fine match, her slow sarcasm playing nicely off his staccato line deliveries, and a mystery surrounding this pair would have been a sure audience pleaser. As it is, watch how Ann takes a part that lasts onscreen only a few minutes and creates such a powerful character that her death believably affects every other character for the rest of the film's running time. It's a fine achievement and should have led to a starring role in a better film for Fox, but Ann never worked for the studio again.

BEHIND THE SCENES

The Spider is very loosely based on a 1926 play of the same name by Lowell Brentano and Fulton Oursler. The play is set completely in a vaudeville theater, where magician Chatrand is presenting a mentalist act using his assistant Alexander. During the performance, a young lady in the audience, Beverly, asks Alexander to identify a spider-shaped locket, while her companion, an older man named Carrington, tries to stop her. The lights go out and Carrington is shot. Alexander, who has suffered from amnesia, is identified as the young lady's long-lost brother, and Carrington was the siblings' cruel guardian, so they're both under suspicion of his murder. However, Chatrand soon discovers that Carrington was a drug lord, and at the climax he identifies the murderer as a member of Carrington's dope ring. The only elements the play shares with its film incarnation are those of the mentalist (who serves as the play's hero and the film's villain) and a lost sibling. There's no private detective in the play, and, in fact, the film doesn't even retain any of the play's character names. Why the film chose to retain the title (which has no meaning without the spider-shaped locket) is more of a mystery than its plot.

The Spider served as something of a screen test for Ann at 20th Century-Fox. Unfortunately, Fox didn't follow up, and she never appeared in another production for the studio.

The *Hollywood Reporter*'s review nonetheless noted that "Ann Savage shines."

The Dark Horse

(Universal) Release Date: July 19, 1946

Screenplay by: Charles R. Marion and Leo Solomon; story by Sam Hellman
Cinematography by: Paul Ivano
Editing by: Paul Landres
Art Direction by: Harold MacArthur and Jack Otterson
Set Decoration by: Russell A. Gausman and Fred B. Martin
Musical Director: Hans J. Salter
Produced by: Will Cowan and Howard Welsch
Directed by: Will Jason

Cast: Phillip Terry (George Kelly); Ann Savage (Mary Burton); Allen Jenkins (Willis Trimble); Jane Darwell (Aunt Hattie); Donald MacBride (John Rooney); Edward Gargan (Eustace Kelly); Raymond Largay (Mr. Aldrich); Ruth Lee (Mrs. Aldrich); Henri DeSoto (Maitre d' Hotel); Si Jenks (Old Man)

Synopsis

George Kelly has just returned to his small town after a stint in the Army and is anxious to become a civilian again; he's staying with his Aunt Hattie and cousin Eustace. Aunt Hattie sends him out one morning to drop off a book on the life of George Washington, and during his walk he runs afoul of a fight brewing around a political rally. George is knocked out, but when political operative Trimble finds him with the Washington biography, he thinks George might have the makings of a hero. He returns to his boss, "Honest" John Rooney, the town's political honcho, and Rooney decides to run George in an upcoming election for a new alderman. When George proves difficult for Rooney to persuade, Rooney pays his lovely secretary Mary to help. George is soon smitten and reluctantly agrees to become George "Washington" Kelly, candidate for alderman.

After being paraded through town on a horse and missing a date to speechify at a picnic, George becomes disenchanted. But he's positively furious when he finds out that Mary is working for Rooney as well. He delivers his own speech, one in which he publicly denounces Rooney and asks the listeners to vote for his rival, Aldrich. Rooney, angry at the speech, tries to have George carted off to the local asylum, but Mary intervenes and helps George escape. They eventually wind up at the home of Aldrich, and are surprised to hear over the radio that George has won the election. When Rooney and Trimble show up

Aunt Hattie (Jane Darwell) goads on Mary (Ann Savage) as she kidnaps George (Phillip Terry) in this scene from *The Dark Horse* (1946).

claiming victory as well, Mary threatens to blackmail them with what she knows about Rooney unless they leave George alone. George looks forward to his new career as an alderman and life with Mary.

COMMENTARY

The Dark Horse is obviously trying to fit itself into the Capra-esque tradition of social commentaries à la *Mr. Smith Goes to Washington* (1939), with an Irish twist. The script offers lots of fast dialogue, but the story occasionally meanders off in strange, even mean-spirited directions (as when Mary tries to convince George to leave the house before Rooney's asylum thugs show up — and gentle old Aunt Hattie hands her a gun). Director Will Jason was a craftsman whose career consisted entirely of B movies and television, and *The Dark Horse* consequently lacks the visual pizzazz and sharp pacing that might have helped the story along. The cast is often uneven (leading man Phillip Terry is handsome enough but no master of comic timing) or far too broad (Donald MacBride and Allen Jenkins as, respectively, Rooney and weasel-faced Trimble). Ann Savage manages to get the best of the script and the lackluster direction, offering a strong, spunky heroine; but even her presence can't overcome the film's lack of direction and too-light script.

BEHIND THE SCENES

The Dark Horse is the only film Ann Savage ever made for Universal.

A review of the film by the *Hollywood Reporter*'s Jack D. Grant called Ann "one of the finer new dramatic actresses," and said she was "tossed away" in *The Dark Horse*.

Director Will Jason was also a prolific music composer and probably contributed to the score of *The Dark Horse*.

The Last Crooked Mile

(Republic) Release Date: August 9, 1946

Screenplay by: Jerry Sackheim; based on a play by Robert L. Richards, adaptation by Jerry Gruskin

Original Music by: Joseph Dubin
Cinematography by: Alfred S. Keller
Film Editing: William P. Thompson
Art Direction by: Frank Hotaling
Set Decoration by: John McCarthy Jr. and George Milo
Directed by: Philip Ford
Cast: Don "Red" Barry (Tom Dwyer); Ann Savage (Sheila Kennedy); Adele Mara (Bonnie); Tom Powers (Floyd Sorelson); Sheldon Leonard (Ed "Wires" MacGuire); Nestor Paiva (Ferrara); Harry Shannon (Police Lieutenant Blake); Ben Welden (Haynes); John Miljan (Police Lieutenant Mayrin); Charles D. Brown (Dietrich); John Dehner (Jarvis); Anthony Caruso (Charlie)

SYNOPSIS

The notorious Jarvis gang pulls off a bank heist and immediately flees to a garage, where the mechanic welds the cash into the body of a car. The gang takes off and tries to elude the police, but after running a blockade they're shot during a chase and the car goes off a cliff, killing all the members of the gang instantly.

A few days later, private detective Tom Dwyer shows up in the offices of the insurance company that's been hired to recover the stolen $300,000. Sorelson, the company president, offers Dwyer 10 percent if he can find the money. Dwyer finds out the car's been sold to an amusement park exhibit, and he heads there to interview Ferrara, who owns the "Crime Museum." Ferrara tells Dwyer the car's already been sold to someone named Maguire. Outside, Dwyer meets his girlfriend, Bonnie, and talks her into a roller-coaster ride; when the ride finishes, a dead man is found in the last car. The dead man turns out to be the mechanic who welded the cash into the car.

Lt. Blake, the local homicide detective, is suspicious of Dwyer and questions him, but finally releases him. Unseen by Blake, Dwyer takes a brochure from the dead man's jacket, and he uses it to track down Sheila Kennedy, a sultry singer at a local club. Dwyer is instantly attracted to Sheila, but she won't tell him why she's being followed and fears for her life.

Dwyer goes back to the Crime Museum to investigate and finds Ferrara knocked out. He also has an encounter with Maguire, and

Nightclub singer Sheila (Ann Savage) performs in *The Last Crooked Mile* (1946).

soon recognizes him as the notorious killer "Wires" Maguire. Dwyer realizes that Maguire killed the mechanic — the only other person who knew about the cash — and will probably try to kill him now. Luckily for Dwyer, Lt. Blake shows up just then, and Dwyer is able to make his escape.

Dwyer sees Sheila Kennedy again, and she finally confesses that she was Jarvis's girlfriend. But she claims she doesn't know anything about the location of the missing cash.

Dwyer uses a contact inside the police force to get more information on the car, and that night he breaks into the Crime Museum again, this time with a welding torch. He pulls the door panel apart and finds the missing cash. He returns with it to his hotel room, calls Sorenson — and is knocked out during the call.

When Dwyer comes to, it's morning, the cash is gone, and Lt. Blake is there, accusing him of having murdered Maguire and his sidekick Haynes. But Sheila Kennedy arrives and alibis Dwyer, claiming she was with him all night. The disappointed cops exit, but soon thereafter Sorelson arrives and tries to kill Dwyer. Sheila knocks his gun aside, and Dwyer subdues him just as Lt. Blake rushes back in. Dwyer tells the cops that Sorelson is the murderer — Dwyer's figured out that the bank heist was an inside job, and Sorelson was working with the Jarvis gang.

With the case apparently solved, Sheila prepares to leave town and asks Dwyer to accompany her, but he turns her down. However, later that day he joins her on the way to the train station, and in the car he reveals that he's finally truly solved the case — he's figured out that Sheila was really the one who murdered Maguire and Haynes and now has the cash. Dwyer's right, and Sheila pulls a gun on him — but he reveals that the car is connected to the police radio, and Lt. Blake has now heard

Sheila (Ann Savage) accepts a light from Tom (Donald Barry) in this scene from *The Last Crooked Mile*.

her confession. As the car is chased by police on winding mountain roads, Dwyer takes a chance and cuffs Sheila. After the car skids to a stop, the police catch Sheila and take her off as Bonnie pops up from the car's rumble seat, ready for a date with Dwyer that doesn't involve a corpse.

COMMENTARY

Like other B crime films of the time, *The Last Crooked Mile* is an entertaining thriller that suffers from some odd casting. Republic may have thought they had their own James Cagney in Don Barry, but, unfortunately, Barry is neither as skilled nor as charismatic as Cagney, and his lack of chemistry with co-star Ann Savage is an obvious detriment to the film.

Fortunately, Barry is surrounded by an excellent supporting cast. Aside from Ann, there's stalwart baddie Sheldon Leonard as "Wires" Maguire and the lovely Adele Mara as Barry's bubbly girlfriend. Ann, in particular, is a standout, giving a sultry, sexy performance as the moll who's actually the boss (this is also one of her few appearances as a brunette). Two scenes in which she performs a torchy ballad in a nightclub are especially well shot, and Ann exudes sensual allure. Some of her dialogue with Barry is equally enticing, and it's a testament to the ability of the B films to slide under the censors' radar that a number of references to overnight stays are present. It's unfortunate that Barry's smug, smirking attempts at love scenes with Ann reduce any potential heat to subzero temperatures.

The Last Crooked Mile also suffers from a

frequently absurd script, and once again demonstrates the low-budget filmmaker's love of poking fun at cops, who are apparently too stupid in this movie to figure out that the money is welded into the car. Police and authorities were often belittled in these films (see, for example, *Dangerous Blondes*, in which a cop named "Gatling" can't name the inventor of the machine gun!), and shown as incompetent and incapable — until their presence was required to save the hero's life. This particular trope of the Bs is probably one of the clearest indicators of their intended audience — working class folk who might have had a run-in or two with Johnny Law.

Probably the most interesting aspect of *The Last Crooked Mile*—aside from the performance of Ann Savage—is the location shooting. Use of real locations was another trope of the B films, since they didn't have the money to build sets; and *The Last Crooked Mile* features an amusement park (complete with actual roller coaster footage rear-projected behind the actors as they pretend to react to the thrilling ride), city streets, and twisting hillside roads of the type that once outlined the Southern California basin before urban sprawl took over and the roads became freeways. *Mile* makes genuinely good use of those locations, and the car chases that open and close the film are tense and exciting.

Behind the Scenes

Don Barry was a popular star at Republic. A college football player, Barry had achieved minor stardom in 1940 in Republic's *Adventures of Red Ryder*, and made mainly westerns for Republic and other B film companies during the next decade. Because of his similarity to Jimmy Cagney, Republic occasionally tried to cast him in crime pictures (like *The Last Crooked Mile*), but Barry developed a reputation for being difficult, and his career began to fade. From 1951 on Barry appeared mainly in television roles, and in 1980 he committed suicide (he was 68).

Like Ann Savage, Adele Mara had worked under contract at Columbia, where she also appeared in one of the Boston Blackie films (*Alias Boston Blackie*, 1942). Mara, whose real name was Adelaide Delgado, was a Spanish-American who eventually dyed her hair blonde and found a small measure of success in Republic's westerns and crime thrillers. She eventually appeared in several big-budget John Wayne films, particularly *Sands of Iwo Jima* (1949).

Sheldon Leonard was a popular character actor who was known for his villains and mobsters (he'd played shady characters in two earlier Ann Savage films, *Klondike Kate* and *Passport to Suez* [both 1943]). After appearing in more than 60 feature films as an actor, Leonard followed a different career path beginning in the '50s when he became one of the most successful television producers in Hollywood, with such classic shows as *The Dick Van Dyke Show*, *The Andy Griffith Show*, and *I Spy* to his credit.

Portrait of a brunette: Ann Savage from *The Last Crooked Mile.*

In a *Hollywood Reporter* review, Jack D. Grant noted: "Miss Savage continues to give the impression that she has a great deal more to offer than any of her screen roles have demanded. Some of her scenes here as the nightclub thrush are really fine."

Lady Chaser

(PRC) Release Date: November 25, 1946

Screenplay: Fred Myton; story by G. T. Fleming-Roberts
Cinematography by: Jack Greenhalgh
Film Editing by: Holbrook N. Todd
Art Direction by: Frank Sylos
Set Decoration by: Elia H. Reif
Produced by: Sigmund Neufeld
Directed by: Sam Newfield
Cast: Robert Lowery (Peter Kane); Ann Savage (Inez Marie Polk); Inez Cooper (Dorian Westmore); Frank Ferguson (Vickers); William Haade (Bill Redding); Ralph Dunn (Brady); Paul Bryar (Garry); Charlie Williams (Apartment House Manager); Garry Owen (Herman); Marie Martino (Anna)

Synopsis

In the lounge of the exclusive Fabian's department store two women are writing letters: Dorian is penning a note to her sweetheart, but Inez is requesting more money in a blackmailing scheme regarding a murder. When Dorian gets a headache, Inez offers her aspirin. Meanwhile, a nosy maid (Anna) spies on Inez's letter and steals her elaborate brooch.

In a rough and rugged logging camp, David receives the letter from his girlfriend Dorian. She mentions her encounter with Inez and the brooch, but is more concerned with her uncle, who is opposed to the idea of her marrying David.

A day later Inez is home when she reads a newspaper article about how Dorian's uncle died after taking a poisoned aspirin, and that Dorian has been arrested for murder. Inez realizes her blackmail victim was aiming to kill her with the aspirin; unfortunately, Inez's boyfriend Bill seems more interested in gambling than Inez's troubles.

At Dorian's murder trial, her defense argues that a strange woman gave her the lethal aspirin; but Anna, the department store maid, lies to cover her theft of the brooch and contradicts Dorian's story of meeting Inez. Dorian is found guilty.

When David hears about the verdict, he immediately leaves the wilds and goes to see Dorian's attorney, Vickers. He shows Vickers the letter he received from Dorian, which mentions Inez, and he claims the police didn't care about the letter.

David decides to conduct his own investigation, so he starts by going to Fabian's, where he encounters Anna and flirts with her. They go out on a date, and she wears the brooch mentioned in Dorian's letter. At Anna's apartment, David threatens her until she reveals that she memorized the address on Inez's letter and is now running her own blackmailing scheme. Just then a man enters the apartment, knocks out David and kills Anna.

When David comes to, he finds himself a suspect in Anna's murder. The lead investigator, Inspector Brady, warns David not to leave town. David also discovers that the brooch is now missing.

David returns to Vickers, who is writing names down on a pad. He almost pulls a gun on David but stops when a detective enters his office and tells David that he's tracked down Inez. David goes to talk to her but finds she's gone. The apartment manager remembers her boyfriend's name and mentions that his bookie was "Herman." Vickers also arrives at the apartment and shoots at David, but misses and flees.

David goes to see Dorian in prison, and she shows him an anonymous letter she's received offering to help David's investigation. David goes to the address given in the letter but is ambushed by two thugs. David beats them off.

David's next move is to track down Bill's bookie. He finds Herman and gets Inez's address—but, unfortunately, so does Vickers. Vickers arrives at her place first and demands the evidence she's been using to blackmail him. She hands over some film.

Inez (Ann Savage) watches boyfriend Bill (William Haade) keep bad guys at bay in ***Lady Chaser*** (1946).

Just then both Bill and David arrive at Inez's apartment, and when David won't answer Bill's questions they begin to fight. David finally subdues Bill, then faces Vickers, who tries to shoot him, but David knocks him down. Inspector Brady arrives and arrests Vickers, and Dorian is freed at last.

Commentary

Lady Chaser is the last of the three films Ann Savage made for PRC. It features the director, writer and star of the spicy and very enjoyable *Apology for Murder*, and is another crime thriller in the classic PRC mold. Newfield's direction is professional, and the art direction is classic PRC—the exclusive department store consists of little more than a few plants on cheap tables.

The cast is a good mix of character types. Robert Lowery is an appealing leading man, and Inez Cooper makes an attractive and sympathetic match for him. Marie Martino's duplicitous and scheming Anna is snake-like, while Frank Ferguson's Vickers is creepy when on the prowl. Ann has a more hysterical edge in *Lady Chaser* than she normally allows her noir characters—we're obviously supposed to care about Inez when Vickers threatens her, even though she's been painted as a blackmailer and possibly an accessory to murder. Ann valiantly attempts to capture both sides of the character, moving effortlessly from anxiety and anger to fear; her considerable talents and appeal are well displayed in this odd roundelay of murder.

Behind the Scenes

The working title for *Lady Chaser* was *Lady Killer*.

Ann would work again with Robert Lowery in *Jungle Flight* (1947).

Frank Ferguson also has a small role in

1953's *Woman They Almost Lynched* (as the bartender).

Renegade Girl

(Affiliated Productions) Release Date: December 25, 1946

    Screenplay by: Edwin V. Westrate
    Director of Photography: James Brown Jr.
    Music: Darrell Calker
    Produced and Directed by: William Berke
    Cast: Ann Savage (Jean Shelby); Alan Curtis (Captain Fred Raymond); Edward Brophy (Bob Crandall); Russell Wade (Jerry Long); Jack Holt (Major Barker); Claudia Drake (Mary Manson); Ray Corrigan (William Quantrill); Chief Thundercloud (Chief Whitecloud)

Synopsis

It's 1864 and the Civil War rages even in the state of Missouri. Jean Shelby and her brother Bob are supplying information to Bill Quantrill's gang of Confederate raiders. Jean is returning home one day when she's captured by Union soldiers and taken to Major Barker. Just as she's brought before the Major, she witnesses a renegade native, Chief Whitecloud, telling the Yankees where the Shelbys can be found; Whitecloud and the Shelbys have a longstanding feud. Anxious to warn her brother, Jean pulls off a daring escape, stealing a soldier's gun and riding off. She reaches the Shelby homestead, where Bob is recovering from a serious injury. They attempt to leave before the Yankees arrive, but Bob doesn't get far before collapsing.

Jean attempts to ride on to Quantrill's camp, but she runs into the handsome Union officer Captain Raymond. She succeeds in capturing him, but finally acknowledges a mutual attraction by releasing him.

In this scene from 1946's *Renegade Girl*, Jean Shelby (Ann Savage) is interrogated by Sergeant James (Edmund Cobb, left) and Major Barker (Jack Holt, right).

Unfortunately, Bob is found and murdered by Whitecloud before Jean can reach him with help. Quantrill arrives with his men as Jean sobs over her brother's dead body. They've also found Captain Raymond and want to hang him, but Jean talks them out of it.

Whitecloud, meanwhile, has returned to his Cherokee tribe, vowing to destroy all of the Shelbys. He leads a band to burn down the Shelby home, killing Jean's parents in the process. Then he encounters Jean, who he seriously wounds with a thrown knife.

A year passes as Jean recovers. She thinks about Captain Raymond but is sure he's forgotten her. She's now living only to go after Whitecloud.

One day several members of Quantrill's old gang, including his second-in-command, Jerry, show up, telling Jean that since the Civil War has ended and Quantrill is dead, the gang is now down to only six. Jerry wants Jean to join them, and she agrees as long as they'll help her get Whitecloud.

Just as Jean leaves with Jerry, Captain Raymond shows up; he's been imprisoned and tried to get letters out to her, but she didn't receive them.

Jean strikes a deal with the remaining members of Quantrill's gang: She'll marry whoever can help her kill Whitecloud. In the meantime, she's changing her name to "Marie Carol" and is taking control of the gang. Under her leadership, the gang achieves criminal success, pulling off raids and robberies. But the day comes when she can no longer hold the quarreling men together. They begin to fight over her, and soon only Jerry is left alive.

Overcome with guilt at the deaths of the five men she once commanded, Jean flees and is found by Raymond's troops. They reunite and he proposes—provided he can capture the notorious criminal Marie Carol. Just then Jean finds out that Jerry has been caught by Raymond's men, and she escapes to go after Whitecloud. Jerry reveals the truth to Raymond, and he rides out after her. He catches up just as she kills Whitecloud, but she's shot by one of Raymond's men and dies in his arms.

COMMENTARY

Renegade Girl is not only one of the most interesting films Ann Savage ever made, but also an extraordinary picture in other ways. Made in 1946 on a budget that was obviously very low, the film is compelling, well acted, and could well be the first B-movie feminist western ever made.

Eight years later Nicholas Ray would make *Johnny Guitar*, and a host of low-budget girl-outlaw movies would follow. However, in 1945 low-budget westerns were designed to appeal to the largely male viewers of these films, so most of the entries in the genre focused on reliable male protagonists. As Don Miller says in his study of B westerns, *Hollywood Corral*, "The place for a woman, according to Hollywood, is in front of a wistful smile and adoring look saved for the finale."

Not so *Renegade Girl*. Although the script mixes in the standard trappings of a handsome Yankee soldier and a romance, the film is plainly more interested in telling the story of a female outlaw leader who snarls at men, "I don't belong to you," before leading them off to rob another town. Director William Berke made literally dozens of low-budget westerns prior to this one (including 1943's *Saddles and Sagebrush*, also starring Ann Savage), but *Renegade Girl* is genuinely unique.

That's thanks largely to the performance of Ann Savage in the eponymous role of Jean Shelby/Marie Carol. Most other actresses in the '40s would have emphasized the romantic aspect of Jean, her love for Captain Raymond and the tragedy of her downfall. But what Savage brings to the role is a genuine forcefulness; the ease with which she can both boss tough outlaws and stand up to Yankee questioning puts her on a par with Crawford or Davis. Savage even goes so far as to suggest that Jean actually enjoys committing violent acts; the twinkle that comes to her eye when she first picks up a gun after her recovery or talks about killing Whitecloud is unmistakable. Even the way she handles the love scenes—she pulls Raymond into every kiss, rather than the usual vice versa—is almost unheard-of for an ac-

Mary (Claudia Drake, right) comforts Jean (Ann Savage) in *Renegade Girl*.

Recovered after being badly wounded, Jean Shelby (Ann Savage) makes sure she can still shoot, as Mary (Claudia Drake) watches in this scene from *Renegade Girl*.

tress in 1946. If *Detour* had created cinema's first feminist monster, then *Renegade Girl* might be said to offer up one of its earliest truly liberated women.

If the rest of *Renegade Girl* isn't quite up to Savage's level, it's not for lack of trying. Director Berke generally keeps the melodrama to a minimum and the action fast. He occasionally moves the camera in unusual ways, has two short but nicely cut montages, and even employs some disturbing tight close-ups to maximum effect. Where he falters is in dialogue scenes that might have benefited from a few snips, and a wooden performance from Alan Curtis as the stalwart Captain Raymond. Also, whether for budgetary reasons or because of the censors at the time, actual punches and hits are kept so completely off-screen that the action occasionally becomes confusing, especially at the end.

But there are other assets on display in *Renegade Girl*, including some fine horsemanship displays, a rousing musical score (by Darrell Calker), and some solid supporting performances, especially from Russell Wade, oozing sleaze and pomade as Jerry Long.

With a slightly larger budget and tighter script, *Renegade Girl* might well be regarded today as a genre-busting classic. Instead, it's a diamond in the rough — buried in a pit of ash, but with enough light glinting through to mark it as a little gem worthy of rediscovery, especially by those who think Ann Savage's career began and ended with *Detour*.

Behind the Scenes

Renegade Girl is one of two Westerns (the other is the 1953 *Woman They Almost Lynched*) Ann Savage appeared in that centered on the true historical figure of William Quantrill, a Confederate guerrilla leader who died in 1865 at the age of 27. In *Woman They Almost Lynched*, Quantrill was played by Brian Donlevy (who had also played the role in the 1950 *Kansas Raiders*); in *Renegade Girl* it's legendary stuntman Ray "Crash" Corrigan. Corrigan earned his nickname for his willingness to act out dangerous stunts, and later made a career of playing apes and monsters. Corrigan came to the role of Quantrill in *Renegade Girl* almost by mistake: The production was shooting on his ranch in Ventura County, and the actor originally hired to play Quantrill got lost trying to find the location, so director Berke talked his old friend Corrigan into taking the part.

Claudia Drake, who plays "Mary Manson," had previously appeared with Ann in *Detour*.

Director William Berke also worked frequently with western star Russell Hayden (they made 16 films together), and directed Ann in the two films she made with Hayden, *Saddles and Sagebrush* (1943) and *The Last Horseman* (1944). He also directed Ann in *Pygmy Island* (1950) and *Pier 23* (1951).

Renegade Girl was loosely based on a 1928 Columbia film called *Court-Martial* about a Union Army officer who is ordered to bring in the outlaw Belle Starr, but instead falls in love with her. The lead in *Court-Martial* was played by western star Jack Holt, who appears in *Renegade Girl* as Major Barker.

Renegade Girl proved to be a difficult film for Ann (the pressbook for the film claims that director Berke auditioned 20 other actresses for the role). Ann insisted on tackling a difficult 15-foot roll down an embankment, and the stunt cost her more than a few bruises. However, because Ann wasn't a horsewoman in real life, all the riding in the film was doubled by an experienced rider who happened to bear a strong resemblance to Ann. Ann was proud of the fact that the same stuntwoman also doubled Jennifer Jones in 1946's *Duel in the Sun*.

The publicity materials for *Renegade Girl* emphasize that the film passed the censors and is suitable for all ages. The pressbook includes a small interview with Ann on how she approached the film's crying scenes, and she notes that crying onscreen needs to be carefully controlled by the performer:

> No woman is attractive when she's crying — unless she's crying for an effect. There was the case of the actress who started to cry for a scene, let herself get out of control and wound up bawling in front of some 200

Renegade Girl: Gang leader "Marie Carol" (Ann Savage) plots with lieutenants Jerry (Russell Wade, left) and Bob (Edward Brophy, right).

people on the set — and all the camera got was a long close-up of her wide-open mouth.

The pressbook biography of the "petite Miss Savage" notes that

> In January, 1946, Miss Savage was married to Bert D'Armand, theatrical agent and producer. They live quietly in a sumptuous apartment off Hollywood's famed Sunset Strip and they devote most of their attention to two Siamese cats and a large collection of classical and popular records.
>
> Except for fishing, Ann is strictly a spectator in sports. She spends at least a month out of every year fishing the waters of a favorite Nevada stream.

Jungle Flight

(Pine-Thomas Productions/Paramount) Release Date: August 22, 1947

Screenplay by: Whitman Chambers; story by David Lang
Cinematography by: Jack Greenhalgh
Film Editing by: Howard Smith
Art Direction by: F. Paul Sylos
Set Decoration by: Elias H. Reif
Produced by: William H. Pine and William C. Thomas
Directed by: Sam Newfield
Cast: Robert Lowery (Kelly Jordan); Ann Savage (Laurey Roberts); Barton MacLane (Case Hagin); Douglas Fowley (Tom Hammond); Douglas Blackley (Andy Melton); Curt Bois (Pepe); Duncan Renaldo (Police Captain Costa)

SYNOPSIS

Kelly Jordan and Andy Melton, former AAF fliers, are operating two planes in a Latin American country, saving money to fly home to Texas to open a commercial line — and for Andy to see his wife and baby.

An eager beaver, Andy tries to double-up

to regain money Kelly lost gambling. Case Hagin is all for it, as the boys are flying for his mine and he desperately needs new machinery.

Against Kelly's wishes, Andy starts out, followed angrily by Kelly. The latter has landing gear trouble and uses it as an excuse to go to town, where he sees Laurey Roberts, a singer, at the hotel. She completely ignores his advances.

Meanwhile, she's having difficulties. Tom Hammond, her divorced husband and a murderer, appears on the scene and threatens her if she doesn't go with him. Wanting to escape, she goes to the airport and tries to thumb a flight with Andy. He's overloaded but suggests she try Kelly.

Andy takes off. His heavy load breaks loose, the plane crashes and he is killed. Laurey tells Kelly, and the latter gives her a hop to the mine. He doesn't know about Hammond.

Laurey is cooking for the mine and falls in love with Kelly. Natives bring Hammond, half dead from traveling through the jungle, to the camp. Native police arrive and arrest Hammond for robbery and murder, and he, seeking revenge, implicates Laurey.

The police plane, with Laurey and Hammond aboard as prisoners, takes off, but the murderer overpowers the officer and causes the ship to crash into the jungle. Kelly goes to the rescue and saves the group. However, Hammond is killed in self defense by Laurey.

Commentary

Jungle Flight was not available for viewing; it seems to be, sadly, a lost film.

The above synopsis was taken from the film's original pressbook.

Jungle Flight (1947): Laurey Roberts (Ann Savage) is held hostage by her ex-husband Tom Hammond (Douglas Fowley, left), while the pilot (Douglas Blackley) tries to keep the plane on course.

BEHIND THE SCENES

Jungle Flight's aerial scenes, led by stunt flier Paul Mantz, were filmed in California over the Sierra Mountains (standing in for the Andes).

The pressbook for *Jungle Flight* claims that Ann "had to turn down an offer of a leading role with Helen Hayes in the New York stage production of *Happy Birthday* in order to complete her co-starring part" in the film.

Ann and co-star Barton McLane were both born in Columbia, South Carolina.

Robert Lowery and Ann Savage from *Jungle Flight*.

Satan's Cradle

(Inter American Films) Release Date: October 7, 1949

Screenplay by: Jack Benton; based on a character created by O. Henry
Original Music by: Albert Glasser
Cinematography by: Jack Greenhalgh
Film Editing by: Martyn Cohn
Art Direction by: Frank Sylos
Set Decoration by: Helen Hansard
Produced by: Philip N. Krasne
Directed by: Ford Beebe
Cast: Duncan Renaldo (Cisco Kid); Leo Carrillo (Pancho); Ann Savage (Lil); Douglas Fowley (Steve Gentry); Byron Foulger (the Preacher); Claire Carleton (Belle); Buck Bailey (Rocky); George DeNormand (Idaho)

SYNOPSIS

The Cisco Kid and his partner Pancho are riding into Silver City, where the Kid is looking forward to meeting legendary frontier beauty Lil. On the outskirts of town they encounter a preacher who's been banished for speaking out against Lil. The preacher tells them that the town and the silver mine were founded and owned by a man named Jim Mason, but after Mason died in a cave-in Lil arrived, claiming to be Mason's widow and thus inheriting all. The Kid and Pancho agree to accompany the preacher back to town.

They arrive at Lil's saloon and announce Sunday services, but the lovely Lil immediately cancels any church proceedings, and her men attack Cisco and Pancho. Lil is impressed by Cisco's fighting skills, and they flirt before Cisco and Pancho leave. After they exit, Lil's partner, Steve Gentry, wants to kill Cisco, but Lil says she'll handle him.

Cisco and Pancho are helping the preacher put his church back together when Lil shows up, suggesting Cisco join her. When he declines, one of Gentry's men tries to gun him down, but Cisco shoots his would-be assassin first.

Cisco suggests to the preacher that they try to prove Lil is not really Mason's widow, but the preacher tells him he's already been informed that the courthouse where the marriage records were kept has burned down.

Stumped, Cisco decides to confront Lil directly, but he's forced to flee when Gentry pulls a gun on him. When Lil complains to Gentry, he reveals that he's forged a quit-claim deed to all of the properties Lil had supposedly inherited from Mason, and so Lil now works for him.

Hiding in the hills at the edge of town, Cisco and Pancho decide to investigate the mine where Mason died. On the way to the mine they're ambushed by Gentry and his gang, but they manage to shoot their way out. They arrive at the mine and find proof that the deadly landslide was man-made; but just then Gentry and his lieutenant Rocky blow up the mine, sealing them in. Fortunately, they're unharmed and find another way out.

Cisco and Pancho return to town, and Cisco visits Lil, who now confesses her part in the scam. Gentry appears and tries to shoot her; then he and Rocky ride off, with Cisco and Pancho in pursuit. Pancho lassos Rocky, and Cisco finally kills the villainous Gentry. They return to Silver City to find that Lil has surrendered.

Commentary

Satan's Cradle is an unpretentious and enjoyable little western, and one that's considerably fueled by Ann Savage at her loveliest. The script asks a lot of her, embodying a woman so beautiful that she's drawn the Cisco Kid across the west in search of her. But she more than fulfills the plot's promise, and her Lil is one of her most alluring and delightful character creations.

Satan's Cradle is a typical B western in most other respects, replete with a heroic, slightly roguish good guy, his comic relief sidekick, a ruthless bad guy, some resplendent locations and a fast plot (with a few requisite logic gaps). By casting Ann as a tough-girl saloon owner with an attraction to Cisco, it adds a healthy dollop of sexuality to the oater mix, even while retaining the bang-bang-you're-dead action that would usually mark a film like this as kiddie fare. There's potent chemistry between Ann's Lil and Duncan Renaldo's Cisco, and it's actually disappointing at the conclusion when she surrenders to church-going goodness instead of bringing out more of Cisco's naughty nature.

Satan's Cradle occasionally runs into trouble when it allows Leo Carrillo's Pancho to abscond with large chunks of running time, and the editor seems to have noticeably left a few scenes on the cutting room floor, including one explaining how Cisco and Pancho escaped from a mine after a deadly cave-in.

But in the final analysis those flaws are minor when compared to the strengths of Ann's Lil (and her interplay with Duncan's Cisco). In the annals of unusual B westerns, *Satan's Cradle* may not be *Renegade Girl*, but Ann's luscious sensuality nonetheless sets it well apart from the rest of the herd.

Behind the Scenes

The Cisco Kid was a character originally created by O. Henry in his 1907 short story "The Caballero's Way." Contrary to the character's cinematic renderings, O. Henry describes him as a 25-year-old outlaw: "The Cisco Kid had killed six men in more or less fair scrimmages, had murdered twice as many (mostly Mexicans), and had winged a larger number whom he modestly forbore to count." The character Pancho does not appear in the story at all, and wasn't introduced in the Cisco Kid legend until a 1942 radio incarnation. More than 30 Cisco Kid movies have been made, with actors Warner Baxter, Cesar Romero, Gilbert Roland and Duncan Renaldo all making multiple movies portraying the character. Renaldo and Leo Carrillo as Pancho went on to appear in 156 episodes of an early color television series that ran from 1950 to 1956.

Duncan Renaldo, who was one of Ann's favorite co-stars, was a Spanish-born actor who first came to the United States in the 1920s, made his living for a time as a portrait painter, and was arrested for illegal immigration before being pardoned by Franklin Delano Roosevelt (fortunately for Duncan, FDR's wife Eleanor owned one of his paintings). Renaldo started in the film industry as a producer, but his good looks and charm soon earned him more work as an actor. Despite appearing in dozens of other films (including 1947's *Jungle Flight*, also with Ann), Duncan (who passed away in 1980) is best known today for his long run as the Cisco Kid.

Leo Carrillo came from one of the oldest families in California, with ancestors who had served as early settlers, governors and mayors (of Los Angeles). Leo, who was also a writer and cartoonist, was active in California conservation and preservation. Eventually, Leo Carrillo State Park (located 28 miles northwest of Santa Monica) was named in his honor.

Director Ford Beebe was a craftsman who was skilled in making serial films; his list of credits includes movies in the Buck Rogers, Jungle Jim, Flash Gordon, Green Hornet and Bomba the Jungle Boy series, as well as stand-alone features.

Satan's Cradle was the seventh of the 8 Cisco Kid feature films starring Duncan Renaldo, and was also known by the alternate title *The Devil's Den*.

Pygmy Island

(The Katzman Corporation/Columbia) Release Date: November 22, 1950

Screenplay by: Carroll Young
Director of Photography: Ira H. Morgan
Musical Director: Mischa Bakaleinikoff
Film Editor: Jerome Thoms
Art Director: Paul Palmentola
Set Decorator: Sidney Clifford
Produced by: Sam Katzman
Directed by: William Berke
Cast: Johnny Weissmuller (Jungle Jim); Ann Savage (Captain Ann R. Kingsley); David Bruce (Major Bolton); Steven Geray (Leon Marko); William Tannen (Kruger); Billy Curtis (Makuba)

Synopsis

At a top-level meeting, Army brass are concerned over a missing officer, Captain Kingsley, who disappeared in a distant jungle while searching for the legendary nagoma plants, which provide a fiber that's unbreakable and impervious to fire. Since Kingsley's dogtags were found by a local guide named Jungle Jim, it's agreed that Jim will be hired to lead an army squad in search of Kingsley.

The army troops arrive in exotic Bugandi and immediately encounter Leon Marko, a local merchant. After Major Bolton hires Jim and reveals that Kingsley is actually a woman, Marko reports to a rival group also seeking the nagoma plants, and the race is on.

Leading Major Bolton's troops in search of Kingsley, Jungle Jim encounters and fights off stampeding elephants, a rampaging gorilla, a treacherous rope suspension bridge, and enemy soldiers. He also discovers that the murderous "Bush Devils" who have been menacing the area are actually Marko's men in disguise. Meanwhile, Kingsley has befriended a tribe of pygmies who've shown her the nagoma plants and now agree to help her return to Bugandi. She and the pygmy chief, Makuba, set off on a raft disguised as driftwood. Kingsley and Makuba are nearly captured by Marko's men, but Jungle Jim saves them and accompanies them to Major Bolton. Makuba agrees to help Bolton find the nagoma plants.

The next morning, Jim, Makuba and Captain Kingsley attack Marko's camp but find the enemy soldiers have already left and are now en route to the swamp where the nagoma plants grow. Unfortunately for Marko and his cohorts, though, the pygmies, led by second-in-command Kimba, are ready for them; as Jim fights off machine-gunners and hand grenades at the rear of Marko's forces, the pygmies subdue the main unit with rocks, clubs and nagoma lassoes. Bolton and Kingsley arrive to claim ownership of the nagoma plants; and as they leave, Jungle Jim stays behind to celebrate with Makuba and the victorious pygmies.

Commentary

Pygmy Island is a serviceable boys' adventure film; in fact, its simplicity and sheer camp appeal practically defy any real criticism. Yes, of course that crazed gorilla is an actor in a thoroughly ridiculous suit; yet the very fact that the suit has clearly seen better days only adds to the charm of the whole ridiculous enterprise. Johnny Weissmuller may be twenty years past his prime (and with no better acting skills acquired in the meantime), but he's still game to leap into any body of water or play with his chimpanzee sidekick "Tamba." As the intrepid army scientist Kingsley, Ann Savage looks smashing in her safari suit, but she seems bored by the proceedings (as indeed do virtually all of the other actors, with the notable ex-

Captain Kingsley (Ann Savage) confers with the title characters (including Billy Barty, lower right) in *Pygmy Island* (1950).

ceptions of Billy Curtis as Makuba and Billy Barty as pygmy lieutenant Kimba). The film relies on locations around Los Angeles (especially the famed County Arboretum) to recreate its exotic jungle locale, and in some sequences merely reversing an angle can change the setting from jungle to high desert. However, the film is paced well and probably kept many a twelve-year-old riveted to the screen in anticipation of the next peril Jungle Jim would encounter and finally triumph over.

Behind the Scenes

Jungle Jim was a character first created in a comic strip begun in 1934 by writer Don Moore and artist Alex Raymond. The newspaper strips were later republished in comic book form, and original Jungle Jim comic books were published intermittently from 1949 to 1970. There was a Jungle Jim radio series (starring Gerald Mohr, who also appeared with Ann in *One Dangerous Night* [1943]), and in 1937 Universal produced a 12-part serial starring Grant Withers.

Jungle Jim would become Johnny Weissmuller's second most popular character after Tarzan (in fact, Weissmuller only played four characters in his career, and one of those was himself). He played Jim in 16 feature films for Columbia, and then for one season of a television series.

In the spring of 1950, Johnny Weissmuller toured the country in a live show called "Aquacade" that included a beauty contest whose winner would supposedly become the leading lady in *Pygmy Island*. What the winners didn't know was that producer Sam Katzman had essentially already cast Ann Savage in the part.

Ann holds her own in the land of *Pygmy Island* and tackles a water sequence very bravely, even though she didn't like any film that required her to leap into water; she had a fear of acquiring pneumonia as a result of being immersed (this same predilection caused far more trouble on the set of 1944's *Two-Man Submarine*).

Pygmy Island is considered a minor camp classic by some fans, and consequently has an amazingly high rating at internet film sites like the Internet Movie Database. The film is full of the sort of gaffes (the best probably being a background waterfall that never moves) that have endeared films from this era to nostalgic baby boomers, and its depiction of the pygmies is good-natured enough to make it relatively inoffensive to modern-day, politically-correct audiences.

Pier 23

(Spartan Productions/Lippert Pictures) Release Date: May 11, 1951

Screenplay by: Julian Harmon and Victor West; story by Herbert Margolis and Louis Morheim
Original Music by: Bert Shefter
Cinematography by: Jack Greenhalgh
Film Editing by: Carl Pierson and Harry Reynolds
Art Direction by: F. Paul Sylos
Set Decoration by: Harry Reif
Produced and Directed by: William Berke
Cast: Hugh Beaumont (Dennis O'Brien); Ann Savage (Ann Harmon); Edward Brophy (Professor Shicker); Richard Travis (Inspector Lt. Bruger); Margia Dean (Flo Klingle); Mike Mazurki (Ape Danowski); David Bruce (Charles Giffen); Raymond Greenleaf (Father Donovan); Eve Miller (Norma Harmon)

Synopsis

Pier 23 is an anthology film consisting of two separate stories, both focusing on San Francisco boat shop owner and gun-for-hire Dennis O'Brien.

In the first story, O'Brien is hired by a man named Cavalli to pick up $1000 at a rigged wrestling match. When O'Brien tries to deliver the money to his contact, Nick Garrison, Garrison pulls a gun on him and O'Brien just barely escapes. He goes in search of Cavalli but runs afoul of "Ape" Danowski, who won the match. Danowski knocks him out, and when O'Brien comes to he finds himself facing Inspector Bruger, who tells him Cavalli is dead. After O'Brien meets up with Flo Klingle, the wife of the dead wrestler, he finds out that Flo is having an affair with Garrison. Garrison tries to kill O'Brien, but "Ape," who is in love with Flo, intervenes. Although Garrison finally kills "Ape," O'Brien escapes. After Flo confesses, Garrison is finally captured by the police.

In the second story, O'Brien receives a visit from a priest, Father Donovan, who hires him to track down an escaped convict. O'Brien finds the escapee, Joe Harmon, but agrees to let him make one stop en route to Donovan. They arrive at a woman's apartment, where O'Brien is knocked out. When he awakens, he finds Harmon stabbed to death. He calls Donovan and describes the mystery woman, who is actually Harmon's sister. He also discovers that the dead man is not Harmon but another man named Greeley. When O'Brien receives a tip from Lt. Bruger that the real Harmon has already killed someone tonight at the Nubian Club, O'Brien heads there and encounters Ann, Harmon's sister, again. She claims that Greeley was fine when she left him, and that she's at the club because she's dating the owner, Charlie Giffen. She also tells O'Brien that her sister Norma made off with all of Joe's money. When O'Brien heads home, he finds Norma awaiting him; she doesn't have any money but wants to know where Joe is. Later, the Professor calls in with the news that Joe got $5,000 tonight from Giffen, only to be found dead just after he left the club, with the money missing. O'Brien realizes that Norma is innocent and is the one who told Father Donovan about her brother's escape. O'Brien arranges a meeting with Father Donovan, but when he and Norma arrive for the rendezvous they find Giffen and Ann waiting for them. Giffen tries to kill them, but Ann has secretly emptied the gun. Lt. Bruger arrests Giffen, and O'Brien finds out that Ann has a terminal disease and wanted the money to live out her remaining six months in style.

Commentary

Pier 23 is consistent with the standards of early 1950s crime films (or television, which this compilation film was actually aiming for). Although the basic concept — Hugh Beaumont as a scruffy jack-of-all-trades who lives on the San Francisco wharf and solves crimes with the aide of his drunken sidekick the Professor — is certainly serviceable, the two stories that make up the film are overly-complicated and depend too much on the protagonist being knocked unconscious in the first act.

As with *The Last Crooked Mile* (which Ann made five years earlier), probably the best thing about *Pier 23* is the location shooting. Shots of Beaumont walking the San Francisco streets at night feel authentically seedy (they were undoubtedly grabbed on the sly), and director William Berke also shoots his interiors well, giving the film(s) a textured *film noir* look.

The entire cast is solid, with Beaumont making a fine low-key, masculine *noir* protagonist, and Ann Savage in fine form as the femme fatale in the second offering (even though her character is saddled with an inexplicable last-minute terminal illness).

Unfortunately, *Pier 23*'s stories attempt to pack too many plot twists into their short running times and end up being so difficult to follow they lose any possibility of developing real suspense. Given some better writing, *Pier 23* could have been an effective and successful television series instead of filler for the bottom half of a low-budget double feature.

Behind the Scenes

At a time when other distributors were repackaging episodes of television shows and selling them as low-budget features, producer/distributor Robert Lippert had the idea of shooting six different short films, all based on episodes of a syndicated radio show called *Pat Novak, for Hire* (which was written by Herbert Margolis and Louis Morheim, who receive "story by" credit on *Pier 23*). Lippert first packaged the six 30-minute stories as three features, and then as six television episodes. The three feature films eventually became *Pier 23*, *Roaring City* and *Danger Zone* (all three were released in 1951).

Hugh Beaumont had previously appeared with Ann in *Apology for Murder* (1945). Six years after *Pier 23*, Beaumont would forever leave behind his *film noir* days by taking on the role of Ward Cleaver in the television series *Leave It to Beaver*.

Pier 23 was the fifth and last film Ann Savage would make with director William Berke (the others were *Saddles and Sagebrush* [1943], *The Last Horseman* [1944], *Renegade Girl* [1946] and *Pygmy Island* [1950]).

An alternate (television) title for *Pier 23* was *Flesh and Leather*.

Woman They Almost Lynched

(Republic) Release Date: March 20, 1953

Screenplay by: Steve Fisher; based on a story in *Saturday Evening Post* by Michael Fessier
Cinematography by: Reggie Lanning
Editing by: Fred Allen
Music by: Stanley Wilson
Art Direction by: James Sullivan
Set Decoration by: John McCarthy, Jr., and George Milo
Costume Design by: Adele Palmer
Produced and Directed by: Allan Dwan
Cast: John Lund (Lance Horton); Brian Donlevy (Quantrill); Audrey Totter (Kate Quantrill); Joan Leslie (Sally Maris); Ben Cooper (Jesse James); Nina Varela (Mayor Delilah Courtney); Jim Davis (Cole Younger); Reed Hadley (Bitterroot Bill Maris); Ann Savage (Glenda); Virginia Christine (Jenny); Marilyn Lindsey (Rose); Nacho Galindo (John Pablo)

SYNOPSIS:

It's the spring of 1865, near the end of the Civil War, and outlaws are running wild. One town in particular, Border City, has been nearly overrun by lawlessness. Set right on the border of Arkansas and Missouri (in fact, the border runs right through the Lead Dollar, the town's saloon), the citizens of Border City have elected a female mayor, Delilah Courtney, who is so tough she hangs men just for trying to stir up trouble with talk.

A stagecoach with a lone female passenger, Sally Maris, is headed for Border City when it's attacked by a gang of outlaws led by the notorious Quantrill and his even more infamous wife, Kate. A small troop of Yankee soldiers holds the robbers off for a few moments, but they're finally slaughtered and Sally is captured. Quantrill allows her to continue on into Border City, accompanied by one of his men, a sympathetic youngster named Dingus. On the ride into town Sally tries to talk the young man out of pursuing the life of an outlaw, but upon arriving in Border City she finds out "Dingus" is actually Jesse James. Although she realizes there's no point trying to talk him out of his criminal life, she's nonetheless had an effect on him.

Sally has come to Border City to see her brother, Bill. She finds him running the Lead Dollar, and is horrified when he at first mistakes her for a new dance hall girl. But when Jesse tells Bill that Sally is his sister, Bill apologizes and offers her his room. Sally soon realizes that Bill's former fiancée is now Kate Quantrill; two years ago Kate was abducted from Border City, and now she's married to Quantrill and has become an outlaw herself. In the saloon, meanwhile, Kate sings Bill's favorite song just to cause him pain. Unfortunately, she's a little too successful, and the enraged Bill tries to shoot her, but is himself cut down by Lance Horton, the local mine foreman and the closest thing Border City has to a sheriff.

When Sally finds her brother dead, she angrily orders Quantrill and Kate to leave, then finds out she's inherited the saloon. She immediately tries to put a stop to the drinking, gambling and prostitution, and the three saloon girls pack their bags to leave. However, when Sally discovers that the mayor is unwilling to help her secure other employment, she's forced to re-open the Lead Dollar. Although the saloon girls are happy to stay, they also give Sally some bad news: Along with the saloon, she's also inherited her brother's gambling debts, which will take some time to pay off.

Meanwhile, Quantrill arranges a meeting with Lance Horton. The outlaw leader reveals that he's in town to obtain lead from the local mines to sell to the Confederacy, and he knows that Horton is actually a spy working for the rebels. Quantrill threatens to unmask Lance unless he agrees to sell Quantrill lead.

Meanwhile, at the saloon, Quantrill's second-in-command, Cole Younger, accosts Sally but is warned away by Jesse James. Suddenly, news arrives that the Southern army is one mile outside of town. Kate tries to sing "Dixie," but Sally challenges her to a fistfight and wins. After Sally closes the saloon, Lance confesses that he's a spy for the rebels, and he kisses Sally. He tries to escape from town to the Confederate Army but is captured by Quantrill's men.

Kate, meanwhile, infuriated by losing the fistfight to Sally, is planning on shooting Sally in the morning. Jesse overhears her plans and goes to warn Sally, suggesting she run. Sally, however, is resolute about facing Kate, and Jesse leaves her a pistol. The next morning Sally easily outdraws Kate and injures Kate's hand.

As Quantrill rides off to the mines with the captive Lance, the Union army appears, and the gang tries to fight them off. Cole Younger goes to kidnap Sally, but Jesse James frees Lance to save her. Lance manages to take out Younger but is himself badly injured.

As the battle between Quantrill's men and the Union troops rages on, Sally hides the wounded Lance and also takes in Kate, who has been hurt during the fight. After the Yankees chase Quantrill's gang out of town, they come to the Lead Dollar, looking for Kate. Kate has disguised herself as one of the saloon girls and even performs a number to entertain the Union soldiers. The ruse works, and after the Yankees leave, Kate begs Sally's forgiveness.

Later, Horton regains consciousness long enough to give Sally his secret map to the lead mines. Just then the Yankees reappear, having been informed that Lance is a Confederate spy. Sally, however, lets herself be caught with the map, and Mayor Courtney orders that Sally be hung.

Just as the noose tightens around Sally's neck, Kate rides in to save her, telling them about Lance Horton. Kate then rides out of town, with the Union soldiers in hot pursuit, but she manages to elude them. In town, Sally is declared innocent and set free.

A month later Sally has paid off her brother's debts and is still running the Lead Dollar. News comes that Kate has left Quantrill and is now in New Orleans, singing under the name Kitty McCoy. Lance Horton finally reappears and tells Mayor Courtney that the war is over. As the citizens of Border City celebrate, Lance proposes to Sally and suggests they start a new life together in the south.

Commentary

Woman They Almost Lynched would be a fairly average mid–50s B western were it not for the unusual focus on the female characters.

Director Allan Dwan (possibly the most prolific director in cinematic history) knows how to efficiently shoot and cut material like this while still giving it a certain amount of polish, and the film's action scenes in particular — whether the opening chase scene or the girl-girl bar brawl — are exciting.

Woman They Almost Lynched is probably most remembered now, though, for Audrey Totter's Kate Quantrill. She makes a striking visual impression, with her tight cowboy duds and blonde ponytail. Her over-the-top portrayal of Kate is well-balanced by Joan Leslie's grounded and matter-of-fact Sally, and the scenes between the two of them have genuine verve (and occasionally a smirk).

Sadly, the rest of the cast, especially the male performers, is less successful. Brian Donlevy is both too old to play real-life youthful outlaw Bill Quantrill and comes across as too contemporary; he'd be far more at home in a fedora than a Stetson. John Lund, as romantic lead Lance Horton, is simply stiff and poorly matched to Leslie. Ann Savage is nearly lost in a supporting role as saloon girl Glenda; it's to her credit that she brings the underwritten role to life.

With a better script, *Woman They Almost Lynched* might have attained cult classic status, but it's hopelessly hamstrung by an overly-complicated plot. Had the film simply focused on a town beset by outlaws, it would have worked far better; trying to intercut Quantrill's gang with lead mining, Lance's subterfuge and the sudden arrival of armies overpacks the story, often confusingly so. The film also features an odd political angle, portraying the Confederate spy as a noble hero who winds up simply wanting to take his girl back home — to a South that surely even 1953 audiences would have remembered as enduring the horrors of Reconstruction. It hardly seems like a triumphant payoff for poor Sally.

Part of the film's confusion may result from Dwan's insistence that he approached it as a comedy. Unfortunately, nothing in the film is genuinely funny; some of it approaches camp, certainly, but only Totter seems to have been in on the joke. Even the purely female gun duel and fistfight are approached with a seriousness that hardly lends itself to camp. *Woman They Almost Lynched* really required a lighter hand at the directorial helm; Dwan was nearly 70 when he made this film, and although it benefits from his skill, it also betrays considerable reluctance in actually exploring the story's humorous potential.

BEHIND THE SCENES

Director Allan Dwan called *Woman They Almost Lynched* a parody, and added, "We had a gun fight between two gals— going down the street like the cowpunchers. If they'd had anything but skirts on, I'd have shot between their legs. I couldn't do that with girls." In commenting on some of Dwan's B pictures, film historian Peter Bogdanovich noted:

> Customarily, when the material struck him as ludicrous enough, Dwan resorted to his own brand of subtle satire, which even the actors were rarely, if ever, aware of. One or two shots of open-mouthed Nelson Eddy singing jovially as he rides through *Northwest Outpost* (1947) are sufficient to destroy him forever, and the Joan Leslie-Audrey Totter confrontations in *Woman They Almost Lynched* (1953) are equally devastating. Consciously and only to amuse himself, Dwan was creating camp twenty years ahead of its time.

As with the earlier Ann Savage-starring western *Renegade Girl* (1946), the action in *Woman They Almost Lynched* centers on the real-life Confederate guerrilla leader William Clarke Quantrill, who raided towns and terrified civilians along the Missouri-Kansas border until he was killed in 1865 at the age of 27. Quantrill's gang, which at one point was nearly 400 strong, included famed outlaws Jesse and Frank James, and Cole and Jim Younger. In 1862 Quantrill took a 14-year-old bride who rode and lived with the men until she was widowed at the age of 17. Quantrill has been a character in a number of films aside from *Renegade Girl* and *Woman They Almost Lynched*, including *Quantrill's Raiders* (1958), *Young Jesse James* (1960), and the 1950 *Kansas Raiders*, in which Brian Donlevy first played Quantrill.

Fire with Fire

(Paramount) Release Date: May 9, 1986
  Screenplay by: Bill Phillips and Warren Skaaren and Paul Boorstin & Sharon Boorstin
  Original Music by: Howard Shore
  Cinematography by: Hiro Narita
  Film Editing by: Peter E. Berger
  Production Design by: Norman Newberry
  Art Direction by: Michael Bolton
  Set Decoration by: Rondi Johnson
  Costume Design by: Enid Harris
  Produced by: Gary Nardino
  Directed by: Duncan Gibbins
  Cast: Craig Sheffer (Joe Fisk); Virginia Madsen (Lisa Taylor); Jon Polito (Duchard); Jeffrey Jay Cohen (Myron); Kate Reid (Sister Victoria); Jean Smart (Sister Maria); Tim Russ (Jerry Washington); David Harris (Ben Halsey); D. B. Sweeney (Thomas Baxter); Ann Savage (Sister Harriet)

SYNOPSIS

Joe Fisk is a fresh arrival at an honor camp in the Pacific Northwest; not far away is an all-girls Catholic school. When Joe has a chance encounter with Lisa Taylor, a star student from the school, he falls for her instantly. When Lisa arranges a dance between the school and the camp, Joe finds out that the attraction is mutual. Soon the young lovers are arranging secret night-time meetings, where Lisa learns that Joe's crime was stealing a cruel stepfather's car, and reveals that Lisa's parents have essentially imprisoned her in the Catholic school.

Unfortunately, a rendezvous in a cemetery is discovered by Duchard, the cruel warden of the honor camp, and Joe and Lisa are captured. Lisa is locked in her room while Joe is held overnight, to be sent to the state penitentiary in the morning. Joe, however, is rescued by his best friend Myron, who provides Joe with a map to an isolated cabin and a car from the camp's auto shop. Joe escapes, stopping only long enough to take Lisa out of the school before heading into the wilderness.

Duchard is obsessed with capturing the escaped Joe, and upon searching Myron's locker he finds a copy of the map. He soon arrives at the mountain cabin with an armed force, intent on gunning Joe down. When the cabin goes up in flames, Joe and Lisa run into the woods, with Duchard in hot pursuit. They reach a cliff's edge and, faced with the murderous Duchard, choose instead to leap into the river hundreds of feet below.

Convinced that the lovers are dead, Duchard gives up the hunt — but Joe and Lisa have survived. Some distance downstream they clamber up out of the river, ready to begin a new life together.

COMMENTARY

Fire with Fire is typical of the teen romances that filled movie screens in the mid–80s, complete with absent parents, cruel authority figures, comic relief best friends and attractive kids with big hair bouncing to the beats of Huey Lewis and the News. The film is notable chiefly for the star-making performance of Virginia Madsen as the vivacious and sensitive Lisa Taylor. However, its earnest take on young love has since earned it a minor cult status.

If *Fire with Fire* didn't quite enjoy the success of any of the John Hughes films that filled movieplexes in the '80s, it has more to do with the script than the young stars, who all deliver solid performances. The script, however, offers subplots that have no pay-off (the fine actor D. B. Sweeney plays Baxter, a sullen bad boy who is set up in the film's beginning as a rival to Fisk, but then Baxter essentially disappears from the film and there's never a confrontation between the two characters) and logic-stretching contrivances, which climax with the two leads miraculously surviving a leap from a cliff that's several hundred feet tall into a shallow river. Jon Polito's portrayal of Duchard, the swaggering, gun-toting honor camp warden, is so over-the-top it's hard to tell if the performance was intended to be comic or not (Polito also sports a Southern accent which is in dire conflict with his Bronx thug looks).

But there's no denying that Sheffer and Madsen make a believable and attractive pair; they imbue their love scenes with real affection and care. Madsen in particular manages to bring life to her underwritten character, and watching her here it's easy to predict a long and successful career for her (it's also interesting to note that — with her blonde hair and aristocratic nose — she coincidentally bears a strong resemblance to the young Ann Savage in a number of shots, especially the profiles).

Ann appears as Sister Harriet, one of the trio of nuns in charge of the Catholic girls school, and essentially the comic relief of the three. She has one lovely comic moment as the deejay at the dance, smiling and bobbing her head slightly to the rock music, completely unaware that she's the only one who can hear it. While it's disappointing to see her reduced to a minor supporting role with only a few scenes, it is a pleasure to see that she can still steal a scene.

BEHIND THE SCENES

Fire with Fire was the first feature film from director Duncan Gibbins. Gibbins, who made his name primarily by directing music videos for such groups as the Eurythmics and Wham!, directed one other feature (1991's *Eve of Destruction*) and one television movie (1993's *A Case for Murder*) before perishing in the 1993 Malibu fires when he returned to his burning home in an attempt to save his cat.

Fire with Fire is the only acting appearance Ann Savage made from 1955 (when she appeared in the television show *City Detective*) to 2008 (*My Winnipeg*).

The film's alternate title was *Captive Hearts*.

My Winnipeg

(Buffalo Gal Pictures/Documentary Channel/Everyday Pictures/IFC Films) Release Date: June 13, 2008

Opposite: **Ann poses in costume during the shooting of *Fire with Fire* (1985).**

Screenplay by: Guy Maddin and George Toles
Cinematography by: Jody Shapiro
Film Editing by: John Gurdebeke
Production Design by: Réjean Labrie
Art Direction by: Katharina Stieffenhofer
Costume Design by: Meg McMillan
Produced by: Phyllis Laing, Guy Maddin and Jody Shapiro
Directed by: Guy Maddin
Cast: Darcy Fehr (Guy Maddin); Ann Savage (Mother); Amy Stewart (Janet Maddin); Louis Negin (Mayor Cornish); Brendan Cade (Cameron Maddin); Wesley Cade (Ross Maddin); Lou Profeta (Himself); Fred Dunsmore (Himself); Kate Yacula (Citizen Girl); Jacelyn Lobay (Gwenyth Lloyd); Eric Nipp (Viscount Gort); Jennifer Palichuk (Althea Cornish)

Synopsis

Guy Maddin's self-described "docu-fantasia" charts a surreal and autobiographical train journey through "snowy, sleepwalking Winnipeg." As the film begins, Guy (played by actor Darcy Fehr, but with Maddin himself supplying the voice-over narration) wants to leave Winnipeg via this "dream train." Maddin's Winnipeg is a city of tremendous supernatural pull, thanks to its location at "the heart of the heart of the continent" and the intersection of the Red and Cinnabar Rivers, which not only create a powerful fork but are rumored to have a second fork buried deep beneath the surface.

But it isn't the forks that rule Maddin's life; it's Mother, who is the "direction from which I can't turn for long." Even on the train, Mother is a powerful force literally overseeing the passengers.

Maddin struggles with his own inability to stay awake, and paints Winnipeg as a city of sleepwalkers—sleepwalkers who long for buildings they once lived in.

Guy is drawn by his own childhood home at 800 Ellice. His family of six — mother, father, Guy, and siblings Ross, Cam and Janet — lived on the second floor of the white block house, while the first floor was taken up by Lil's Beauty Shop, run by his mother and his aunt. Guy grew up enveloped in the sounds and scents of the "gynocracy," smelling of "female vanity and desperation." In an attempt to "film" his way out of Winnipeg, the adult Guy sublets the house at 800 Ellice, moves in furniture from 1963, and hires actors to play his two brothers and sister, while his mother will play herself. He recalls sitting in the living room with his family watching the only dramatic television series ever produced in Winnipeg, *LedgeMan*. The show, which still runs every day at noon, has starred his mother for fifty years as a woman who talks her son out of jumping from a building every day. Mother, Guy notes, has never missed a day in all that time.

Winnipeg is a city fueled by powerful mothers. Guy recalls how these women once banded together to (unsuccessfully) stop the city from cutting down the elm tree in "the world's smallest park."

The city has also been home to other protests, including a 1919 labor riot that took place in front of Saint Mary's Academy for Girls. The exclusive school has become the "Academy of the Ultravixens" in Guy's memory, as he recalls an incident when, at the age of 3, he accidentally wandered onto the school grounds and was caressed and cuddled by the girls. In modern times the girls are likelier to act like delinquents, leaving the school for cigarettes in the park across the street.

Delinquent girls were a particularly sore subject for Mother. Guy's sister, Janet (who later became a sports star), was once returning from a track team party when she hit a deer. "I'll bet!" responds Mother. When shown the bloodstained car, Mother demands to know what really happened, and accuses Janet of having used the accident as a ruse to have sex in the back seat of the car. When Janet breaks down and confesses, Mother continues to harangue her, finally wishing she'd never even had Janet.

Guy then recalls Winnipeg's long fascination with the supernatural, particularly séances. In 1939 a woman named Gwenyth Lloyd both founded the city's ballet company and held a legendary séance in the city hall building, which also happens to be the world's largest Masonic temple. Possessed by the spirits of gods and goddesses (both Greek and local Cree

Indian), Lloyd and two others danced a story of tragic love.

Winnipeg is a city of "unspoken byways," secret streets that run behind the official avenues and are not allowed to be shown on city maps. One taxi company in Winnipeg will only use these back streets, and strange frequencies can be heard on these streets-behind-the-streets.

Secret byways aren't the only oddities in Winnipeg's urban sprawl, however. The architecture is frequently haphazard, like the Arlington Street bridge, which was constructed by a London company to span the Nile in Egypt but was sold to Winnipeg when it wouldn't fit the Nile. Or there's Garbage Hill, a huge mound of garbage which has now become a park — despite the dangers to sledding kids (who are occasionally impaled on an errant piece of old metal).

The magnificent Eaton's Department Store once defined Winnipeg shopping, but the huge old building was razed a few years back, and a new sports arena was erected in its place. The old Winnipeg arena was condemned when the new structure was built, and Guy still mourns its loss. His father worked for the hockey teams at the old arena, and Guy was literally born (during a hockey game) and raised there. Now he imagines a hockey team made up of aging greats, still playing as the arena is demolished around them.

Guy wants to reenact one last incident at 800 Ellice, one in which his mother was almost sympathetic: The kids try to awaken her one day to demand that she cook for them. When she claims that her "cooking days are over," the children release a parakeet, knowing that Mother has a morbid fear of birds.

Mother's terror leads to an incident that occurred in 1926 when the local racetrack's paddock went up in flames; all the panicked horses fled into the Red River, where they were frozen in place. The icy landscape of dozens of frozen horse heads extending up from the river became a favorite walk for lovers that year and led to a tremendous baby boom the following autumn.

With their racetrack gone, Depression-era Winnipeggers created new wagering events, including the "Golden Boy" pageants, in which handsome young men were paraded before the town's women and judged by the mayor. The pageants, which took place in the Hudson Bay department store, were eventually dismantled when they provoked a hotbed of corruption. Nowadays the department store hosts little more than the Manitoba Sports Hall of Fame, which includes memorabilia from the great hockey players as well as a photo of Guy's champion sister.

Winnipeg's public swimming pool was another building that featured prominently in Guy's childhood. Once, when Guy was a child, he was lured to the pool by his friends, who forced him to strip and share their pre-adolescent arousal.

The word "if" leads to a remembrance of "If Day," which took place in 1942. 5,000 Nazis invaded Winnipeg, renaming the main street "Hitlerstrasse" and the city itself "Himmlerstadt." The Nazis were actually Rotary Club volunteers, however, and were very successful in frightening the Winnipeggers into purchasing war bonds.

Guy finally imagines a "Citizen Girl," a labor goddess who restores Eaton's and the old arena, and who keeps both horses and schoolgirls safe. He could leave Winnipeg if he knew it was safe with her.

As it is, though, he must finally ask himself: How can one live without his ghosts? He tells us, for example, that Mother has developed an attachment to Brendan, the actor he hired to play his brother Cameron, who died at the age of 16. Mother now rests in Winnipeg's snow, cradling Brendan tenderly — and we sense that Guy himself will never leave his own Winnipeg ghosts.

COMMENTARY

At one point in *My Winnipeg*, director and narrator Guy Maddin talks about "creating an entirely new genre" of film, and that isn't just arrogant boasting or wishful thinking, because this "docu-fantasia" is unlike almost any other film ever made. It's neither the personal essay form of documentary (as exemplified by the work of Michael Moore) nor the semi-autobiographical fiction of some of Woody Allen's work. It's not even especially similar to the two earlier films in Maddin's autobiographical trilogy (*Cowards Bend the Knee* [2003] and *Brand Upon the Brain!* [2006]), both of which were more traditionally narrative in structure. It's a completely unique work of art, and as such can't be properly termed as a new genre because its style and content cannot be recreated without producing mere imitation.

It is, however, a brilliant exploration of cinematic time and space, and a magnificent finale for the career of Ann Savage, a career now bookended by two prime examples of the power of the true cinema auteur.

In some respects, *My Winnipeg* does feel like a natural extension of Maddin's earlier work. With the two previous films, *Cowards Bend the Knee* and *Brand Upon the Brain!*, Maddin had begun naming his protagonists "Guy Maddin" and employing personal details from his own life, including his love of hockey, his domineering mother, the strained relationship between his mother and his athletic sister, and the experience of growing up in a beauty salon. *Cowards* tells the story of a young man named "Guy Maddin" who plays for the Winnipeg hockey team, which is managed by his father. His mother is dying, but Guy is too preoccupied with hockey and his girlfriends to visit her, so she remains a largely off-screen presence. As in his 2003 *The Saddest Music in the World* (in which his female lead has lost her legs in a car accident and had them replaced with beer-filled glass prosthetics), dismemberment becomes a central motif — Guy's girlfriend demands that her dead father's hands be sewn onto Guy's arms (the doctor, who works in a hidden surgery at the rear of the beauty salon, secretly refuses, merely painting Guy's own hands to suggest the replacement). In *Brand Upon the Brain!*, Guy is a morose middle-aged house painter who returns to his childhood home upon the death of his mother. That home is revealed to be a lighthouse on an isolated island, where Guy's parents ran an orphanage with a hidden agenda: His mad-scientist father sucked "nectar" from the children that restored youth to his domineering mother. Meanwhile, his older sister defied mother's iron-fisted control when she entered into a relationship with an androgynous young female "detective" who came to the island to investigate the mysterious fate of the orphans.

My Winnipeg eschews any traditional narrative structure and in the process creates the most original and personal of Maddin's films. Maddin's assignment was to create a documentary about Winnipeg, but he's fused documentary, personal essay, family drama and fantasy films into a singular work that simultaneously obscures Winnipeg and reveals Guy Maddin. His Winnipeg is largely a fabrication, a city ruled by endless snow, sleepwalkers, "unspoken byways" and frozen horses. His style, as always, is an artful (but refreshingly unpretentious) blend of black-and-white, silent film techniques, low-budget aesthetics and black humor. There's not another director working today who can make a film with 16mm, and even 8mm, cameras and have them stand side-by-side with anything else in global cinema. He can find beauty in the most mundane or ugliest settings (witness, for example, *My Winnipeg*'s haunting train trip through downtown Winnipeg), and sexuality in his work can go well beyond mere polymorphous perversity. He also has the true artist's gift of making each film part of a greater whole but unique unto itself, and he continues to explore new directions. In *Winnipeg*, he uses cut-out animation for several sequences, a technique that's new to his work (but works splendidly here — the animation, in the early style of the films of Lotte Reiniger, is whimsical and dynamic). Even his music is usually a marvelously idiosyncratic mixture of pop, classical and original score (listen to how the fabulous vocal piece "Winnipeg, Wonderful Winnipeg" segues into the film's haunting instrumental soundtrack).

However, some of the most memorable and disturbing sequences in *My Winnipeg* center on Maddin's recreations of his family; these scenes bristle with painful truth (even as that pain is tempered slightly by Maddin's humor).

Mother cradles her dead son in *My Winnipeg*: Ann and Brendan Cade (as Cameron) prepare to shoot the scene (2006).

Watching the ludicrous television show *Ledge-Man*, we understand that he's describing his own strained relationship with a domineering parent; his amusing monologue about being a little boy growing up over a beauty salon is laced with bitter self-awareness. Curiously, Maddin doesn't visually appear in any of the flashback scenes; unlike *Brand Upon the Brain!*, he hasn't hired an actor to portray his own pre-pubescent self, becoming almost a ghost by dispassionately observing the rest of his family from behind a camera. Maddin is a fan of literary biographies (particularly those of Bruno Schulz), and by choosing to distance himself from the memoir, he achieves a sense of literature (think third-person biography), perhaps suggesting that *My Winnipeg* has also combined written reminiscence with narrative and documentary film.

One of the best scenes in *My Winnipeg* is that in which Mother accuses Guy's teenaged sister Janet of using a car accident to cover backseat sex. In a film which also includes gruesome shots of severed horse heads, a bizarre séance sequence (complete with ectoplasm) and an entire displaced subculture living on the roofs of Winnipeg, the confrontation between mother and daughter is the most uncomfortable scene in the film — due in no small part to Savage's terrifying performance. "Who did it?" she demands in a voice limned with ice. "Was it the boy on the track team — or the man with the tire iron?" She reduces the girl to tears in seconds, and her final condemnation — "It only took him five minutes to find out what you are!" — is delivered with such withering fury that it's likely to have the audience squirming as much as the onscreen Janet. And yet by the end of the film Maddin also shows us the sympathetic side of this human monster when she clings in the snow to her dead son Cameron.

In the film (and in some of the film's press materials), Maddin claims that he's cast his actual mother to play herself, and while that seems like a slightly narcissistic in-joke on the surface, a closer examination of the film might suggest that he's telling a cinematic truth — because he's plainly cast an actress who embodies the terror and reverence his own mother inspired in him. Ann Savage could be considered Maddin's movie mother: He undoubtedly watched *Detour* as a young artist, and took in both its low-budget black-and-white, deliberately artificial style and its uniquely terrifying depiction of femininity. Savage was the only actress he approached to play his mother in *My Winnipeg*, and her casting is both a high point of Maddin's considerable body of work, and the richly deserved grand finale in the career of an actress whose talents were too often overlooked.

Behind the Scenes

My Winnipeg was originally commissioned by the Documentary Channel. In an interview with Steve Erickson, Maddin said, "I heard a rumor they were going to approach me, and I was so broke that I phoned them to ask if it was true." The channel's Michael Burns emphasized that they wanted Maddin to take a personal approach to the film, and Guy later said, "I quickly realized that I couldn't separate my home, my family, my hometown; they are inextricably tangled up."

It's easy to see why the Documentary Channel would have approached Maddin about making a feature devoted to his hometown. Over a career that has now spanned twenty years, Maddin has become Canada's resident auteur, a kind of far north David Lynch who has made considerable use of Winnipeg in his films. (He's also frequently compared to two other highly regarded Canadian filmmakers, David Cronenberg and Atom Egoyan.) Maddin made his first short film, *The Dead Father*, in 1986, and followed that in 1988 with his first feature, *Tales from the Gimli Hospital* (co-written with film scholar George Toles, who would go on to be involved with nearly every subsequent Maddin production). *Gimli* already showed Maddin's trademark style — stark black-and-white photography, a

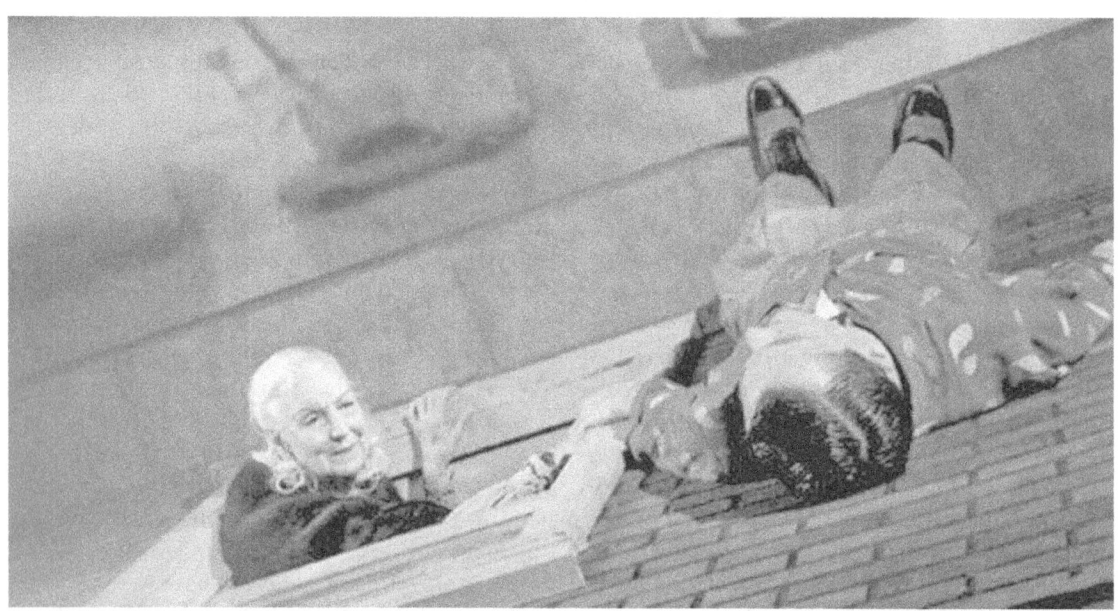

Mother (Ann Savage) tries to talk her son (Darcy Fehr) out of jumping in this scene from "LedgeMan," the television series within the movie of *My Winnipeg*.

use of silent film techniques, black humor, deliberately cheap sets and effects — and became a cult hit around the world. By 2000, he'd made the feature films *Archangel, Careful,* and *Twilight of the Ice Nymphs,* as well as a substantial number of shorts, and his work was well known on the film festival circuit. He achieved his biggest commercial success with 2003's *The Saddest Music in the World,* which starred Isabella Rossellini and Mark McKinney. In 2006, his feature *Brand Upon the Brain!* toured the U.S. and Canada with a live orchestra and guest star narrators, including Rossellini, Udo Kier and Barbara Steele, and *Brand* led directly into *My Winnipeg.*

However, the movie also had its roots in a magazine article Maddin wrote for the British art magazine *Frieze.* In a letter to Ann Savage, Guy said the article "has the kind of fable-like tone I want this movie to have." Some of this article does indeed read like an early draft of the film's narration:

> Winnipeg has a pathologically alarming rate of somnambulism — up to 250 times the normal rate for urban centers. Our streets are full of drowsy and forgetful wanderers, and the city is divided into the two worlds, almost indistinguishable, of the sleeping and the barely awake.... By law Winnipeggers are permitted to visit any house they have ever lived in, no matter how long ago. When you vacate a flat or house in this town, you keep your keys in case you need them while out in the night.

The article also mentions the Arlington Street Bridge, the "vast network of back lanes," and "mattresses bent over with fatal stains." An emphasis on the forgetfulness of Winnipeg's residents and how they use scent to revive their memories feels like a deleted scene from the film.

Thanks to the financing provided by the Documentary Channel, Maddin had a decent budget to work with. Compare the budget of *Cowards Bend the Knee* ($10,000), and you'll see how he was able to afford to fly an American star in and expand his use of rear projection.

However, one expense Maddin did without was traditional 35mm motion picture cameras. He'd shot previous features almost entirely with 8mm cameras, and for *Winnipeg* he used Super16, 16, Super8, miniDV video, HD video and even a cell phone camera (as well as stock footage, animation and still photographs). This mix of footage made editing interesting: "I know I present problems for the lab and postproduction all the time," Guy said in an interview with Kurt Halfyard, "because I've shot in so many different formats."

Once the financing for the film (which at one point was titled *Love Me, Love My Winnipeg* after the city's one-time motto) was in place and Maddin had the film's structure sketched out, he went after his leading lady. While chatting with Los Angeles–based film expert Dennis Bartok, he happened to mention that he thought Ann Savage was the only actress who could play his mother, but he assumed she was dead. Bartok knew Ann through American Cinematheque, an organization that stages screenings and revivals in Hollywood, and he put Maddin in touch with her. At first Ann was perplexed by Maddin's unique way of working — he doesn't use traditional scripts — but upon screening his one-of-a-kind ballet/horror film *Dracula: Pages from a Virgin's Diary* (2002), she realized he was a filmmaker possessing the sort of vision she'd been wanting to work with. Maddin tried to create some sort of script for her, and his first pass was a 15-page section entitled "Episode VI: 800 Ellice Ave." The script begins with this description: "This episode is clearly meant to be the depiction of a dream — a dream misshaped by my inept memory" (Maddin's memory is clearly anything but inept, as the script goes on to describe buildings around his childhood neighborhood in astonishing detail). Unlike the narration in the finished film, this earlier conception indicates that Mother has rented the house for one month, rather than Guy. Other scenes are remarkably similar to the finished film, and there's one long additional scene for Mother in which she halfheartedly tries to make meatloaf for the children but has almost completely forgotten how.

This early section of script resembles a play more than a movie, and for Ann's convenience the script was run through software to re-format. Ann then copied her own lines by hand, a technique commonly employed by actors to assist with memorization.

The film's other main role to cast was the part of Guy Maddin. For the sequences on the train — the only time "Guy Maddin" appears onscreen — he cast actor Darcy Fehr, who had played "Guy Maddin" in the earlier feature *Cowards Bend the Knee*. For the voice-over narration, he considered casting another actor, favoring someone with the sophisticated tones of a James Mason, but he finally opted to read the narration himself. "I've hated the sound of my voice," he told Steve Erickson, "but after a week of mixing, where you have to listen to every line about a hundred times, I not only learned to like the sound of my voice, but I got kind of a crush on myself." (Maddin does also make a brief onscreen appearance in the film as the man glimpsed urinating for the last time in the Winnipeg arena men's room.)

The film was completed in 2007, and in September it showed in Toronto, with a live narration by Guy Maddin. It went on to win the Rogers Best Canadian Feature Award at the Toronto Film Festival (a prize accompanied by a $10,000 cash award) — in competition against the features *Continental, a Film Without Guns* (directed by Stephane Lafleur) and *Up the Yangtze* (directed by Yung Chang). It was chosen as an official selection for both the 2008 Berlin International Film Festival and the 2008 Tribeca Film Festival, and won the Audience Award at the Boston Independent Film Festival, 2008. *My Winnipeg* also won the 2008 San Francisco Film Critics Circle Award for Best Documentary. It received a limited American theatrical release in 2008, and appeared on the top ten list of *Time* magazine's Richard Corliss (he ranked it 3rd on his list), *The Austin Chronicle*'s Marc Savlov (4th on his list), *The Globe and Mail*'s Rick Groen (5th), *The Austin Chronicle*'s Marjorie Baumgarten (6th), *The Globe and Mail*'s Liam Lacey (7th), and *The A.V. Club*'s Noel Murray (10th).

Maddin continued the charade of claiming to have cast his actual mother throughout the first phase of publicity, leaving a few reviewers deliberately confused; but word soon spread that the star of *Detour* was the real performer, and Ann was favorably mentioned in numerous reviews. In *Time*, Richard Corliss said, "She has the melodramatic sulfur of the mad mom in one of David Sedaris' 'memoir' stories, the domineering vindictiveness of a shrew-mother from 40s movies," and called the movie "the finest, funniest, saddest film I've seen in Toronto or at any festival this year." Roger Ebert summed up his review simply with, "Savage! See this film!" And in his wrap-up of the best films of 2008, Ebert awarded the film his "Special Jury Prize." In the *Los Angeles Times*, Kenneth Turan noted "a wonderful turn by legendary actress Ann Savage."

In the IndieWire Critics' Poll of 2008, both Ray Pride and J. Hoberman listed Ann Savage in *My Winnipeg* as the number 1 Best Supporting Performance of 2008.

In 2009, Canadian publisher Coach House Books published Guy Maddin's book on the making of *My Winnnipeg*.

Minor Film Roles

The films listed here are those in which Ann Savage either appeared as a non-speaking extra or was cut from.

The Great Waltz   (MGM, 1938)

Directed by Julien Duvivier; starring Luise Rainer, Fernand Gravey, Miliza Korjus, Hugh Herbert and Lionel Atwill.

While still a teenager, Ann worked as an extra in this acclaimed story of composer Johann Strauss II.

The More the Merrier
(Columbia, 1943)

Directed by George Stevens; starring Jean Arthur, Joel McCrea and Charles Coburn.

Ann worked as an extra (her character is sometimes listed as "Miss Dalton") in this well-received comedy of apartment-sharing in wartime Washington. Director Stevens liked Ann enough to feature her in a lengthy two-shot (during a bar scene); she originally had dialogue as well, but a press release from Columbia indicates that Ann fell ill during filming and Stevens had to "shoot around her," so her part was, unfortunately, curtailed. Columbia issued a number of press releases regarding Ann's appearance in this film; some of the articles actually compare her comedic talents to those of Carole Lombard. Later press biographies of Ann listed *The More the Merrier* (or *Merry-Go-Round*, the film's shooting title) as her film debut, but both *One Dangerous Night* and *After Midnight with Boston Blackie* opened prior to this film's American premiere (on March 26, 1943), and Ann had probably shot both those films earlier as well. In a 1988 interview, Ann referred to working on *The More the Merrier* as "a treasured experience."

Murder in Times Square
(COLUMBIA, 1943)

Directed by Lew Landers; starring Edmund Lowe, Marguerite Chapman, William Wright and Bruce Bennett.

Ann appeared in this somewhat dull murder mystery as "Miss Ruth," but was cut from later television prints (distributed by Hygo Television Films). She went on to work again with Edmund Lowe in *Dangerous Blondes* (1943) and the television series *Front Page Detective*; she also appeared with William Wright

Bert D'Armand (left) and Ann share a moment with *The More the Merrier* star Charles Coburn (right), 1946.

in *Saddles and Sagebrush* (1943) and, more memorably, her final film for Columbia, *Dancing in Manhattan* (1944), in which she and Wright played a pair of con artists.

Destroyer (COLUMBIA, 1943)

Directed by William A. Seiter; starring Edward G. Robinson, Glenn Ford and Marguerite Chapman.

Ann was initially cast in this film, and Columbia released a number of press releases with quotes like "able to hold her own against Robinson." However, in this wartime drama of an older officer clashing with a cocky young chief aboard an untested ship, she does not appear in the final film. It's entirely possible that she may have been originally cast in the Marguerite Chapman role (as Robinson's daughter and Ford's love interest) but was reassigned to another Columbia film. Other announcements for the casting of *Destroyer* list Janet Blair, who also does not appear in the film.

Appointment in Berlin (COLUMBIA, 1943)

Directed by Alfred E. Green; starring George Sanders, Marguerite Chapman, Onslow Stevens and Gale Sondergaard.

At one point Ann was cast in this wartime drama, but she does not appear in the film (she may have been replaced by Marguerite Chapman, as she apparently was in *Destroyer*).

Good Luck, Mr. Yates (COLUMBIA, 1943)

Directed by Ray Enright; starring Claire Trevor, Edgar Buchanan, Tom Neal and Frank Sully.

Ann was initially cast in this wartime drama of a teacher who falsely claims to be a war hero (the film was shot under the title *The Right Guy*), but she doesn't appear in the film. Columbia may have originally cast her just to provide another pairing with Tom Neal.

Sahara (COLUMBIA, 1943)

Directed by Zoltan Korda; starring Humphrey Bogart, J. Carrol Naish, Bruce Bennett and Lloyd Bridges.

News articles from 1943 indicate that Ann had worked on location as part of the cast of this well-reviewed wartime drama, but she does not appear in the film.

What's Buzzin', Cousin? (COLUMBIA, 1943)

Directed by Charles Barton; starring Ann Miller, Eddie "Rochester" Anderson, Freddy Martin, Jeff Donnell, Leslie Brooks and John Hubbard.

Ann was originally slated to star in this light musical but was replaced at the last minute by Ann Miller, whose dancing skills were more suited to the role.

Nine Girls (COLUMBIA, 1944)

Directed by Leigh Jason; starring Ann Harding, Evelyn Keyes, Jinx Falkenburg, Jeff Donnell, Anita Louise, Leslie Brooks and Nina Foch.

Casting notices on this comedy-mystery indicate that Ann was part of the original cast, along with Jeff Donnell, Leslie Brooks and Marguerite Chapman. However, neither Ann nor Ms. Chapman appears in the film.

Any Number Can Play (MGM, 1949)

Directed by Mervyn LeRoy; starring Clark Gable, Alexis Smith, Wendell Corey, Audrey Totter, Frank Morgan and Mary Astor.

In this somewhat tepid and unlikely story of conflicted casino owner Charley Kyng (Gable) losing touch with his family, Ann appears near the beginning as a prostitute who's asked to leave because Kyng hasn't hired her himself. Although Arthur Freed cast Ann as a favor to her husband/manager, Bert D'Armand, Ann only has two lines (with Gable, at least), and even those were dubbed by another actress.

On the Right Side
(FAMILY FILMS, INC., 1949)

Directed by S. Roy Luby; starring Steve Flagg, Ann Savage and Harry Cheshire.

In this inspirational short film, Ann plays Mary, a "girl next door" whose husband Bill has developed a gambling addiction. After Mary is forced to deal with bill collectors by taking money from their daughter's piggy bank, and Bill is beaten by loan sharks, Mary seeks the help of a family friend, who convinces Bill to attend church. Through faith, Bill secures a good job, overcomes his gambling problem and saves his marriage. The film was probably intended for sale to television, but poor production values and a heavy-handed script confined it to obscurity.

Television Appearances

Fireside Theatre   (1949–1955)

Ann appeared in two episodes: "Judas," the first episode of Season 2 (first broadcast on January 7, 1950), and "Polly," the first episode of Season 3 (originally broadcast on August 29, 1950).

An anthology series, *Fireside Theatre* is now considered the first successful filmed series on American network television (as opposed to the live programming that was the standard at the time).

Front Page Detective   (1951–1952)

Ann appeared in the 1951 episode "Clean Sweep."

Front Page Detective (which also appeared in magazine form) starred Edmund Lowe as investigative journalist David Chase and George Pembroke as his police friend Lt. Andrews. In "Clean Sweep," a drug peddler named Mickey Clayton has broken out of prison and come back to town gunning for Chase, whose testimony helped put him away. Chase goes to interview Mickey's girlfriend, Patti Carrol, and finds Mickey hiding in her apartment. Chase manages to escape, and Mickey is gunned down by his former partner Pete Farmer, who tries to implicate Chase in the murder. Chase overcomes Farmer just as Lt. Andrews shows up.

Ann, playing Patti, offers up a terrific turn as the classic jaded gangster's moll in this fast-paced and well-acted little thriller.

Gang Busters   (1952)

Phillips H. Lord's *Gang Busters*, one of the earliest television crime dramas, lasted less than a year. Its stories were purportedly based on actual cases from FBI and police files, and the series also featured profiles of the FBI's "Most Wanted."

Ann appeared (with Tom Neal) in the episode "The Red Dress." She plays Juanita, a woman who has been awaiting the release of her convict boyfriend Crain (Neal). When Crain returns home, he finds not only his old cronies Shakey and Bunch, but a small arsenal and a police radio; Juanita tells him that she's been planning for five years to take over the gang. Unfortunately, her plan goes awry when she demands that the boys rob a dress shop because she wants a red dress she's seen there; the robbery goes bad, and a night watchman is killed. As the police close in, the three men are caught, and Juanita overdoses on pills and is dead by the time she's found.

Although "The Red Dress" does offer the final onscreen pairing of Ann Savage and Tom Neal (who do what they can with their ridiculous dialogue), the show is very cheaply made, with poor writing and laughable direction.

Schlitz Playhouse of Stars
(1951–1959)

Ann appeared in the sixth episode of Season 2, "Tango" (first broadcast on November 7, 1952).

Like *Fireside Theatre* and *Ford Television Theatre*, *Schlitz Playhouse of Stars* was a popular anthology series.

Death Valley Days (1952–1975)

Ann appeared in the first episode of Season 2, "The Diamond Babe" (originally broadcast on September 29, 1953).

Death Valley Days began life as a radio series (created by Ruth Woodman) that ran from 1930 until 1945. As a television series, it ran 558 episodes and is now considered to be the most successful syndicated television western in history.

City Detective (1953–1955)

Ann appeared in two episodes: the 22nd episode of Season 1, "Cruise Ship," as "Lisa," and the 15th episode of Season 2, "In Sickness and in Stealth" (originally broadcast on January 25, 1955), as "Natalie."

City Detective was a syndicated crime drama that starred Rod Cameron as New York detective Bart Grant.

Ford Television Theatre
(1948–1957)

Ann appeared in the 14th episode of Season 3, "Magic Formula" (first broadcast on January 6, 1955).

Ford Television Theatre was a dramatic anthology series that is now considered one of the key programs from the "Golden Age of Television Drama."

In "Magic Formula," Claudette Colbert plays Lorna Gilbert, a famed actress who has always put career before her marriage (her husband is played by Patric Knowles). When her small plane crashes on an isolated beach, Lorna has a tense night trapped in the cabin, giving her time to realize the error of her ways before she's rescued.

Ann plays her efficient secretary Maggie. Ann is attractive and competent, but the part is little more than a walk-on and was probably a key factor in Ann's decision to leave the television industry.

Saved By the Bell (1989–1993)

Saved By the Bell was a popular sitcom chronicling the exploits of a group of students at Bayside High School in the fictitious town of Palisades, California.

Ann appears in the episode "Boss Lady" (the 10th episode of Season 3, originally aired October 19, 1991). Left to run her father's beach club for a weekend, Stacey (Leah Remini) discovers that both a "Sweet Sixteen" party and a 50th Anniversary party have been booked for the same Saturday night. Stacey and the gang successfully salvage the situation by convincing the two parties to join together.

Ann plays the wife in the 50th Anniversary party, and gets to perform a tango with then-hot teen idol Mario Lopez. Even though her role is small, she offers an attractive and sweet performance, and looks quite spry dancing with Lopez.

Appendix 1.
Detour Script with Ann Savage's Notes

Fortunately for film historians and biographers, Ann Savage was an inveterate collector of material relating to her career. She kept everything from press clippings to posters to contracts to scripts, and even documented much of her life in handwritten journals and notes.

Her personal copy of the original script for *Detour* was among Ann's most highly prized possessions. The script was originally presented to her in a leather binder that PRC head and *Detour* producer Leon Fromkess had custom-made; the binder, which aptly displayed Fromkess's high regard for his leading lady, featured her name embossed on the front cover. The script itself was a shooting draft that ran 140 pages and was bound between orange covers; one of the most curious things about the screenplay was the listing of replaced PRC regular Lew Landers as director on the cover and title page. Writer Martin Goldsmith, adapting his own book, was a novice screenwriter and went to unusual lengths breaking the script down into detailed shots, many of which final director Edgar Ulmer recreated almost exactly in the final film.

Ann made some working notes in the script during rehearsal and shooting, mainly in a thick green pencil; these notes provide insight into her technique as an actress, and also reveal how Ulmer worked with his performers. Equally interesting, however, is that Ann continued to annotate the script throughout her life. In her later years, as *Detour* gained cult status and Ann was a favored speaker at screenings of the film, she added post-it notes throughout the script regarding her performance as Vera. Although she turned down parts that she felt simply traded on her portrayal of Vera, these notes demonstrate that, in some ways, Ann happily lived side-by-side with Vera for over 60 years.

Included here are only those sections of Ann's *Detour* screenplay which include scenes with Vera and Ann's notes; these start as Al, driving the car of the dead Charles Haskell, chances upon the hitchhiking Vera on the desert fringe of Los Angeles, and end as Al flees Vera's death. Footnotes in the script indicate where Ann has made a notation, either in original green pencil, a black pen (it's unknown when Ann made these notes), or post-it notes.

Appendix 1

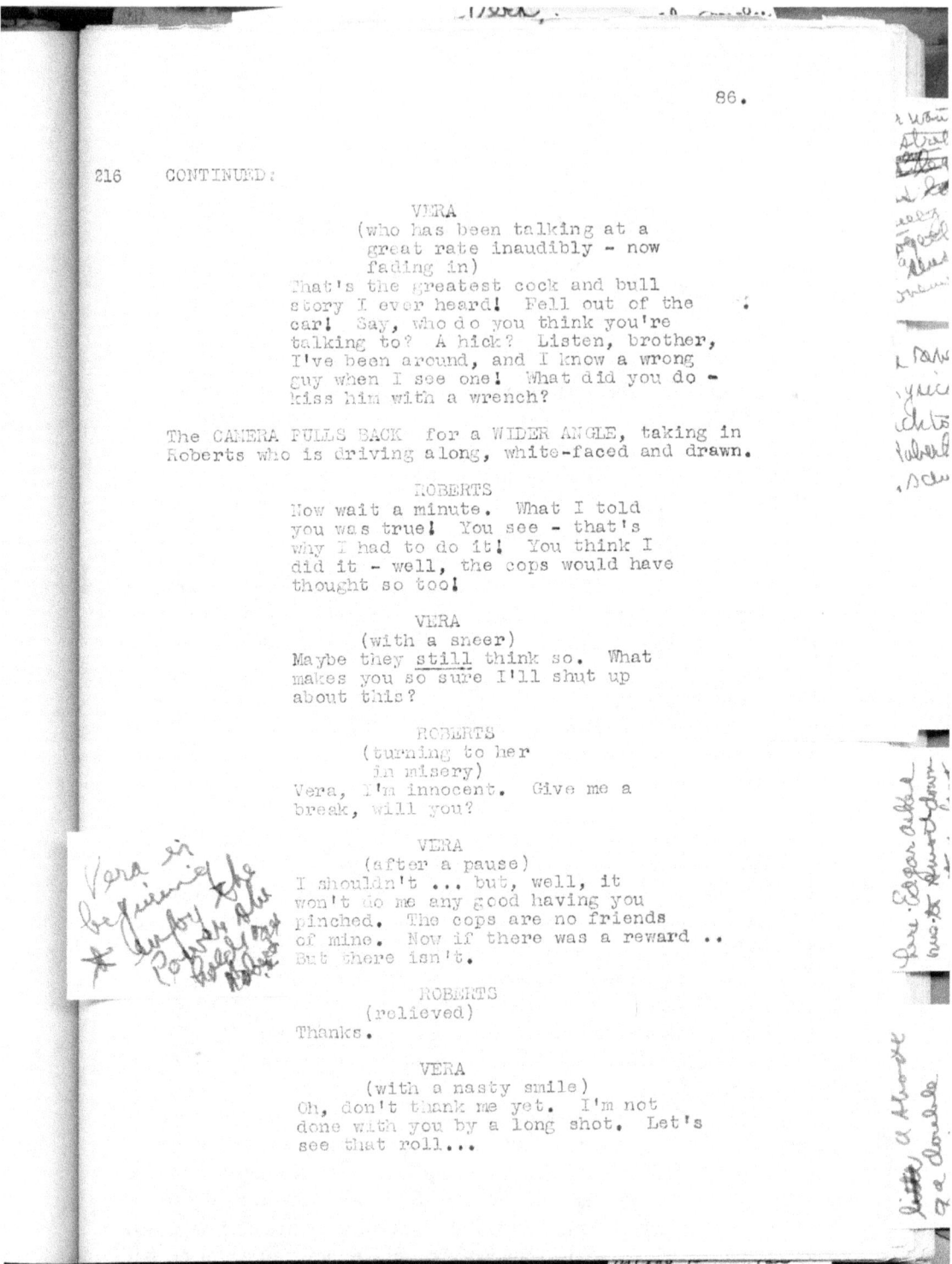

216 CONTINUED:

          VERA
     (who has been talking at a
     great rate inaudibly - now
     fading in)
That's the greatest cock and bull story I ever heard! Fell out of the car! Say, who do you think you're talking to? A hick? Listen, brother, I've been around, and I know a wrong guy when I see one! What did you do - kiss him with a wrench?

The CAMERA PULLS BACK for a WIDER ANGLE, taking in Roberts who is driving along, white-faced and drawn.

          ROBERTS
Now wait a minute. What I told you was true! You see - that's why I had to do it! You think I did it - well, the cops would have thought so too!

          VERA
     (with a sneer)
Maybe they still think so. What makes you so sure I'll shut up about this?

          ROBERTS
     (turning to her
     in misery)
Vera, I'm innocent. Give me a break, will you?

          VERA
     (after a pause)
I shouldn't ... but, well, it won't do me any good having you pinched. The cops are no friends of mine. Now if there was a reward .. But there isn't.

          ROBERTS
     (relieved)
Thanks.

          VERA
     (with a nasty smile)
Oh, don't thank me yet. I'm not done with you by a long shot. Let's see that roll...

A page from Ann Savage's *Detour* script, complete with one of Ann's hand-written post-it notes.

"DETOUR"

Screenplay
By
Martin M. Goldsmith

ASSOCIATE PRODUCER:
    Martin Mooney

DIRECTOR:
    Lew Landers*

PRODUCTION #493
FINAL SHOOTING SCRIPT
May 24, 1945

This Script is the property of PRC Productions Inc. It is loaned with the understanding that it will be returned to the production office upon completion of shooting.

187 INT. ROADSTER, TOP DOWN — MED. CLOSE SHOT THRU WINDSHIELD — PROCESS — DAY

Roberts is driving along at a moderate rate of speed through desert country. It is a beautiful day. The tension has gone from his face. The SOUND of the motor, subdued, SUSTAINS throughout the sequence.

ROBERTS' VOICE
(narrating)

There were quite a number of fellows hitch-hiking along the road, but I passed them all by. If I was picked up, the cops would grab them, too — as accomplices, accessories after the fact, or whatever they wanted to hold them on...

188 EXT. SERVICE STATION ON HIGHWAY — FULL SHOT — DAY†

A very small service station with one pump in the left f.g. The convertible comes down the highway toward the camera and pulls in with a steaming radiator. Roberts is driving. VERA can be seen standing on the shoulder of the road in front of the station, thumbing the cars that pass from time to time. She is young, thin and dirty. A small overnight case is at her feet.

ROBERTS' VOICE
(narrating)

But near the airport at Desert Center, I pulled up for water. There was a woman...

189 MED. CLOSE SHOT — ROBERTS AT CAR — DAY‡

Roberts stops the car and gets out. As he starts putting water into the steaming radiator, he looks o.s. toward the highway.

ROBERTS
(calling o.s.)

Hey, you...

---

*On the front cover of the script, the name "Lew Landers" has been marked out in black pencil (although it still appears on the title page of the script).
†A post-it note added here reads simply "Entrance Vera."
‡Ann has drawn a line in heavy green pencil down the page beginning at this scene. The line ends at the bottom of Scene 193.

190   FULL SHOT OF VERA — DAY

Vera, standing on the shoulder of the road, turns her head o.s. toward the station.

                              VERA
                            (calling)
Me?

191   MED. SHOT — DAY

Roberts screws the radiator cap back on as a mechanic emerges from the station.

                            MECHANIC
                           (in doorway)
Trouble with your radiator, partner?

                            ROBERTS
                        (getting back in car)
No — just hot.

                            MECHANIC
Need gas?

                            ROBERTS
No, thanks.
            (turning toward the highway again and calling to Vera o.s.)
Say, come on — if you want a ride.

192   FULL SHOT — DAY

Vera picks up her overnight case and walks to the car — not hurrying. The mechanic goes back inside the station.

193   MEDIUM SHOT — DAY

Vera reaches the car and opens the door. Roberts takes her little overnight case and throws it behind the seat. He puts the car in gear and drives o.s.

194   INT. ROADSTER — MED. TWO SHOT THRU WINDSHIELD — ROBERTS AND VERA — PROCESS — DAY

The two are driving along at a moderate rate of speed through desert country. Roberts keeps his eyes on the road as they converse.

                            ROBERTS
How far are you going?

                              VERA
                      (without looking at him)
How far are *you* going?*

195   CLOSE SHOT — ROBERTS THRU WINDSHIELD — PROCESS — DAY

Roberts turns his head to look at her (o.s.) in mild surprise. He narrates above the subdued hum of the motor which SUSTAINS throughout the sequence.

                         ROBERTS' VOICE
                           (narrating)
That took me by surprise, and I turned my head to look her over...

---

*Ann made a note here apparently during shooting which she has crossed out (it's unreadable).

196   CLOSE SHOT — VERA — PROCESS — DAY

For this shot, the CAMERA IS PLACED at the height of Roberts' eyes, and Vera is photographed in profile as she sits staring straight in front of her, the wind blowing her hair back from her head. There is a curious, tight expression on her face.

ROBERTS' VOICE
(narrating)

She was facing straight ahead, so I couldn't see her eyes, but she was young, not more than twenty-four...

Vera's hair is unkempt and her hands dirty. She may, perhaps, have a slight ring around her neck. But she should not be overdone in any respect.

197   INSERT: CLOSE SHOT — VERA'S DIRTY HANDS ON HER LAP — DAY

As she sits in the car. The SOUND of the car's motor comes over.

198   INSERT: CLOSE SHOT — VERA'S RUN-DOWN SHOES CAKED WITH MUD — DAY

As they rest against the floor of the car. The SOUND of the car's motor comes over.

ROBERTS' VOICE
(narrating)

Man, she looked as if she'd just been thrown off the crumbiest freight train in the world...

199   INSERT: CLOSE SHOT — VERA'S CALVES SHEATHED IN STOCKINGS WITH RUNS AND HOLES — DAY

As she sits in the car. The SOUND of the car's motor comes over.

200   INT. ROADSTER — CLOSE SHOT — VERA — PROCESS — DAY

Vera is photographed in profile with the CAMERA PLACED the height and approximate position of Roberts' eyes. The SOUND of the motor continues to come over. The same tight expression is on her face.

ROBERTS' VOICE
(narrating)

Yet, in spite of the condition she was in, I got the impression of beauty. Not the beauty of a movie actress, mind you, or the beauty you dream about when you're with your wife, but a *natural* beauty — a beauty that's almost homely because it's so real.

(pause)

Then, suddenly, she turned to face me — and I took it all back...

201   TWO SHOT — ROBERTS AND VERA, FEATURING VERA — PROCESS — DAY.

Vera turns away from the windshield to face Roberts as they drive along. There is an icy look about her and the tight lines around her mouth are still there.*

VERA

How far did you say you were going?

Roberts turns back to the road quickly and hesitates before answering. A slight, but troubled, frown comes onto his face.

ROBERTS
(reluctantly)

Los Angeles.

---

*Somewhere around here Ann has added two post-it notes reading all together; "You can bet she does! She knows this is the same car that she rode in and was thrown out of! But where is the other (guy) man."

VERA
(returning her attention to the road)

L.A.? L.A. is good enough for me, mister.

202 CLOSE SHOT — ROBERTS — PROCESS — DAY

Roberts looks most uncomfortable as he continues to drive.

ROBERT
(muttering)

I was afraid of that...

VERA'S VOICE
(o.s.)

What did you say?

ROBERTS
(quickly, trying to cover up)

Huh? Oh, nothing. I was just thinking out loud.

VERA'S VOICE
(o.s. — mockingly)

People get in trouble for doing that.
Roberts turns his head to look at her, and the CAMERA PULLS BACK to a TWO SHOT, framing them both. Vera is looking at him curiously — almost as though looking *through* him.*

ROBERTS
(to make conversation)

What's your name?
He returns his attention to the road.

VERA

You can call me Vera, if you want to.

ROBERTS

You live in Los Angeles?

VERA

No.

ROBERTS

Where are you coming from?

VERA

Oh ... back there.
She nods her head toward the rear.

ROBERTS

Blythe?

VERA

No.

ROBERTS

Oh, sure. Phoenix. You look like a Phoenix girl.

VERA

Are the girls in Phoenix *that* bad?

---

*In the original green pencil. Ann has written just after this description: "Smile."

SLOW DISSOLVE TO:

203   INT. ROADSTER — TWO SHOT — ROBERTS & VERA — PROCESS — DAY

The CAMERA, SHOOTING FROM BEHIND AND SLIGHTLY ABOVE, photographs Roberts and Vera as they drive along at a moderate rate of speed through desert country. Vera is sleeping, resting her head against the door on her side of the car.

>ROBERTS' VOICE
>(narrating)

The girl must have been pretty tired, because she fell asleep not twenty minutes after she stepped into the car...

204   CLOSE — VERA — PROCESS — DAY

Vera is apparently asleep as the car moves along through the desert.

>ROBERTS' VOICE (CONT'D)
>(narrating)

She lay sprawled out, with her head resting against the far door — like Haskell. I didn't like that part of it much, but I didn't wake her up.

205   MED. TWO SHOT — ROBERTS AND VERA THRU WINDSHIELD — PROCESS — DAY

The car is still moving along at a moderate rate of speed. The HUM of the motor, of course, SUSTAINS.

>ROBERTS' VOICE
>(narrating)

It wasn't that this girl still worried me; I'd gotten over that funny feeling I had when she looked at me — which I put down as just my jangled nerves. With her eyes closed...

206   CLOSE SHOT — VERA — PROCESS — DAY

Vera still has her eyes closed but the lines around her mouth have softened.

>ROBERTS' VOICE
>(narrating)

...and the tenseness gone out of her, she seemed harmless enough; and instead of disliking her, I began to feel sorry for her. The poor kid probably had had a rough time of it...

207   MED. TWO SHOT — ROBERTS & VERA THRU WINDSHIELD — PROCESS — DAY

>ROBERTS' VOICE
>(narrating)

Who was she, anyway? And why was she going to Los Angeles? And where had she come from in the first place? The only thing I knew about her was her name.

Roberts, his eyes on the road, drives along, the CAMERA MOVES IN for a CLOSE SHOT of him. Vera is now o.s.

>ROBERTS' VOICE
>(narrating)

Not that it made any difference. A few hours more and we'd be in Hollywood. I'd forget where I parked the car and look up Sue. This nightmare of being a dead man would be over ... who this dame was, well, it was no business of mine.

Roberts casually removes his eyes from the road and looks over in the direction of Vera (o.s.) and is a bit startled. The CAMERA PANS to Vera, who now has her eyes wide open. She is staring at Roberts (o.s. now) with that peculiar, hard, calculating glint in her eyes.

After HOLDING for a moment, the CAMERA PULLS BACK for a WIDER ANGLE, TAKING THEM BOTH IN. Roberts' troubled eyes are looking into Vera's cold ones. With an effort, he returns his attention to the road ahead.

                        VERA
                (staring at him hard)
Where did you leave his body?
The CAMERA ZOOMS IN for a BIG CLOSEUP of both as he freezes and his eyes widen. HOLD ON ROBERTS as he sits immobile for a second.

208   CLOSE SHOT — VERA — PROCESS — DAY

Vera sits up erect and faces Roberts, o.s. The HUM of the motor is all that is heard for a few seconds.*

                        VERA
            (after having given Roberts time to reply)
Where did you leave the owner of this car? You're not fooling anyone.† This buggy belongs to a fellow named Haskell. That's not you, mister.

209   TWO SHOT — ROBERTS AND VERA THRU WINDSHIELD — PROCESS — DAY

Roberts is visibly shaken but tries to control himself as the car continues to travel along through the desert.

                       ROBERTS
                (forcing a laugh after a moment)
You're out of your mind. That's *my* name, Charles Haskell. Look! I can prove it...
Roberts reaches into his inside pocket and pulls out Haskell's wallet. He offers it to her, taking care to keep his eyes on the road, for he is afraid to let her read the fear in them.

                       ROBERTS
You'll find my driver's license in there.

                        VERA
            (paying no attention to the wallet and
             not removing her eyes from Roberts' face)
Save yourself the trouble, Mister. Having Haskell's wallet only makes it worse.‡
CAMERA MOVES IN FOR A CLOSER SHOT OF VERA. Roberts is now o.s.

                        VERA
It just happens I rode with Charlie Haskell all the way from Louisiana. He picked me up outside of Shreveport.

210   CLOSE SHOT — ROBERTS — PROCESS — DAY

Roberts is genuinely frightened now. His mouth drops open a little. He does not dare look over toward Vera, just keeps his eyes on the road.

                       ROBERTS
                       (blankly)
You ... rode ... with...?

                    VERA'S VOICE
                        (o.s.)
You heard me.
There is a pause, during which Roberts wets his dry lips. Only the HUM of the motor is heard.

---

*Just to the right of this description, in the original green pencil is circled "F" (the meaning of this is unknown).
†This line is circled in green pencil.
‡The words "makes it worse" are circled in green pencil.

ROBERTS' VOICE
(narrating)

Then it all came back to me. All that talk about dueling and scars and scratches...

(pause)

There was no doubt about it. Vera must be the woman Haskell had mentioned. She must have passed me while I slept.

Vera speaks as CAMERA PULLS BACK for a WIDER ANGLE, taking her into the scene.

VERA
(impatiently)

Well?

Roberts turns to her, opens his mouth but finds it impossible to say anything.

VERA
(persistently, not removing her gaze from his face for an instant)

Well? I'm waiting.

The CAMERA TRACKS IN for a CLOSER SHOT of Roberts. Vera is o.s. again. Roberts can find nothing to say. Sweat stands out on his forehead.

ROBERTS' VOICE
(narrating)

My goose was cooked. She had me. That Haskell guy wasn't dead yet. He wasn't stretched out stiff and cold in any Arizona gully. He was sitting right there in the car, laughing like mad while he haunted me...

VERA'S VOICE
(o.s.)

Well?

The CAMERA KEEPS MOVING IN on Roberts.

ROBERTS' VOICE
(narrating)

There was nothing I could say. It was her move...

DISSOLVE THRU TO:

211–212–213 OMITTED

214   INT. LAS VEGAS DINER — CLOSE SHOT REVOLVING RECORD IN JUKE BOX PLAYING "SOPHISTICATED LADY" — NIGHT

DISSOLVE THRU TO:

215   INT. LAS VEGAS DINER — CLOSE SHOT — ROBERTS AT COUNTER MOROSELY SIPPING COFFEE — NIGHT. — EVENING

The music is louder now, as Roberts narrates.

ROBERTS' VOICE
(narrating)

Vera whatever-her-name-was. It was just my luck picking her up on the road. It couldn't have been Helen, or Mary, or Evelyn, or Ruth. It had to be the very last person I should ever have met.... That's life. Whichever way you turn, Fate sticks out a foot to trip you up...

DISSOLVE THRU TO:

216   INT. ROADSTER — CLOSE SHOT — VERA THRU WINDSHIELD — PROCESS — DAY

The music is lost in the HUM of the car motor Vera, facing Roberts o.s. is talking heatedly in pantomime as Roberts' voice continues the narration. When she does speak, her voice FADES IN as

Roberts' voice (narrating) FADES OUT. This technique holds for all such transitions in the script, making a kind of Lap Dissolve of the sound track.

ROBERTS' VOICE
(narrating)

I told her everything, but she didn't believe my story. I should have saved my breath...

VERA
(who has been talking at great rate inaudibly — now fading in)

That's the greatest cock and bull story I ever heard! Fell out of the car! Say, who do you think you're talking to? A hick? Listen, brother, I've been around, and I know a wrong guy when I see one! What did you do — kiss him with a wrench?

The CAMERA PULLS BACK for a WIDER ANGLE, taking in Roberts who is driving along, white-faced and drawn.

ROBERTS

Now wait a minute. What I told you was true! You see — that's why I had to do it! You think I did it — well, the cops would have thought so too!

VERA
(with a sneer)

Maybe they *still* think so. What makes you so sure I'll shut up about this?

ROBERTS
(turning to her in misery)

Vera, I'm innocent. Give me a break, will you?

VERA
(after a pause)

I shouldn't ... but, well, it won't do me any good having you pinched. The cops are no friends of mine. Now if there was a reward.... But there isn't.*

ROBERTS
(relieved)

Thanks.

VERA
(with a nasty smile)

Oh, don't thank me yet. I'm not done with you by a long shot. Let's see that roll...

217 ANOTHER ANGLE — PROCESS — DAY

The HUM of the motor SUSTAINS as Roberts looks over at Vera. He notes that she is not fooling, for she holds out her hand. In silence, Roberts digs into his pocket and puts the roll of bills into her hand. Vera starts counting the money as the car continues to travel through desert country — more populated than before, however.

218 ANOTHER ANGLE — TWO SHOT, ROBERTS AND VERA THRU WINDSHIELD — PROCESS — DAY

Vera finishes counting the money and looks up at Roberts with narrowed eyes.

VERA

Is that all Haskell had?

ROBERTS
(grouchily)

Isn't it enough?

---

*Next to this dialogue is a post-it note: "Vera is beginning to enjoy the power she holds over Roberts."

                    VERA
                (suspiciously)

I thought he had more.

                    ROBERTS

Not that I know of. You can search me if you think I'm holding out on you.

                    VERA
            (stuffing the money into a purse)

Well, maybe I will at that. He told me he was going to bet three thousand dollars on a horse named Paradisical on Wednesday at Santa Anita.

                    ROBERTS

He must have been stringing you. He meant three hundred.

                    VERA

Maybe.

                    ROBERTS

Sure, three hundred. Or three bucks. He was a piece of cheese. Big blowhard.

                    VERA

Listen, Mister. Don't try to tell me anything about Charlie Haskell. I knew him better than you did.
WARNING: Avoid sexy interpretation of above speech.

                    ROBERTS

Okay, then you know he was a fourflusher. That explains his three grand bet.

                    VERA

I'm not so sure he didn't *have* that three grand. Why should I believe you? You've got all the earmarks of a cheap crook.
Roberts turns his head to protest this remark.

                    ROBERTS

Now wait a minute...

219 CLOSE SHOT — VERA — PROCESS — DAY

Vera's eyes blaze. She speaks swiftly, bitingly, facing Roberts o.s.

                    VERA

Shut up. You're a cheap crook and you killed him. For two cents I'd change my mind and turn you in. I don't like you.

220 CLOSE SHOT — ROBERTS — PROCESS — DAY

In this REVERSE ANGLE SHOT, Roberts turns his head toward Vera o.s. starts to open his mouth in protest, then closes it and returns his attention to the road ahead.

                    ROBERTS
                (softly — to soothe her)

All right, all right. Don't get sore.

221 TWO SHOT THRU WINDSHIELD, ROBERTS AND VERA, FEATURING VERA — PROCESS — DAY

                    VERA

I'm not sore. But just remember who's boss around here. If you shut up and don't give me any arguments, you have nothing to worry about. If you act wise — well, mister, you'll pop into jail so fast it'll give you the bends.

> ROBERTS
> (humble)

I'm not arguing.

> VERA

See that you don't. Crooked as you look, I'd hate to see a fellow as young as you wind up sniffing that perfume Arizona hands out free to murderers.*

> ROBERTS

I'm not a murderer...

> VERA
> (laughing humorlessly)

Of course you're not. Haskell knocked his own head off.

> ROBERTS

He fell. That's how it happened. Just like I told you.

> VERA

And then he made you a present of his belongings.

> ROBERTS

Look I explained why I had to...

> VERA

Oh, skip it. It doesn't make any difference one way or another. I'm not a mourner. I liked Haskell even less than I like you.

> ROBERTS

Yeah. I saw what you did to him.

> VERA

What do you mean?

> ROBERTS

Those scratches on his wrist.

> VERA

Oh, sure. I scratched him.

> ROBERTS

I'll say you did!

222 INT. ROADSTER — ANOTHER ANGLE — ROBERTS AND VERA IN CAR — PROCESS — LATE AFTERNOON

The Process Screen should reveal that the car is traveling slowly through the outskirts of a California town.

> VERA
> (with a sniff)

So your idea was to drive the car for a little way, maybe into San Bernardino, and then leave it?
> (pause)

You weren't going to *sell* it?

> ROBERTS
> (turning to Vera in amazement)

Sell it! Do you think I'm crazy? A — car that belongs to somebody else? Say, all I want is to leave it somewhere, and forget I ever saw it!

---

*In green pencil, Ann has placed commas after "Arizona" and "hands out," and she has circled "hands out, free to murderers."

VERA
(yawning contemptuously)

Hmmm... Not only don't you have any scruples, you don't have any brains.

ROBERTS

I don't get you.

VERA

Maybe it's a good thing you met me. You would have got yourself caught, sure. Why, you dope, don't you know a deserted automobile always rates an investigation?

ROBERTS

Huh?

VERA

The police find a car. Then they get curious. They wonder where the owner is. So, all right, they don't trace Haskell. They trace *you*.

ROBERTS

I never thought of that.

VERA

The only safe way to get rid of the car is to sell it to a dealer. Get it registered under a new name.
(pause)
Say, pull in to the curb by that drug store. I want to get a bottle and do some shopping before we hit Los Angeles.
(nodding toward something o.s.)
There's a parking place.

The Process Screen reveals that they are in the main drag of a fair sized town.

223   EXT. TOWN STREET — MED. SHOT TOWARD CURB — DAY

The convertible, bearing Roberts and Vera, pulls in to the curb and stops. Traffic passes in the roadway and pedestrians in light summer attire keep coming by. Roberts parks the car in front of a drug store. There is a dress shop next door, and in the show window is the dress that Vera wears at some later point in the picture.

ROBERTS

This is a red zone, Vera. You run in. Then if a cop comes, I can move.

VERA

Nothing doing. You're coming in, too. From now on, you and I are the Siamese twins.

ROBERTS
(shrugging)

Have it your way. But I don't get the point.

VERA
(opening the door on her side of the car)

The point is I don't want you to get lost.

ROBERTS

I'm not going to beat it, if that's what you're afraid of.

VERA

I'll say you're not. I'm going to see that you sell this car, so you won't get caught.

ROBERTS
(sarcastically)

Thanks. Of course your interest wouldn't be financial, would it? You wouldn't want a small percentage of the profits?

VERA
Well, now that you insist, how can I refuse? A hundred per cent will do.

ROBERTS
Fine. I'm relieved. I thought for a moment you were going to take it all.

VERA
I don't want to be a hog.

Vera and Roberts get out of the car, cross the curb and enter the drug store.

FADE OUT:

FADE IN:

224 MONTAGE OF (STOCK) SHOTS OF HOLLYWOOD — NIGHT
Thru
229 (224) Hollywood and Vine.
    (225) The Brown Derby
    (226) Hollywood Boulevard
    (227) Grauman's Chinese
    (228) Neon sign reading: All Roads Lead to Hollywood.
    (229) The above shots SUPERIMPOSED upon a MED. TWO SHOT OF ROBERTS AND VERA from behind their heads, shooting toward the windshield.

Roberts' voice narrates over the entire Montage.

ROBERTS' VOICE
(narrating)

A few hours later we were in Hollywood, and I was recognizing places Sue had written about. I scarcely saw them. It struck me that far from being at the end of the trip, now there was a greater distance between Sue and me than when I started out.

DISSOLVE THRU TO:

230 EXT. HOLLYWOOD APARTMENT HOUSE — FULL SHOT — NIGHT

The convertible drives up and parks in front of an average California apartment building; Roberts and Vera get out and start unloading some bags and packages.

ROBERTS' VOICE
(narrating)

Vera wasn't kidding with that Siamese twins crack, and she made me rent a little apartment — as Mr. Charles Haskell.

WIPE TO:

231 INT. LOBBY OF HOLLYWOOD APARTMENT — FULL SHOT — NIGHT

A smallish lobby with a desk behind which a stout landlady is waiting. Roberts and Vera enter from the street and, the CAMERA TRUCKING THEM, they carry their bags and packages over to the desk. Roberts sets his (Haskell's) suitcase down and registers. Vera hands the landlady some money and the landlady hands her a key. Then Vera and Roberts go o.s. lugging their lares and penates. This scene, and Scene 230, are played without sound.

ROBERTS' VOICE
(narrating)

When I objected to this, she explained that it was on account of the car. A dealer might think something was funny if he called and found we were using different names...

WIPE TO:

232 INT. HOLLYWOOD APARTMENT LIVING ROOM — FULL SHOT — NIGHT*

CAMERA SHOOTING TOWARD the entrance door. As the scene opens, the place is dark. Vera and Roberts enter, carrying their bags. Vera snaps on the lights. The place is a typical Hollywood apartment; there is a breakfast nook in evidence, and a door opens into a bedroom. Behind another door in the room is a Murphy bed. A telephone on a long cord stands on an end table by the couch, close to the bedroom door.

VERA
(setting down her overnight case and the few packages she is carrying)

Home sweet home. And not bad, either. In case there's any doubt in your mind, I'll take the bedroom.

ROBERTS
(moving toward a window)

It sure is stuffy in here.

VERA

The old crow downstairs said there's a folding bed behind those doors there.
Roberts throws open a window and goes over to the French doors concealing a Murphy bed. He opens them revealing a bed.

VERA (CONT'D)

You know how to work it?†

ROBERTS
(letting down the bed, then putting it back again)

I invented it.
At this point the SOUND of a saxophone amateurishly running scales comes over — as though through the open window. Roberts and Vera exchange looks.‡

ROBERTS
(in dismay)

Home sweet home.

VERA#
(picking up her paraphernalia and disappearing into the bedroom)

Well, one can't have everything. I'm first in the bathtub.§

ROBERTS
(sarcastic)

I don't know why, but I figured you would be.
The saxophone continues to run sour scales as we:

DISSOLVE TO:

233 INT. HOLLYWOOD APARTMENT LIVING ROOM — MED. SHOT — NIGHT

Vera, with her hair up and bound in a bath towel, and wearing Haskell's dressing gown, is sprawled in an easy chair with a bottle of whiskey beside her on an end table. She lights a cigarette

---

*A green line starts at the top of this scene and continues for several pages, all the way to the end of scene and continues for several pages, all the way to the end of scene 237.
†A post-it note here reads: "There's a transition in her around here. Edgar asked me to smooth down my sweater in front."
‡Post-it note: "Per Edgar* Vera pulls her sweater down tight on her body (a sexually suggestive gesture) and says 'I'm first in the bathub!' (an invitation to Roberts)."
#Post-it note: "'I'm first in the bath tub!' That line was said with a double meaning. She's attracted to him & coming on to him."
§This line has been underlined in green pencil. A later post-it note beside the line reads: "Besides the literal meaning of the line, there's another meaning there."

and pours herself a stiff drink as the scene opens. Roberts is seated on the window-sill, looking out. He is in shirt sleeves. The SOUND of the saxophone comes over, running scales.

> VERA
>
> Boy, it feels good to be clean again. I must be ten pounds lighter.*

> ROBERTS
> (without turning)

You must be.
Vera looks at him angrily for a moment, then lashes out.

> VERA
>
> Well, hitching rides isn't exactly the way to keep your schoolgirl complexion.

> ROBERTS
>
> I wish that guy with the sax would give up. It gets on my nerves.

> VERA
>
> Forget it, and have a drink.

> ROBERTS
> (still with his back to her)
> Aren't you afraid I'll take you up on it?

> VERA
>
> If I didn't want to give you a drink, I wouldn't have offered it.

The CAMERA TRACKS IN SLOWLY for a CLOSE SHOT of Vera.

> VERA
>
> Why be a sore-head, Roberts? You got yourself into this thing. You should be grateful I'm not turning you in. Why, if I wasn't regular, you'd be in the pen this minute being photographed and fingerprinted and pushed around by the cops. So cheer up. Get rid of that long puss.
> (pause)
> Or is your conscience bothering you?

234   CLOSE SHOT — ROBERTS AT WINDOW — NIGHT

Roberts turns around swiftly from the window to face camera. The saxophone stops playing. For a second he stares in the direction of Vera (o.s.) angrily. Then he says:

> ROBERTS
>
> No, it isn't.

The CAMERA TRUCKS HIM as he leaves the window and comes over to Vera. She pours him a drink and hands it to him. Both are now framed in a CLOSE TWO SHOT.

> VERA
>
> Fine. That's the spirit. He's dead, and no moaning around will bring him back. I never could understand this worrying about something that was over and done with.

> ROBERTS
>
> Listen, Vera. For the last time. I didn't kill him. Haskell was a sick man. Maybe he was dead *before* he fell out of the car, I don't know.

> VERA
> (sarcastic)
>
> Sure, he died of old age.†

Roberts looks at her in disgust and Vera laughs.

---

*A post-it note next to this line reads: Edgar wanted me to stretch and cross my legs together — it was a sensuous movement.

†Post-it note: "Vera reveals a physical attraction for Roberts in this scene."

              VERA (CONT'D)
All right. If it'll make you sociable, you didn't kill him.

Roberts tosses off his drink and Vera pours him another. The CAMERA PANS DOWN to the whiskey bottle on the end table and MOVES IN ON IT for CLOSE SHOT. It is almost full.

                                              DISSOLVE THRU TO:

235 INT. HOLLYWOOD APARTMENT LIVING ROOM — CLOSE SHOT — WHISKEY BOTTLE — NIGHT

From a CLOSE SHOT of the whiskey bottle, which is now empty, the CAMERA PULLS BACK to a MED. SHOT OF THE ROOM, shooting toward the chair in which Vera is lounging. Roberts is pacing back and forth across the floor in front of her. She follows him with her eyes.

                        VERA
We're out of liquor, Roberts.*

                        ROBERTS
                    (pacing by)
Yeah.

                        VERA
Too bad. I felt like getting tight tonight.

                        ROBERTS
Well, I think you succeeded.

                        VERA
Am I tight?

                        ROBERTS
As a prima donna's corset.

                        VERA
That's nice. I wanted to get tight.

                        ROBERTS
                    (grouchily)
Why? What have you got to get tight about?

                        VERA
Oh, I don't know. A few things...

                        ROBERTS
Hmph! You should have my worries.

Vera looks at him as he paces for a moment, then laughs.

                        VERA
If I had your troubles, I'd stay sober.

                        ROBERTS
Yeah. Maybe you're right.

                        VERA
I'm always right.

Roberts gives Vera a disgusted look.

236 CLOSE SHOT — VERA IN CHAIR — NIGHT

Vera follows the pacing Roberts (o.s.) with her eyes. They are a bit glassy with alcohol and they narrow a trifle.

---

*Post-it note: "Edgar told me — Vera takes the last drop of whisky out of the glass with her finger."

                                VERA

I don't like your attitude, Roberts.

                           ROBERTS' VOICE
                               (o.s.)

Well, there's a lot of things *I* don't like.

                                VERA
                (following him with her eyes as he paces o.s.)

*Sure. But life is like a ball game. You have to take a swing at whatever comes along before you wake up and find it's the ninth inning.†

                           ROBERTS' VOICE
                               (o.s.)

I bet you read that somewhere.

                                VERA
                              (frowning)

That's the trouble with you, Roberts. All you do is bellyache, instead of taking it easy and trying to make the best of things.
                              (slowly)
Maybe that's what's wrong with the whole world.

                           ROBERTS' VOICE
                               (o.s.)

Get the professor!

                                VERA

People knock themselves out trying to buck Fate. Now you, for instance. You're lucky just to be alive! Suppose *Haskell* had pulled open *your* door. You'd be playing a harp now. Thank of that.

                           ROBERTS' VOICE
                               (o.s.)

You think of it. I'm tired of thinking.

237   MED. SHOT‡ — NIGHT

Roberts is pacing up and down restlessly while Vera sprawls in the chair, following him with her eyes.

                                VERA

#There's plenty of people dying this minute that would give anything to trade places with you. I know what I'm talking about.§

                               ROBERTS
                       (looking around for something)

I'm not so sure. At least they *know* they're done for. They don't have to sweat blood *wondering* if they are.

                                VERA
                             (with a yawn)

Your philosophy stinks, pal! We all know we're going to kick off some day. It's only a question of when. But what got us off on this anyway? We'll be discussing politics next.

---

*There is a star in black ink at the beginning of this line.
†Post-it note: "Vera reaches up to Roberts."
‡"MED. SHOT" has been crossed out in green pencil.
#There's a star in black ink at the beginning of this line, and the note "Vera reaches for Roberts."
§Post-it note: "Vera knows that she is not long to live (she is drunk and maudlin)."

ROBERTS

Or spiritualism. Where did you hide the butts?

VERA

(nodding toward the far end table by the couch)

On the table, sucker...

Roberts moves over to the end table indicated and takes a cigarette from the pack. The CAMERA TRUCKS IN until we get a BIG CLOSEUP OF THE ASHTRAY by the opened pack. There is almost a full pack of cigarettes and there are only two butts in the tray.

DISSOLVE THRU TO:

238 –SERIES OF INSERTS: BIG CLOSEUP OF ASH TRAY AND PACK

239 –OF CIGARETTES ON END TABLE

240

(238) Ash-tray with six butts in it — pack half full.

DISSOLVE THRU TO:

(239) Ash-tray with twelve butts in it — pack almost empty.

DISSOLVE THRU TO:

(240) Ash-tray full — pack crumpled up in it.

Roberts' voice narrates throughout the series.

ROBERTS' VOICE

We bored each other with conversation for a couple of hours longer, every five minutes one of us wishing we had another bottle or a radio or something to read. Then, when we finally ran out of chatter, I suggested the hay...

241   INT. HOLLYWOOD APARTMENT LIVING ROOM — MED. SHOT — NIGHT*

The CAMERA PULLS BACK from a BIG CLOSEUP of the ash-tray (as in Scene 240 of the series) to a MED. SHOT OF THE ROOM. Roberts is slumped on the couch. Vera is still in the easy chair, but the bath towel is off her head and she is combing her hair.†

ROBERTS

(his voice fading in as his voice — narrating — fades out)

...I know it's only eleven o'clock. But I want to get up early and make the rounds of the used-car lots.

VERA

No hurry about that. We've got all the time in the world.

ROBERTS

Maybe *you* have, but if you think I want to stay cooped up in this place any longer than I have to, you're batty.

VERA

(shrugging)

It's not a bad place. You'd pay plenty for diggings like this in New York.‡

ROBERTS

I wouldn't care if it was the Ritz.

Vera starts to cough and the CAMERA TRUCKS IN for a CLOSER SHOT of the two, featuring Vera. The coughing spell lasts a few seconds.#

---

*A green pencil line starts here and goes through until the end of scene 248.
†A post-it just below this reads: "Vera is sitting at the table, brushing her hair."
‡A green pencil note just past line reads: "(start coughing)."
#This line is underlined in green pencil.

VERA
(wiping her eyes)

That rotten liquor.

ROBERTS

You got a mean cough. Ought to do something about it.

VERA

Oh, I'll be all right.

ROBERTS

That's that Camille said.

VERA

Who?

ROBERTS

Nobody you know.

VERA

Anyway, wouldn't it be a break for you if I did kick off? You'd be free — and with all Haskell's dough and the car.

ROBERTS

I don't want to see anybody die.

VERA

Not even me?

ROBERTS

Especially not you. One person died on me. If you did — well, that's all I need.

242   CLOSE SHOT — VERA IN CHAIR — NIGHT

Vera, who has quite recovered from her coughing spell, resumes combing her hair. She looks up at Roberts (o.s.) with a half malicious smile.

VERA

You don't like me, do you, Roberts?

243   REVERSE ANGLE — CLOSE SHOT — ROBERTS ON COUCH — NIGHT

ROBERTS
(with a sardonic twist of the mouth)

Like you? I love you. My favorite sport is being kept a prisoner.

244   REVERSE ANGLE — CLOSE SHOT — VERA IN CHAIR — NIGHT

VERA
(rising to her feet)

After we sell the car, you can go to blazes, for all I care ... but not until then. I'm going to bed. Good night, Roberts. Don't try to sneak away during the night. You can't get that chain off the door without making a lot of noise and I'm a light sleeper. Anyway, if I find you gone, I'll notify the police and they'll pick you up.

245   MED. SHOT — NIGHT

Vera starts from the chair to the bedroom door. Roberts does not move from his position on the couch.

ROBERTS
(gloomily)

Don't worry. I know when I'm in a spot.

VERA
(turning at the bedroom door with a malicious smile)

Well, good night. I hope that portable rack won't be too uncomfortable for you.

246 CLOSE SHOT — ROBERTS ON COUCH — NIGHT

Roberts slumps on the couch, the picture of dejection. He looks over in the direction of Vera o.s.

ROBERTS

Don't lose any sleep over it, will you, Vera?

The SOUND of a door closing comes over. After a moment, Roberts rises, stretches and starts to remove his shirt. Then his eye is caught by something o.s. and he stops dead.

247 INSERT: TELEPHONE WITH LONG CORD, ON THE TABLE — NIGHT

248 MED. CLOSE SHOT — ROBERTS — NIGHT

Roberts stares over at the telephone on the end table, then turns to stare at the bedroom door, which is closed. There is a moment of indecision, then he goes quickly over to the phone, the CAMERA PANNING HIM. He picks up the receiver.

ROBERTS
(muttering as he dials)

Crestview ... six...

Roberts continues to dial as the CAMERA MOVES IN SLOWLY for a CLOSE SHOT OF HIM. His face registers apprehension. The SOUND of the operator buzzing the number comes over, then a click, and the SOUND of Sue's voice.

SUE'S VOICE
(through phone)

Hello ... hello...

Roberts starts to answer, then realizes he can never explain his present predicament. He closes his mouth — frustrated.

SUE'S VOICE
(through phone)

Hello... hello...

Roberts slowly and sadly hangs up the receiver, a click that cuts off Sue's voice.

ROBERTS
(whispering)

No, not yet, honey ... tomorrow...

(pause)

Maybe...

FADE OUT:

FADE IN:

249 INT. HOLLYWOOD APARTMENT BEDROOM — DAY — CLOSE SHOT: VERA

THE CAMERA, SHOOTING OVER VERA'S SHOULDER into the bureau mirror photographs her as she makes up her face. On the bureau may be seen several empty cartons of cosmetics, dress boxes with only tissue paper in them, etc.

As the scene opens, she has no makeup on at all but, bit by bit, she beautifies herself (to the surprise of the audience, it is to be hoped). The final touch comes when she lets down her hair. She is really a very pretty girl. While all this is going on, Roberts' voice (narrating) comes over.

                                  ROBERTS' VOICE
                                      (narrating)

If this were a movie, I would fall in love with Vera, marry her and make a respectable woman of her.... Or else she'd make some supreme Class A sacrifice for me and die — leaving me free to marry Sue. She would experience a complete and totally unwarranted change of heart, wipe out her past by a dramatic death, pleasing me, and you, and the sweethearts in the balcony. Sue and I would bawl a little over her grave, make some crack about there is good in all of us, and fade out. But this isn't a movie, and Vera, unfortunately, was just as rotten in the morning as she'd been the night before....

FADE OUT Roberts' voice (narrating) as the SOUND of KNOCKING FADES IN.

Vera turns her head toward the bedroom door (o.s.)

                                          VERA
                                  (snapping peevishly)

All right! I'm coming!

250   INT. HOLLYWOOD APARTMENT LIVING ROOM — DAY — CLOSE SHOT: ROBERTS AT BEDROOM DOOR

Roberts, fully dressed in Haskell's suit that he wore the day before, looks impatient. He addresses the door:

                                        ROBERTS

Look Vera. It's almost noon!

251   INT. HOLLYWOOD APARTMENT BEDROOM — DAY — CLOSE SHOT: VERA

The CAMERA PULLS BACK from a CLOSE SHOT OF VERA before the bureau mirror to a MED. SHOT OF the bedroom, taking in the bed. There are more cardboard boxes and mountains of tissue paper on it, evidence of the shopping Vera did the previous afternoon. The bed is, of course, unmade. Vera turns away from the mirror where she has been putting on the finishing touches to her makeup, and takes a light weight coat from one of the boxes.

                                          VERA
                      (glancing over toward the door ill-humoredly)

So what? The dealers will be there all day.

                                        ROBERTS
                                    (o.s., through door)

They'll be there all year, too — but that doesn't mean I'm going to wait that long.

Vera walks to the door, the CAMERA TRUCKING HER, and throws it open, revealing Roberts.

                                          VERA

Oh, shut up. You're making noises like a husband.

The CAMERA, SHOOTING OVER VERA'S SHOULDER, records the slow astonishment on Roberts' face as he sees the transformed Vera.

252   INT. BEDROOM DOORWAY — DAY — REVERSE ANGLE: VERA

The CAMERA, SHOOTING OVER ROBERTS' SHOULDER, photographs Vera in her new dress, carrying her new coat. She is in the doorway and she laughs and strikes a pose like a model.

                                          VERA

Do I rate a whistle?

ROBERTS

You sure do—but let's go.

The pleased smile vanishes from Vera's face, and she pushes past Roberts, a trifle annoyed.

VERA
(mocking him)

Let's go, let's go! I spend eighty-five bucks and two hours preparing bait, and all you can say is 'Let's go!'

253 INT. LIVING ROOM — FULL SHOT — DAY

Vera, followed by Roberts, exits, closing the front door after them. The Murphy bed is down and unmade. As the door closes behind them, the SOUND of the saxophone comes over, running sour and monotonous scales.

DISSOLVE TO:

254 INT. ROADSTER — DAY — (PROCESS) — TWO SHOT THROUGH WINDSHIELD — ROBERTS AND VERA

The two drive slowly through Hollywood streets, Vera proud in her new outfit.

ROBERTS

We passed a few used car lots last night down this way.

VERA
(primping)

What do you think we'll get for this heap?

ROBERTS

I don't know. Plenty. You just let me handle everything.

VERA

You think we can get a thousand dollars?

ROBERTS

I don't know. But don't worry, I'll squeeze as much out of the guy as I can. If I let it go cheap without a fight, he might think the car was stolen. And listen — don't make any slips and call me Roberts. That'll cook us.

VERA

I don't need you to tell me that.

ROBERTS

You better just sit by and keep your mouth closed. Remember, we're both in the soup if anything happens.

VERA

Oh, forget it and drive.

ROBERTS

You're my wife — Vera Haskell.

VERA

After the deal's closed, we can go back to that place on Hollywood Boulevard where I saw that fur jacket. I want to buy it.

ROBERTS

After the deal's closed, I'm saying goodbye to you.

VERA

That's right. I forgot. I guess I'm getting kind of used to you.

                                   ROBERTS
Well, that's a habit you can start breaking. Here's a joint. Keep your fingers crossed and your mouth closed...
Roberts turns the wheel sharply to the right and the Process Screen reacts accordingly.

255   EXT. USED CAR LOT — DAY — FULL (ESTABLISHING) SHOT

Just a vacant lot with lines of cars for sale. There is a driveway with a sign over it — USED CARS — BOUGHT AND SOLD. A little bungalow with the sign: OFFICE painted on it is soon in b.g.
As the scene opens, the convertible bearing Roberts and Vera turns into the driveway and proceeds as far as the bungalow office.

256   EXT. USED CAR LOT — DAY — MED. SHOT OF OFFICE

The convertible pulls up before the office and Roberts punches the horn. The dealer, a shrewd-faced man in his forties, comes out of the bungalow. Roberts does not shut off his motor.

                                   DEALER
Good afternoon, folks. Interested in buying a nice car?

                                    VERA
We're interested in *selling* one.

                                   ROBERTS
                    (with a warning side-glance at Vera)
We're interested in selling — if the price is right.
Roberts gets out of the car, as the dealer walks closer to appraise it.

                                   DEALER
                            (frowning judiciously)
If it's in good shape mechanically, the Blue Book is eight hundred.
                         (calling o.s. over his shoulder)
Tony, come over here and have a look at the motor!

                                    VERA
                                (disgustedly)
Eight hundred! Are you kidding?
As she speaks, a grease-covered mechanic enters the scene from behind the office. He lifts the hood of the car and peers inside.

                                   DEALER
                              (with knit brows)
Well, maybe eight-fifty....

                                    VERA
Before I let it go for eight-fifty, I'll wreck it and collect the insurance!
She is very excited, and commences to cough. But only once or twice.

                                   DEALER
                               (solicitously)
There's some water inside.

257   EXT. USED CAR LOT — DAY — MED. LONG SHOT FROM HIGH PARALLEL

This scene is done entirely in pantomime as Roberts' voice (narrating) comes over scene. The CAMERA, SHOOTING DOWN on the car as it stands in front of the office. Photographs Roberts and the dealer arguing; Vera getting out of the car to join in; and Tony, the mechanic, crawling underneath the car.

ROBERTS' VOICE
(narrating)

While the mechanic appraised the car, we haggled. At last, when we were all worn out, we hit a compromise, his price...

258–259 OMITTED

260   EXT. USED CAR LOT — DAY — GROUP SHOT — VERA, ROBERTS AND DEALER BEFORE OFFICE — AFTERNOON

As the scene opens, Roberts and the dealer are shaking hands. Vera looks disgustedly on.

ROBERTS
(shaking hands, resignedly)

Eight hundred and fifty dollars.

DEALER

Come inside and we'll sign the papers.

ROBERTS

Okay. I've got the ownership right here.
(to Vera)

Look, Vera, you clean out the dash compartment in the meanwhile, will you? We may have left some stuff in there.

VERA

All right—*darling*.

Vera shoots Roberts a nasty look and goes o.s. toward the car. The dealer and Roberts go into the office, Roberts taking out his wallet as he does so.

261   INT. ROADSTER — DAY — CLOSE SHOT — VERA

A profile shot of Vera as she opens up the dash compartment of the car and pulls out a handful of papers, as well as Haskell's cigarette case.

VERA
(grumbling)

Eight hundred and fifty dollars. The dirty chisler.

She turns Haskell's expensive cigarette case over in her hands, admires it, then puts it in her purse.

262   INT. USED CAR OFFICE — DAY — MED. SHOT: ROBERTS AND DEALER AT DESK

Roberts and the Dealer are seated opposite each other at the desk inside the office. The Dealer is studying the papers Roberts has given him.

DEALER

Hmm. New York, eh?

ROBERTS
(a bit nervous)

That's right.

DEALER

But you bought the car in Miami.
The CAMERA DOLLIES IN SLOWLY for a CLOSE TWO SHOT of Roberts and the dealer, featuring Roberts, who registers acute nervousness.

ROBERTS

Er — yes.

DEALER

From the — what was it? West Coast Motors?

ROBERTS

Yes, that's it. The West Coast Motors.

DEALER

No — the East Coast Motors.

ROBERTS

Of course.

DEALER

Now — let me see — about the insurance. We'll have to get that transferred or cancelled. I don't see ... what insurance do you carry, Mr. Haskell?

Roberts looks more nervous than ever. He swallows visibly.

ROBERTS
(weakly)

Aren't — aren't the papers all there?

DEALER

I don't see them. But surely you know what kind of insurance you have on the car, and the name of the company?

ROBERTS

Er — surely.

DEALER

If you give me the name of the Company, I can take care of all the details.

ROBERTS

Well....

Roberts is suffering horribly. He is almost at the point of breaking and running.

263   INT. USED CAR OFFICE — DAY — FULL SHOT TOWARD DOOR

Vera comes quickly into the office, interrupting Roberts and the Dealer. She carries a long strip of paper rolled up in one hand.

VERA
(to Roberts)

Did you sign the papers?

ROBERTS

Not yet.

VERA

Well, don't ... we're not selling the car.
(seizing him by the arm)

Come on.

DEALER

But, wait a minute, Mrs. Haskell...

VERA

Come on...

DEALER
(a bit put out)

Well, I'll be....

                    VERA
                    (to the Dealer)
Shut your mouth. I guess I can keep my own car if I want to.
                    ROBERTS
But, Vera...
                    VERA
                    (pulling him toward the door)
You shut up, too—let's go.

264   EXT. USED CAR LOT — DAY — FULL SHOT

Vera and Roberts come out of the office, get into the convertible and drive off the lot and down the street. The Dealer follows the pair out of the office and stands on the threshold, looking after them and scratching his head.

265   INT. ROADSTER — DAY — (PROCESS) — TWO SHOT THROUGH WINDSHIELD

The pair drive slowly through Hollywood streets.
                    ROBERTS
You got me out of a tight spot, Vera — but I still don't understand all this....
                    VERA
                    (unrolling the paper with the list)
You will in a minute. I almost threw away a gold mine.
                    ROBERTS
Eight-fifty isn't to be sneezed at. The car doesn't book for as much as I thought.
Vera has a nasty little smile hovering around her lips as they drive along through the streets of Hollywood.
                    VERA
We're not going to sell the car.
Roberts turns quickly to face Vera, puzzled.
                    ROBERTS
You want to keep it? Now, wait a minute, Vera. You said yourself I wouldn't be safe until the car was in someone else's name. I'd like to be free of this mess when I go.
                    VERA
That's just it, Roberts. You're not going.
Roberts stares at Vera blankly.
                    VERA
There's a drive-in at the next corner. Pull in there. We'll get a bite to eat and I'll explain.
                    ROBERTS
                    (angrily)
What is this? Another one of your brilliant ideas?

266   to and including

290 — OMITTED

291   EXT. HOLLY DRIVE-IN — DAY — FULL (ESTABLISHING) SHOT

An ordinary California-type drive-in with cars parked head-in. It is busy, and waitresses in uniforms run back and forth to the cars. The convertible, bearing Roberts and Vera, pulls in a vacant space.

292 INT. ROADSTER — DAY — (PARKED IN DRIVE-IN) — MED. SHOT

Roberts and Vera are in the car. A CAR-HOP comes up with the menus. She is young and pretty and wears the uniform of the Holly Drive-in.

CAR-HOP

May I take your order?

VERA

Make mine a hamburger and some coffee.

CAR-HOP

And for you, sir?

ROBERTS
(looking grumpy)

Oh — I don't care. The same.

CAR-HOP

Thank you.
The car-hop writes on her little pad and goes o.s.

ROBERTS
(turning to Vera)

Get this, Vera. I've been pretty patient so far. I've done whatever you asked me to do. But no more.

VERA

Shut up.

ROBERTS

You've taken Haskell's money, and you can have the dough when we sell the car, but you're not going to keep me a prisoner.

VERA
(handing him her newspaper)

Take a look at the paper. It's a good thing I bought it.

ROBERTS

Vera, I'm in no mood....

VERA
(pointing at an item with her fingers)

Read that...
Roberts' eyes reluctantly drop to the paper. Vera still wears that half-smile which presages trouble.

293 INSERT — NEWSPAPER ITEM (NO HEADLINES) — "HASKELL NEAR DEATH" REMAINDER READING: "Millionaire Exporter in Hospital, victim of pneumonia. April 17. Charles J. Haskell, Sr., noted sports enthusiast and President of the Wilmington and San Pedro Exports, Inc. lies close to death after a three-week siege of bronchial pneumonia. Doctors have little hope of recovery...."

294 INT. ROADSTER — PARKED IN DRIVE-IN — DAY — TWO SHOT: ROBERTS AND VERA

Roberts looks up from reading the newspaper item. For a second, Vera and Roberts look into each other's eyes. Comprehension registers slowly on Roberts' face.

ROBERTS

No....

VERA

Yes...

                        ROBERTS

No, I won't do it!

                         VERA
                    (her eyes cold)

You will.

                        ROBERTS
                     (frightened)

You think I'm crazy? It's impossible, I tell you.

                   CAR-HOP'S VOICE (O.S.)

Excuse me?
THE CAMERA PULLS BACK FOR A WIDER ANGLE, taking in the Car-hop. She is standing on Vera's side of the car with a tray on which are sandwiches and coffee. Vera moves a trifle, and the Car-hop fastens the tray over the door.

                        CAR-HOP

Thank you. Punch the horn when you're through.
The Car-hop goes o.s. While the girl has been there, both Roberts and Vera have taken pains to appear composed. But as soon as she is gone, they turn to each other again.

                        ROBERTS

No one could get away with an act like that! They'd be wise to me in a minute!

                         VERA
                      (scornfully)

Don't be yellow. You look enough like him. Same coloring, same build.
                  (waving toward Roberts' suit)
See how his clothes fit you? No kidding, you almost had *me* fooled for a while.

                        ROBERTS
                      (in disgust)

Oh, Vera, grow up. Don't you think a father would know his own son? And there must be other relatives.

                         VERA
        (taking her hamburger and biting into it as she speaks)

The father won't have to know you. We'll wait until he gives up the ghost. He's an old geezer. He won't pull through. And as far as other relatives are concerned, they haven't seen you in fifteen or twenty years.
Vera takes the other hamburger and thrusts it into Roberts' hand.

                         VERA

Eat.

                        ROBERTS
              (putting sandwich back on the tray)

I'm not hungry—and I won't do it.

                         VERA

It's not as tough as it sounds. Remember, you've got all kinds of identification—the car, letters, his licenses–

                        ROBERTS

I could never get away with it.

                         VERA

That dame forgot salt. Well, never mind.

ROBERTS
It's the stupidest idea I ever heard.

VERA
The old boy has scads of dough. Look in the paper here. Personal fortune assessed at over fifteen million. He'll leave plenty, I tell you.

ROBERTS
He may have cut off his son. How do we know? No, it's out, Vera. I won't have anything to do with it.

295   INT. ROADSTER — DAY — CLOSE SHOT: VERA

Vera continues to eat her sandwich calmly.

VERA
I think you will.
There is a threat in her tone — and a cold confidence.

296   OMITTED

297   INT. ROADSTER — PARKED IN DRIVE-IN — DAY — MED. TWO SHOT: VERA AND ROBERTS

For a moment the two sit silently in the car. Then Vera places the remnants of her sandwich on the tray and turns to Roberts.

VERA
(very bitterly)

*Look. Why do you think I was heading West? Because I wanted to break into the movies, be a glamour girl? I'll tell you, if you want to know. I'm out here for my health. The doctor in Jersey City said I wouldn't last a year if I didn't get out to the right kind of climate. And even if I did, he said he couldn't promise much. Yes. My lungs. They're like Swiss cheese.

ROBERTS
Gee, that's too bad, Vera. But....

VERA
(violently)

†Oh, I'm not crying about it. But you can bet your sweet life I'm going to live before I croak. I'm going to have all those things you read of in books....
The CAMERA MOVES IN FOR A BIG CLOSE-UP OF VERA as she speaks, a far-off, almost crazed gleam coming into her eyes.

VERA
‡...diamonds and fur coats and breakfasts in bed.

ROBERTS' VOICE (O.S.)
I'll do anything within reason, Vera. But not that. So forget it — or find yourself another stooge.
The gleam sharpens in Vera's eyes as she turns toward Roberts, (o.s.) in a rush of emotion. She almost spits out her words.

VERA
You sap! You lily-livered coward! You'll be fixed for life as Charles Haskell! You can take your inheritance and go away! No more worrying about the rent. No more sweating and scheming and wondering where your next meal's coming from! Think of that, Roberts!

---

*A note next to this in black ink reads: "This speech was cut out."
†Next to this black ink reads: "This speech was cut out (never used)."
‡Next to this in black ink: "Speech cut out."

> **ROBERTS' VOICE (O.S.)**
> Vera, please.... You're talking too loud.

> **VERA**
> On this I'm splitting fifty-fifty with you. Sure. Why not? We're both alike. We were both born in the same gutter.

> **ROBERTS' VOICE (O.S.)**
> Hey, take it easy, Vera! Remember where we are!
> (this in a hushed voice, frightened)
> People can hear!

298 INT. ROADSTER — PARKED IN DRIVE-IN — DAY — MED. SHOT

Vera recaptures control of herself, reaches over and punches the horn-button. She drains her cup of coffee in one gulp and puts it on the tray. She also tosses the newspaper on it. Roberts has eaten nothing.

> **VERA**
> We'll wait until we read that old man Haskell's dead. Then you show up — as if you read in New York that he was sick.

> **ROBERTS**
> No. And suppose he don't die?

> **VERA**
> He will. I know he will. Something tells me.

At this point the Car-hop returns—coming up on Vera's side of the car.

> **CAR-HOP**
> Anything else?

> **VERA**
> No.

> **CAR-HOP**
> That will be seventy-two cents.

Vera peels off a dollar-bill from her roll and lays it on the tray. The Car-hop takes it and is about to make change when Vera waves her away.

> **VERA**
> Oh, keep it.

Roberts starts the motor as the Car-hop unfastens the tray.

> **CAR-HOP**
> Thank you. Call again.

The Car-hop, carrying the tray, moves away a step as Roberts backs the convertible out of the parking space.

299 EXT. HOLLY DRIVE-IN — DAY — MED. CLOSE SHOT — TRUCKING — TRAY IN UPRAISED HAND OF CAR-HOP

The Car-hop carries the tray to the drive-in service counter, the CAMERA TRUCKING HER. As it does so, it CLOSES IN ON THE NEWSPAPER ON THE TRAY. When the car-hop reaches the service counter, she sets down the tray and the CAMERA MOVES IN for a BIG CLOSE-UP of the following:

> MAN'S BODY FOUND IN ARIZONA DITCH
> BY TELEPHONE LINESMEN
> New York Musician Victim of Foul Play

Yuma police today reported the finding of the body of one Al Roberts, of New York City, by telephone linesmen working along U.S. 70 in the vicinity of Lockhart. Marks on the head lead authorities to believe he was clubbed to death, or possibly hurled from a speeding car. A battered valise containing several press clippings, found near the body, made identification certain...

THE CAMERA PULLS BACK from the newspaper to MEDIUM SHOT RANGE of the service counter as SUE, dressed in the uniform of the drive-in, enters the scene through the swinging doors leading to the kitchen. She commences to clear and dump the trays on the counter. She dumps two or three, then picks the tray with the newspaper on it. She takes the paper off the tray and puts it aside, dumps whatever else is on the tray into the receptacle for that purpose, then, having no more trays to empty at the moment, idly picks up the newspaper. She glances at it casually as the CAMERA BEGINS TO PULL BACK RAPIDLY.

The CAMERA CONTINUES TO PULL BACK, and Sue is blocked off by parked automobiles. The SOUND of an awful scream comes over and, as the CAMERA KEEPS PULLING BACK TO A FULL SHOT of the drive-in, a crowd collects around the service counter. People leap out of cars, etc., and hurry in that direction.

DISSOLVE THROUGH TO:

300 INT. HOLLYWOOD APARTMENT LIVING ROOM — NIGHT — FULL SHOT THRU WINDOW FROM OUTSIDE

The window thru which this shot is made is closed. Roberts and Vera are on the couch playing gin-rummy as the scene opens. Roberts is in his shirt-sleeves and Vera is wearing the dress that was modeled in the show-window in Scene #223. There is a half-filled bottle of whiskey on an end-table near them, and they give the impression of having been at their game for a long time. Both talk (in pantomime) as Roberts' voice (narrating) COMES OVER SCENE.

ROBERTS' VOICE
(narrating)

But as much as I insisted I would have no part of her scheme, Vera was taking it for granted I would...

Roberts, it is observed, is doing most of the talking as they play.

ROBERTS' VOICE (CONT'D)
(narrating)

Neither of us had our mind on the cards as we played that night. I know we were just trying to kill time between newspaper editions. This was a death watch for Vera. Maybe it was for me, too...

301 *INT. HOLLYWOOD APARTMENT LIVING ROOM — NIGHT — MED. TWO SHOT: ROBERTS AND VERA ON COUCH†

Vera and Roberts continue to play cards rather absently.

ROBERTS

...don't you realize that if I'm caught they'll want to know where I got the car and stuff? Then they'd have me on a murder charge.

VERA
(laying down her cards)

If you're smart, you won't get caught. I knock with eight.

ROBERTS
(laying down his hand)

And if I am caught, don't you realize you'll be out, too?

VERA
(marking the score)

Eighteen points. That gives me thirty. How will I be out?

---

*Post-it note: "The beginning of the death scene for Vera!"
†A green pencil line starts at the top of this scene and goes through to the bottom of scene 309.

ROBERTS

You'll be out the eight hundred and fifty dollars we could have got on the car.

(as Vera shuffles for a new deal)

Really, Vera, you'd be an awful chump to throw away all that dough on a dizzy long-shot. Let me sell the bus tomorrow. With the money it'll bring, and with what you've already got, a clever kid like you can run it up in no time. Then we'd both be in the clear.

VERA

(dealing)

I'd be in the clear anyway.

ROBERTS

(picking up his new hand)

Maybe, maybe. If I got caught I'd be good and sore at you, you know...

302 CLOSE SHOT — VERA — NIGHT

Vera starts to pick up her cards, but pauses to raise her eyes to Roberts, o.s. There is a cold, cruel glint in them.

VERA

You mean you'd squeal?

303 CLOSE TWO SHOT — ROBERTS AND VERA ON COUCH — NIGHT

Roberts drops his eyes before Vera's penetrating stare. He fumbles with his cards nervously.

ROBERTS

Well — no, not squeal — exactly. I meant...

VERA

Never mind what you meant. Even if you *did* tell the cops I was in it with you, what could they do to me? They might give me the same medicine they gave you — a rope* — but I'm on the way anyhow. All they'd be doing would be hastening it.

ROBERTS

All right. But think of the eight-fifty you'd lose. You'd kick yourself around the block if you let it get away from you.

VERA

(after a pause)

I'll take the chance. Want another drink?

Roberts shakes his head glumly and Vera tips up the bottle for a long slug. It makes her cough a little.

ROBERTS

You're being a goon. That's how people wind up behind the eight-ball. Once they get a few dollars they become greedy and want more.

VERA

My, my!

She replaces the bottle.

304 ANOTHER ANGLE — FEATURING ROBERTS

Vera and Roberts continue to play their game without much interest on either side. Roberts does not look at her as he speaks:

---

*Post-it note: "'A rope' Edgar asked me to use the gravel quality in my voice on the words, a rope."

                            ROBERTS

Caesar — you know, that Roman general — got his for being greedy. He wasn't satisfied, and the final wind-up was he took the count.

Vera merely sniffs at this. She looks as if she is getting very drunk.

                            ROBERTS

A couple of days ago, you didn't have a dime. Why, you were so broke you couldn't have paid cash for a postage stamp. Now you've got almost seven hundred dollars with eight hundred and fifty more in the offing. Take my advice and don't try for more.

                            VERA
            (throwing down her cards, reaching for the whiskey bottle)

I'm tired of this game. Let's have some blackjack.

Roberts throws down his cards too.

305   MED. SHOT — NIGHT

Roberts rises from the couch sullenly as Vera takes another drink, replaces the bottle, then puts the cards together.

                            ROBERTS

Play solitaire.

                            VERA

Okay, if that's the way you feel about it.

                            ROBERTS

That's the way I feel about it.

Roberts crosses the room to a chair, takes hold of a pillow that is on it and flings it disgustedly across the room. He drops miserably into the chair.

                            VERA
                      (now quite drunken)

Getting sore and throwing things won't help Roberts. I'm really doing you a *favor*. I help you out of a jam by keeping my mouth shut. I show you how to make some soft money. And what thanks do I get?

                            ROBERTS
                       (with a bitter note)

Thanks?

                            VERA

Sure. Would you rather I call the cops and tell them you killed a man and stole his money?

                            ROBERTS
                           (angrily)

I didn't kill anybody!

                            VERA

You did.

                            ROBERTS

I didn't, and you know it.

                            VERA

All right, then. Suppose ... suppose I call the police? If you're innocent, what have you got to be scared of?

Vera unsteadily takes the telephone from the end-table and picks up the receiver. The SOUND of a dial tone COMES OVER.

306 MED. CLOSE SHOT — ROBERTS IN CHAIR — NIGHT

Roberts lifts himself a little as he stares at Vera, o.s. The SOUND of the dial tone COMES OVER faintly. Then Roberts settles back in the chair with an effort and tries to look unconcerned.

ROBERTS

Okay, call them, you mutt!! Go ahead, call them! See if I care! At least they'll give me a square deal.

307 CLOSE SHOT — VERA ON COUCH — NIGHT

Vera holds the telephone in one hand and the receiver in the other. She sways slightly. The dial tone COMES OVER.

VERA
(threateningly)

You want me to call them?

308 CLOSE SHOT — ROBERTS IN CHAIR — NIGHT

Roberts continues his bluff. The dial tone is still heard.

ROBERTS

You heard me. But I'm warning you. If I'm pinched, I'll swear you were in on it. I'll say you helped me. If I fry, I'll get even with you!

VERA'S VOICE (O.S.)

You wouldn't dare. You're chicken.

ROBERTS

No? Then try it and see. Call them.

VERA'S VOICE (O.S.)

Okay, I will.

As the SOUND of the dialing of three digits COMES OVER, Roberts' faked confidence fades.

VERA'S VOICE (O.S.)

Information? I want the number of the Hollywood police station.

(pause)

The page is torn out of the book.

(pause)

What's that?

(pause)

Okay, I got it. Thanks.

The SOUND of the number being dialed COMES OVER.

309 FULL SHOT — NIGHT

Roberts leaps from his chair and races across the room to the couch where Vera is dialing a number. He takes the phone out of her hands.

ROBERTS

Wait a minute, Vera. You wouldn't do that....

VERA
(reaching for the phone drunkenly)

Oh, wouldn't I? Give me that. I'll show you if I would!

Roberts restores the instrument to the end-table by the bedroom door and returns to Vera's side. He gently eases her back onto the couch, Vera still protesting, ad lib.

ROBERTS

Take it easy, now. Let's talk this over...

310 INT. HOLLYWOOD APARTMENT LIVING ROOM — FULL SHOT THROUGH WINDOW FROM OUTSIDE — NIGHT

Roberts can be seen arguing with Vera (in pantomime). She is on the couch, he standing over her.

ROBERTS' VOICE

(narrating)

This was early in the evening, and the conversation, while hectic, was at least pitched low. But as the minutes passed and more obstacles to her plan popped into my head, the air got blue. Each word coming from our lips cracked like a whip...

Roberts hands Vera the bottle, as if pressing her to take a drink, but Vera drunkenly pushes his hand aside and tries to get the telephone. Roberts takes the phone away from her and puts it back on the end-table by the bedroom door.

ROBERTS' VOICE

(narrating)

I reminded her that as Charles Haskell I didn't even know my mother's name, where I had gone to school, the name of my best friend, whether I had an Aunt Emma or not, my religion, and if I had ever owned a dog. I didn't even know what my middle initial stood for.... I also pointed out that the real Haskell had a scar on his forearm...

311 INT. HOLLYWOOD APARTMENT LIVING ROOM — MED. SHOT — NIGHT*

VERA

(thickly)

His people never saw that scar. He told me he ran away right after putting out the kid's eye.

312 TWO SHOT — ROBERTS AND VERA ON COUCH — NIGHT

Vera, on closer inspection, looks very drunk indeed. Her eyes are bleary. Roberts is sober, but nervous. He drops to the arm of the couch.

ROBERTS

Yes. But his father knew he was cut. There would have to be some kind of mark.

VERA

So what? The old man's dead — or will be, I hope, by tomorrow morning's paper. Anyway, you could cut yourself a little, couldn't you? Boy, for that kind of money I'd let you cut my leg off.

ROBERTS

You're drunk — and you're crazy-mad, Vera. Turn me in, if you want, but I won't get mixed up in this. Besides, how do we know? Haskell was such a phony. Maybe he wasn't the man's son at all. Maybe he dreamed up all this.

313 CLOSE SHOT — VERA — NIGHT

Vera stares drunkenly at Roberts. She is a sight. Her hair is in disarray and her eyes are bleary.

VERA

Well, dream it or not, you won't be dreaming when the law taps you on the shoulder. They've got a cute gas-chamber waiting for you, Roberts — and I hear extradition to Arizona is a cinch...

(looking around)

Where's that phone?

Her eyes light on something o.s. in the direction of the telephone, and she reaches for it.

---

*A green pencil line starts here and goes through to the bottom of scene 318.

314 MED. SHOT — NIGHT

Roberts seizes the arm Vera has stretched out for the telephone. Vera snarls at him drunkenly.

VERA

Let me alone, do you hear?

ROBERTS

Vera....

VERA

I want to phone — call police — I hate you ... yellow stinker you — let me alone.
But Roberts does not let her arm go. They struggle a minute.

ROBERTS
(struggling to hold her)

I'll let you go if you'll promise to leave the phone where it is. You're drunk. You don't know what you're doing....

VERA

You're — hurting — me.

ROBERTS

Will you promise?

VERA
(after a pause)

All right.
Roberts lets her free and puts the phone back on the end-table. Vera tries ineffectively to straighten herself up.

315 MED. TWO SHOT — NIGHT

Vera straightens out her dress as Roberts drops onto the couch alongside of her. Vera takes another drink from the whiskey bottle. Roberts looks utterly worn out.

VERA

You hurt me.

ROBERTS

I'm sorry. But....

VERA

And it's hot in here. Open a window.

ROBERTS

It's not hot.

VERA
(furiously)

Don't tell me. Now, do you do it — or do I do it — you're no gentleman — see?

ROBERTS
(with a sigh)

Oh, all right.
Roberts rises from the couch and the CAMERA PULLS BACK as he walks to a window at the far end of the room. The CAMERA, SHOOTING FROM IN FRONT OF ROBERTS, photographs Vera getting drunkenly to her feet behind his back and taking the phone. Vera stumbles a little, though, and Roberts turns.

ROBERTS

Vera!

Roberts races toward Vera but before he can reach her she staggers into the bedroom with the phone, slamming the door after her.

316   INT. HOLLYWOOD APARTMENT LIVING ROOM — FULL SHOT OF BEDROOM DOOR — NIGHT

Roberts races up to the door and tries to open it. It is locked. He pounds on it as he speaks:

ROBERTS
(pleading)

Vera, open the door. Please open the door.

317   INT. HOLLYWOOD APARTMENT BEDROOM — FULL SHOT OF THE DOOR — NIGHT

Vera stands by the door with the key in one hand and the phone at the end of a long cord in the other. Roberts' VOICE, THROUGH THE DOOR, COMES OVER.

ROBERTS' VOICE (O.S.)
(KNOCKING)

Vera, open the door. Don't use the phone! Listen to me....

VERA
(drunkenly)

I don't like you, Roberts. You're — no gentleman — you hurt my hand. I'm going to get rid of you....

Vera starts to walk toward the CAMERA but trips. The hand holding the phone reaches up high to catch hold of the wall and the telephone wire twists around her neck as she falls.

ROBERTS' VOICE (O.S.)

If you don't open the door, I'm going to kick it down! Vera....

318   INT. HOLLYWOOD APARTMENT LIVING ROOM — FULL SHOT OF BEDROOM DOOR — NIGHT

Roberts sees part of the long telephone cord sticking out under the door.

ROBERTS

Vera, don't call the cops. Listen to me. I'll do anything you say...

He stoops down, seizes the cord of the phone and gives it a yank. Sweat stands out on his forehead as he tugs at the wire.

ROBERTS

Vera, let me in...

As he pulls on the wire, the SOUND OF THE SAXOPHONE COMES OVER. It runs a scale, then starts amateurishly playing the first notes of "Sophisticated Lady." Roberts does not even hear this.

ROBERTS

I'll break the phone.

Finally, he gives up pulling. He cannot yank the cord loose. He moves back from the door a pace and bangs his shoulder against it. The door snaps open. Roberts stares into the room.

ROBERTS
(on the threshold — whispering)

Vera!...

With the CAMERA photographing only the broad expanse of his back, Roberts stops dead and looks down at this feet. There is a dead silence, broken only by the SOUND of a dial tone — and, presently, the SOUND OF THE SAX playing "Sophisticated Lady," very slowly and with many sour notes.

319 INT. HOLLYWOOD APARTMENT BEDROOM — MED. CLOSE ANGLE SHOT — ROBERTS — NIGHT

The CAMERA shoots Roberts from below as he stares down at something. His face registers shock. He is panting. The SOUND of the dial tone and the SAX COMES OVER, then the SAX STOPS in the middle of a bar.

320 INT. HOLLYWOOD APARTMENT BEDROOM — MED. SHOT — NIGHT

Roberts is standing on the threshold staring down at Vera's body, twisted *on the floor*. The telephone wire is tight around her throat. He pants as the dial tone COMES OVER.
The CAMERA DOLLIES IN for a CLOSE SHOT OF VERA. Her eyes stare vacantly out of their sockets. She is obviously dead from strangulation. When the CAMERA REACHES CLOSE SHOT RANGE, it PANS UP TO ROBERTS. He is horrified.

ROBERTS' VOICE
(narrating softly, after a long pause)

The world is full of skeptics. I know. I'm one myself. In the Haskell business, how many of you would have believed he fell out of the car? And now, after killing Vera without really meaning to do it, how many of you would believe it wasn't premeditated? In a jury room, every last man of you would go down shouting that she had me over a barrel and my only out was force....
WARNING: Hold CLOSE SHOT of the dead Vera to a minimum.

321 ANOTHER ANGLE — CLOSE SHOT — ROBERTS — NIGHT

Roberts seems frozen to the spot, staring down at Vera's body (o.s.). The dial tone continues to COME OVER.

ROBERTS' VOICE
(narrating)

The room was still — so quiet that for a while I wondered if I had suddenly gone deaf. It was pure fear, of course. And I was hysterical — but without making a sound.
(pause)
Vera was dead — and I was her murderer.*
(pause)
Murderer — what an awful word that is! But I had become one. And I had better not get caught.

322–323–324–325–326–327 — SERIES OF QUICK CLOSE-UPS — NIGHT
  (322) CLOSE SHOT of phone in Vera's still hand.
  (323) CLOSE SHOT of door knob on bedroom door.
  (324) CLOSE SHOT of polished edge of end-table.
  (325) CLOSE SHOT of glass in bathroom with toothbrush in it.
  (326) CLOSE SHOT of whiskey bottle.
  (327) CLOSE SHOT of a line in the hotel register reading: "Charles Haskell, Jr. and wife — New York, N.Y."

During this SERIES OF QUICK CLOSE-UPS, Roberts' view (narrating) continues to COME OVER, as well as a faint dial tone.

ROBERTS' VOICE
(narrating)

What evidence there was about the place had to be destroyed. And from the looks of things, there was plenty. What first?

---

*Ann flagged this page in the script with a simple blank post-it note.

328   INT. HOLLYWOOD APARTMENT BEDROOM — FULL SHOT — NIGHT

The DIAL TONE still COMES OVER. Roberts, standing by Vera's body, suddenly galvanizes himself into action. He stoops swiftly, wrests the phone receiver from Vera's dead hand and replaces it on the cradle. The dial tone ceases at once. Then Roberts looks right and left, pitiable, not knowing what to do. He is under a tremendous inner pressure.

ROBERTS' VOICE
(narrating)

But then it dawned on me. It was useless. I could destroy evidence for the next five years. There'd always be witnesses. The landlady, for one.

329   CLOSE SHOT — ROBERTS — NIGHT

Roberts is stopping. Only a small portion of Vera's body can be seen. A realization is being born in his frightened eyes.

ROBERTS' VOICE
(narrating)

She could identify me. And the car dealer. And the late Joe Bristol's butler. And that peroxide blonde at Mr. Richards' house. And Tony Dillon. And about a million other people. That waitress in the drive-in. The newsboy where Vera bought her paper. They could all identify me...

Roberts slowly rises to his feet, a panic growing in his eyes.

330   INT. HOLLYWOOD APARTMENT BEDROOM — FULL SHOT TOWARD BEDROOM DOOR — NIGHT

Roberts stands there in momentary indecision, panicky, but still undecided what to do. Vera's body is at his feet.

ROBERTS' VOICE
(narrating)

I was cooked. Done for. I had to get out of there.
Roberts backs away a step toward the threshold of the door leading into the living room.

ROBERTS' VOICE
(narrating)

While once I had remained beside a dead body, planning carefully how to avoid being accused of killing him, this time I couldn't.... This time I was guilty — knew it and felt it...

331   INT. HOLLYWOOD APARTMENT LIVING ROOM — FULL SHOT — NIGHT

The CAMERA is placed so that both the door to the bedroom and the front entrance door are in the scene. As the scene opens, the SOUND OF THE SAX COMES OVER, running scales. Roberts backs into the living room slowly, his eyes still focused on Vera's body (o.s.) on the bedroom floor.

ROBERTS' VOICE
(narrating)

Stupid or not, I couldn't help doing the thing which once before I had managed not to do...
Suddenly, Roberts turns, snatches up his jacket from a chair and runs out of the front entrance door, not even closing it in his hurry. The SOUND OF THE SAX sourly running scales continues to COME OVER — only LOUDER — ironically.

FADE OUT.

Appendix 2.
Detour Pressbook

The following brief articles are excerpts from the original PRC pressbook for *Detour*. In addition to the newspaper articles, the booklet also includes the usual synopsis, newspaper ads, poster reproductions, and suggestions for promotions surrounding the film. The pressbook is unusual in also including line art of the leads and a reproduction of a six-sheet poster (a very large poster that's about a quarter of the size of a billboard); it also includes a full page suggesting cross-promoting the film with Bing Crosby's and Dinah Shore's covers of "I Can't Believe You're in Love with Me." These last few items do imply that PRC had an unusual amount of faith in *Detour* and treated it as a higher quality production than all of their other films.

Wherever possible, these pieces have been authentically reproduced, including misspellings and significant embellishments (suggesting, for example, that "I Can't Believe You're in Love with Me" was written specifically for *Detour*).

"Novelist Does Own Screenplay"

Few novelists have the chance to carry their novels from the written page to the screen, but Martin Goldsmith, author of the novel "Detour" had this opportunity when PRC asked him to do the screenplay of his well-known book.

Goldsmith had never before tried his hand as scenarist. As a novelist, he knew the dramatic highlights of his book. These, he knew, would be heightened drama on the screen. To translate the story from words to action was now his job.

For one week he read every good script he could get hold of. Then he started the screenplay on "Detour." Without changing the theme of his novel or his characters, he turned in such an excellent script that PRC immediately signed him to a contract. Further, a Hollywood agent offered PRC $70,000 for the completed script!

"Detour" stars Tom Neal and Ann Savage. Edgar Ulmer directed. The picture comes to ... theatre, next.

"Catchlines for Ads..."

He went searching for love ... but Fate forced a DETOUR to revelry ... violence ... mystery....

She was dangerous to love ... more dangerous to hate!

From Broadway to Hollywood ... with drama every mile of the way!

Take this DETOUR for a new type of thrills!

Too mean to love ... too vicious to hate ... too dangerous to leave alone! 3,000 miles of thrills and terrifying human drama!

DETOUR! ... where the road turns and life begins!

"Do You Know That..."

During the filming of PRC's "Detour," Ann Savage's face had to be smeared with dust and dirt for most of her scenes? ... that she had to wear old, torn clothing and stockings with runs? ... that she got separated from the company while on location and was completely lost in the middle of the blazing hot Mojave Desert for three hours? ... that she was not permitted to have her hair washed and set for more than ten days because her role in the picture required that she present a grimy, untidy appearance? ... that she had to do scene after scene with a telephone cord pulled tightly around her throat? ... that she lost her voice temporarily due to the irritation resulting from this? ... that some people still say they'd rather be a movie star than anything else in the world? Because it's such fun, and hardly any work at all???

"Came the Deluge!"

That rainstorm you will see in PRC's "Detour," coming to the ... theatre, next..., was manufactured on Stage 4.

The water came from a five-hundred gallon tank on the PRC studio lot and the tank was emptied four times before Director Edgar Ulmer called "Cut!" on the last of the rain scenes.

Tom Neal, starring with Ann Savage, took the season's wettest drenching. He says you can never prove it by him that those scenes were filmed during one of California's dry spells!

Edgar Ulmer directed the new PRC dramatic hit.

"Hard Work—No Fun—Make a Good Movie!"

Tom Neal's athletic prowess and strong constitution stood him in good stead during the making of "Detour," the PRC smash hit starring him with Ann Savage, due at ... theatre, next...

Neal's hard work began when PRC moves the "Detour" company to the Mojave Desert for exterior scenes. For days, Neal trudged uncounted miles in the blazing sun, as the cross-country hitch-hiker of the story.

He couldn't shave for four days. Just when his face stopped itching, the company moved back to the PRC Studios, where Neal put in a day making scenes in a shower bath and shaving. Take after take of the shaving scene netted him skin that was painfully raw.

Then the rains came. It was a Hollywood-made rainstorm on Stage 4, but it was just as wet as if it had been authorized by the Chamber of Commerce.

During the storm, which was whipped to fury by powerful wind machines, Tom had to roll down a muddy embankment carrying and pulling the supposedly dead body of Ed MacDonald. MacDonald is six feet two and weighs about 200 pounds. This went on all day.

It was hard work—every foot of the film. But the results made it worth while for an actor interested in good performance in a good picture—and Tom is definitely interested in both.

Ann Savage co-stars with Neal as the girl who causes him all his troubles. Claudia Drake plays the girl he loves. Edgar Ulmer directed from the original novel and screenplay by Martin Goldsmith.

"WPB Order Stymies Big Detour Scene"

When the WPB [War Production Board] served notice that no more extended wires for telephones could be obtained, no one realized that the directive would hold up screen production. But it did!

One of the most dramatic scenes in PRC's "Detour," now at the ... theatre, calls for Ann Savage to grab a phone, and run into the adjoining room where, in a fight with Tom Neal, she is accidentally strangled.

When the time to shoot the scene arrived, the property department notified Director Edgar Ulmer that such a telephone extension couldn't be obtained. Necessity being the mother of invention, an electrician on the set rigged up a wire which looked like the real thing!

"Camera Fan"

Edgar Ulmer is glad he's an amateur camera fan! His hobby served him in good stead when the still photographer's car broke down en route to location for "Detour," the new PRC hit now at the ... theatre.

Ulmer who directed the new thrill drama, used his own camera and "covered" every scene with professional accuracy!

Ann Savage and Tom Neal co-star in "Detour."

"Ann's a Nice Girl—Off the Screen!

Beautiful, auburn-haired Ann Savage, co-starred with Tom Neal in PRC's stirring drama, "Detour," due at the ... theatre next ..., loves to play meanies on the screen.

Such roles as her current one in "Detour" and her recent one in "Apology for Murder" are Ann's meat, because they are a challenge to her talent as a dramatic actress.

But let no one confuse the reel Ann of "Detour" with the real Ann Savage! In the picture, Miss Savage plays a girl who hates mankind and who finally pays her debt to society with her life. No two people could be more unlike than Miss Savage and the girl she brings to life on the screen.

Of French-Irish descent, Miss Savage was born in Columbus, South Carolina. When the family moved to Los Angeles, Ann took a job as secretary at the Max Reinhardt Workshop. She turned her post in for a chance at acting. A talent scout spotted her in a performance of "Golden Boy" with the result that she got a contract from Columbia Pictures. Her first role was with Warren William in "One Dangerous Night."

Ann is an interesting combination of charming femininity and ardent sports woman. She rides, plays tennis and golf and once taught bowling in Hollywood.

Her weaknesses are fine perfume and jewelry, and the latter is natural since her family has, for generations, been in the jewelry business. She's no mean musician and plays the piano well. And wonder of wonders—she can also cook.

As for men, Ann's very definite about that! She prefers 'em tall, dark and handsome!

"Tom Neal an Earn-Your-Own-Way Fan"

Tom Neal, star of PRC's new drama, "Detour" coming ... to the ... theatre, was born with a golden spoon in his mouth—professionally and personally. His great-uncle was John Drew. His father is a prominent Illinois banker.

Despite all this, however, Tom is an ardent earn-your-own-way fan. He's always found the business of earning his own living exciting.

Long before he ever graduated from Northwestern University a B.A. degree, Tom was a "business man." In fact, he was just about seven when he earned $1.35 selling soda pop. Even now, when he is well established as a screen actor, he has a business interest — real estate.

Tom began acting with the Straw Hat Circuit in New England and eventually reached Broadway in a role with Ina Claire in "If This Be Treason." A number of stage successes preceded his arrival in Hollywood.

Neal stands five feet eleven inches tall and weighs 180 pounds. He has brown hair and black eyes. He is married to Vicky Lane, an actress.

To date, his screen appearances includes such hits as "Behind the Rising Sun," "Klondyke Kate," "Unwritten Code," "Crime, Inc.," and "Club Havana."

Ann Savage co-stars with him in the new PRC hit, "Detour."

Shorts

Tom Neal, starring with Ann Savage in PRC's "Detour," at the ... theatre, is the great-nephew of the late John Drew, famous American stage star and uncle of the Barrymores.

But Tom never depended on his family connections to forge his acting career. He started out in stock, won his spurs on Broadway and went to Hollywood. Roz Russell, whose family has known Tom's family years, interested him in a screen career.

When Clarence Gaskell and Jimmy McHugh wrote "I Can't Believe You're in Love With Me" as the theme song for PRC's "Detour," now at the ... theatre, they felt they'd written a good number! And they have! Not only does Claudia Drake put the number over with a bang in the picture, but also Bing Crosby and Dinah Shore have just finished making recordings of the number. Miss Drake heads the featured cast in "Detour," with Tom Neal and Ann Savage in the starring roles.

Edgar Ulmer, who directed PRC's "Detour," currently at the ... theatre, is a very versatile gent! Aside from his success as stage designer and director, he has, since coming to Hollywood, become a screen director of note. In addition, he's a playwright. And when it comes to the camera — he's not only an ardent candid camera fan, but an artist with the lens as well.

"Detour" stars Tom Neal and Ann Savage in the Martin Goldsmith screenplay based on his famous novel.

"I've played screen meanies in my career," says Ann Savage, currently co-starring with Tom Neal in PRC's "Detour," at the ... theatre, "but this new role is the meanest of the lot!"

In "Detour," Miss Savage plays a girl hitch-hiker who forces Neal to the verge of crime. Edgar Ulmer directed the film from the Martin Goldsmith novel and screenplay.

50 and 25 Word Blurbs for Your Local Radio Stations

ANNOUNCER: Follow Tom Neal as he hitch-hikes across the country, Fate at his heels ... in PRC's startling screen hit DETOUR at the (Theatre name and playdate).

BUSINESS: Dramatic Music

ANNOUNCER: Do you believe in circumstantial evidence? If you do, you'll accuse Tom Neal of murder! If you don't, you'll accuse Ann Savage of crime! See DETOUR — the new PRC dramatic thriller of a man pursued by a relentless fate, starring Tom Neal, Ann Savage, at (Theatre and play date).

ANNOUNCER: A cross country hitch-hike ... a man, a dangerous woman — and Fate! They're all part of PRC's thrilling new drama, DETOUR at (Theatre and playdate).

BUSINESS: Fanfare of Trumpets

ANNOUNCER: Love was his mission — but Fate forces him into a Detour from happiness onto the road of a man hunted for two crimes he did not commit! Never before has the screen offered more thrilling drama than in PRC's DETOUR. See DETOUR at (Theatre name and playdate).

ANNOUNCER: Fate followed him from New York to Hollywood, turning a love journey into tragedy. Don't miss PRC's sensational DETOUR at (Theatre name and playdate).

Bibliography

Allyn, J. "*Double Indemnity*: A Policy That Paid Off," *Literature/Film Quarterly* (6), 1978.

Bogdanovich, Peter. *Allan Dwan: The Last Pioneer*. New York: Praeger, 1971.

_____. *Who the Devil Made It?* New York: Alfred A. Knopf, 1997.

Borde, Raymond, and Étienne Chaumeton. *Panorama du Film Noir Américain*. Les Éditions de Minuit, 1955.

Briggs, Colin. *The Way to the Stars*. Queensland: All Star Publishing, 1999.

Caulfield, Deborah. "So What Ever Happened to Bad Girl Ann Savage?" *Los Angeles Times*, February 17, 1985.

Chanin, A. L. *Art Guide/New York*. New York: Horizon Press, 1965.

Cohen, Mickey. *Mickey Cohen: In My Own Words as Told to John Peer Nugent*. New York: Prentice Hall, 1975.

Corliss, Richard. "Detour — All Time 100 Movies," *Time Magazine*, http://www.time.com/time/2005/100movies/0,23220,detour,00.html.

_____. "10 All-Time Best Movie Villains," *Time Magazine*, Vol. 169, No. 19 (May 7, 2007).

_____. "Two Weird Canadian Geniuses at Toronto," *Time Magazine*, September 10, 2007.

Damico, James. "*Film Noir*: A Modest Proposal," *Film Reader*, No. 3, 1978.

Dixon, Wheeler. *Producers Releasing Corporation: A Comprehensive Filmography and History*. Jefferson, NC: McFarland, 1986.

Ebert, Roger. "The Best Films of 2008 ... and There Were a Lot of Them," *Chicago Sun–Times*, December 5, 2008.

_____. "Great Movies: Detour," http://rogerebert.suntimes.com/apps/pbcs.dll/article?AID=/19980607/REVIEWS08/401010312/1023.

_____. "My Winnipeg," *Chicago Sun–Times*, June 26, 2008.

Erickson, Steve. "Guy Maddin on My Winnipeg: Shooting a Documentary-Fantasy on 16mm, Super-8, MiniDV, HD — and a Cell Phone," *Film and Video*, June 12, 2008.

Flinn, Caryl. *Strains of Utopia: Gender, Nostalgia, and Hollywood Film Music*. Princeton: Princeton University Press, 1992.

Gillmor, Alison. "Guy Maddin Takes a Dreamlike Tour of Winnipeg," *CBC News*, September 7, 2007.

Goldsmith, Martin. *Detour*. New York: Macauley, 1939.

_____. *Detour*. Final Shooting Draft Screenplay, PRC, 1945.

_____. *Detour* (script), *Scenario: The Magazine of Screenwriting Art*, Vol.3, No. 2.

Halfyard, Kurt. "Guy Maddin Talks My Winnipeg, Self-Mythologizing, Psychological Honesty, and Even the Host," www.twitchfilm.net, October 2, 2007.

Heimann, Jim. *Sins of the City: The Real Los Angeles Noir*. San Francisco: Chronicle Books, 1999.

Henry, O. *Heart of the West*. New York: Doubleday, 1904.

Hoaglin, Jess. "Blond B-Film Beauty Made Transition to Television," *Los Angeles Independent*, February 17, 1988.

Hoberman, J. "IndieWIRE Critics' Poll '08," http://www.indiewire.com/movies/2008/12/indiewire_criti_45.html.

Isenberg, Noah. *Detour (BFI Film Classics)*. London: Palgrave Macmillan, 2008.

Kerr, Paul. "Out of What Past? Notes on the B *Film Noir*," *Screen Education*, Nos. 32/33, Autumn/Winter, 1979–80.

Keyes, Evelyn. *Scarlett O'Hara's Younger Sister*. New York: Lyle Stuart, 1977.

Krohn, Bill. "King of the B's: A Retrospective of the Films of Edgar G. Ulmer," UCLA, 1983.

Lucia, Ellis. *Klondike Kate: The Life and Legend of Kitty Rockwell, the Queen of the Yukon*. New York: Ballantine Books, 1972.

Maddin, Guy. *From the Atelier Tovar: Selected Writings of Guy Maddin*. Toronto: Coach House Books, 2003.

_____. *My Winnipeg*. Toronto: Coach House Books, 2009.

Matson, Kate Rockwell (as told to May Mann). "I

Was Queen of the Klondike," *Alaska Sportsmen*, August 1944.

McCarthy, Todd, and Charles Flynn. *Kings of the Bs: Working Within the Hollywood System*. New York: E. P. Dutton, 1975.

Meisel, Myron. "Edgar G. Ulmer: The Primacy of the Visual," 1972, in *Kings of the Bs: Working Within the Hollywood System*. New York: E. P. Dutton, 1975.

Miller, Don. *Hollywood Corral*. New York: Popular Library, 1976.

Muller, Eddie. *Dark City: The Lost World of Film Noir*. New York: St. Martin's Press, 1998.

_____. *Dark City Dames: The Wicked Women of Film Noir*. New York: HarperCollins, 2001.

Naremore, James. *More Than Night: Film Noir in Its Contexts*. Berkeley: University of California Press, 1998.

Oursler, Fulton, and Lowell Brentano. *The Spider*. New York: Samuel French, 1926.

Peary, Danny. *Cult Movies: The Classics, the Sleepers, the Weird, and the Wonderful*. New York: Dell Publishing, 1981.

Persons, Dan. "Guy Maddin Makes My Winnipeg Everyone's Winnipeg," www.cinefantastiqueonline.com, June 11, 2008.

Polan, Dana. "Senses of Cinema: Detour," http://archive.sensesofcinema.com/contents/cteq/02/21/detour.html.

Price, Michael H., and John Wooley. *Forgotten Horrors 4: Dreams That Money Can Buy*. Baltimore: Midnight Marquee Press, 2007.

Pride, Ray. "indieWIRE Critics' Poll '08," www.indiewire.com, December 23, 2008.

Reinhardt, Gottfried. *Genius: A Memoir of Max Reinhardt*. New York: Alfred A. Knopf, 1979.

Sarris, Andrew. *The American Cinema: Directors and Directions 1929–1968*. New York: E. P. Dutton, 1968.

Silver, Alain, and James Ursini. *Film Noir Reader*. New York: Limelight Editions, 1996.

Slide, Anthony (editor). *De Toth on De Toth: Putting the Drama in Front of the Camera*. London: Faber and Faber, 1996.

Spicer, Andrew. *Film Noir*. England: Pearson Education Limited, 1992.

Taylor, John Russell. *Cinema Eye, Cinema Ear: Some Key Film-Makers of the Sixties*. New York: Hill and Wang, 1964.

_____. *Strangers in Paradise: The Hollywood Emigres, 1933–1950*. New York: Holt, Rinehart and Winston, 1983.

Thomas, Kevin. "UCLA Focuses on 'The King of the B's,'" *Los Angeles Times*, October 6, 1983.

Turan, Kenneth. "My Winnipeg," *Los Angeles Times*, June 20, 2008.

Ulmer, Shirley, and C. R. Sevilla. *The Role of Script Supervision in Film and Television*. New York: Hastings House, 1986.

Wager, Jans B. *Dangerous Dames: Women and Representation in the Weimar Street Film and Film Noir*. Athens: Ohio University Press, 1999.

Wilkerson, W.R., III. *The Man Who Invented Las Vegas*. Ciro's Books Publishing, 2000.

Index

Numbers in ***bold italics*** indicate pages with photographs.

Abbott, John 100
The Actor's Studio 35, 37
Adams, Henry 123, 126
Adler, Stella 37
Adrian 78
The Adventures of Ichabod and Mr. Toad 83
Adventures of Red Ryder 154
Affiliated Productions 157
After Midnight with Boston Blackie 47, 81, 83–86, ***85***, 112, 123, 125–126, 181
Aginsky, Burt 73
Aginsky, Ethel 73
Aherne, Brian 106, 108
Airport 52, 117
Alias Boston Blackie 154
Alibi 86
All That Heaven Allows 52
Allen, Fred 169
Allen, Lester 101
Allen, Woody 176
The Amazing Spider-Man 123
The American Cinema 146
American Cinematheque *see* Grauman's Egyptian Theatre
Anderson, Eddie "Rochester" 55, 182
The Andy Griffith Show 154
Andy Hardy series 30
Any Number Can Play 68, 182–183
Apology for Murder 61–63, 117, 122, 128–135, ***130, 132, 133***, 145, 156, 168
Appointment in Berlin 182
Archangel 179
Arliss, George 27
Arnow, Max 40–42, 47, 52
art (trading and investment) 46, 68, 70–71
Art Guide/New York 70
Arthur, Jean 47, 50, 64, 128, 180
Ashe, Warren 80
Astor, Mary 182
Atoll, Gen 75
Atoll, Harry 75
Attala County *see* Bear Creek, Mississippi
Atwill, Lionel 180
Auntie Mame 108
Austin Chronicle 180
The A.V. Club 180
Aylesworth, Arthur 124

Bacon, Irving 96
Bailey, Buck 163

Bakaleinikoff, Mischa 118, 165
Bankhead, Tallulah 128
Banks, Lionel 80, 83, 86, 89, 91, 96, 98, 101, 106, 109, 112, 114
Baptist religion 17
Barrie, Mona 80
Barry, Donald "Red" 66, 151, 153–154, ***153***
Barry, Joan 39, 40
Barry, Mona 135
Barrymore, John 27
Barsha, Leon 86, 112
Bartok, Dennis 179
Barton, Charles 182
Barty, Billy 166, ***166***
Baumgarten, Marjorie 180
Baxter, Warner 164
Bear Creek, Mississippi 16
Beaumont, Hugh 62–63, 129, 133–135, ***133***, 167–168
Beddoe, Don 129
Beebe, Ford 163, 165
Behind the Rising Sun 106
Bennett, Bruce 106, 181–182
Benton, Jack 163
Berger, Peter E. 171
Berk, Roy 123, 126
Berke, William 66, 86–89, 112, 114, 157–158, 160, 165, 167–168
Berkeley, Busby 145
Berlin International Film Festival 180
The Best Years of Our Lives 65
Beverly Hills Bowl 32, 38, 45
Beware of Blondie 98
Biberman, Abner 109, ***111***
Birell, Tala 80, ***81***
Bischoff, Samuel 98
Black Beauty (Mercedes Benz 280 SL) 76
The Black Cat 144
Blackley, Douglas 161–162
Blackstone the Magician 50
Blair, Janet 182
Blonde Ice 135
Blondie (first film) 98
Blondie (series) 47, 97–98
Blondie: Footlight Glamour 47, 78, 83, 91, 96–98, ***97***
Blore, Eric 80, 82–83, 92, 95
Bluebeard 144
Boetticher, Budd 47
Bogart, Humphrey 182
Bogdanovich, Peter 144, 171
Bois, Curt 161

Bolton, Michael 171
Bomba the Jungle Boy series 165
Bonnie and Clyde 89
Boorstin, Paul 171
Boorstin, Sharon 171
Border Badmen 134
Borg, Veda Ann 123
"Boss Lady" *see* Saved by the Bell
Boston Blackie series 83–84, 86, 125
Boston Blackie's Chinese Venture 86
Boston Independent Film Festival 180
Bowery Boys series 128
bowling 32, ***34***
Boyd, William 88, 145
Boyle, Jack 83–84, 114
Boys Town 30
Brady, Fred 121
Branch, Houston 101
Brand Upon the Brain! 77, 176–177, 179
Brayton, Margaret 148
Brentano, Lowell 148–149
Bridges, Lloyd 83, 92, 182
Briskin, Irving 40–41, 101
Briskin, Sam 41
Britton, Andrew 141
Broadway movie theatres (Los Angeles) 26–27
Brooke, Hillary 106
Brooks, George 121
Brooks, Leslie ***34***, 89, 182
Brophy, Edward 157, ***161***, 167
Brothers (nightclub) 57–58
Brown, Charles D. 129, 151
Brown, James, Jr. 157
Brown Derby 27
Bruce, David 165, 167
Bryar, Paul 155
Buchanan, Edgar 182
Buck Rogers series 68, 165
Buffalo Gal Pictures 172
Burns, Bob 105
Burns, Lillian 33, 44
Burns, Michael 178
Buster, Budd 129
Buttolph, David 148

"The Caballero's Way" 164
Cade, Brendan 174, ***177***
Cade, Wesley 174
Cagney, James 36–37, 66, 153–154
Cain, James M. 131, 142
Calker, Darrell 157, 160
Cameron, Rod 184

233

Index

Canter's Deli 29, 76–77
Cantor, Eddie 48
Capra, Frank 151
Captive Hearts see *Fire with Fire*
Careful 179
Carleton, Claire 163
Carr, George Mill 16
Carr, Marcus Alonzo 16–17
Carr, Nancy 16
Carrillo, Leo 163–164
Carroll, Mary 101
Carter, Janis 72–74
Carthay Circle Theater 27
Caruso, Anthony 151
Casablanca 92
A Case for Murder 172
The Case of the Howling Dog 83
Castle, Nick 89
Castle, William 41, 48, 101–102, 104–106
Cavanaugh, Hobart 98, 106
C.C. Browns 27
Central Avenue (Los Angeles) 24, 52, 57–58
CFI Laboratories 59
Chambers, Wheaton 129
Chambers, Whitman 161
Chandler, Raymond 131
Chanel No. 5 78
Chanin, A.L. 70
Chaplin, Charles 39–40
Chapman, Marguerite **34**, 80, 181–182
Charell, Erik 106
Charles, Ray 58
Chatkin, David 80
Cheshire, Harry 183
Christine, Virginia 169
Christmas 71, 78
Ciro's 57, 64, 66
The Cisco Kid series 164–165
City Detective 172, 184
Clark, Al 106
Claxton, William 86
"Clean Sweep" see *Front Page Detective*
Cleveland, George 101
Clifford, Sidney 165
Club Havana 59, 60, 144–145
Clurman, Harold 37
Cobb, Edmund 86, **157**
Coburn, Charles 47, 180, **181**
Coburn, Robert 41–42
Coconut Grove 57
Cohen, Jeffrey Jay 171
Cohen, Mickey 67
Cohn, Harry 41, 47, 50–51, 68, 78, 82, 96, 108
Cohn, Martyn 163
Colbert, Claudette 184
Colbert, Norman 148
Colman, Ronald 64
Columbia, South Carolina 17, 163
Columbia Pictures 29, 40–48, 50–54, 56–57, 59–61, 64, 66, 68, 70, 72, 78, 80–84, 86, 89, 91, 94, 96–98, 100–101, 105–106, 108–109, 112, 114, 116–118, 120–121, 123, 127, 139, 144, 154, 160, 165, 167, 180–182
Conte, Richard 148–149

Continental, a Film Without Guns 180
cooking 18, 20, 65, 73
Cooper, Ben 169
Cooper, Inez 155–156
Cooper, Jackie 33
Le Cordon Bleu 73
Corey, Wendell 182
Corliss, Richard 147, 180
Corrigan, Lloyd 83, 86
Corrigan, Ray 66, 157, 160
Court-Martial 160
Cowan, Will 149
Cowards Bend the Knee 176, 179–180
Cramp, Harold 148
Craven, Frank 98
Crawford, Joan 48, 158
Crehan, Joseph 86
Cronenberg, David 178
Crosby, Bing 57, 106, 128
"Cruise Ship" see *City Detective*
Cukor, George 64
Cult Movies 146
Cummings, Irving 106, 108
Cummings, Irving, Jr. 148
Currier, Mary 118
Curtis, Alan 157, 160
Curtis, Billy 165–166
Curtiz, Michael 92

Daffy Duck 117
Dallas, Texas 16–20
Damico, James 131
dancing 18, 38, 48, 55, 64, 76, 90, 184
Dancing in Manhattan 55, 88, 121–123, **122**, 182
Danger Zone 168
Dangerous Blondes **44**, 48, 98–101, **99, 100**, 154, 181
Dark City Dames 76
The Dark Horse 64, 149–151, **150**
Darling, W. Scott 148
D'Armand, Bert 33, 35, **35**, 37, 38–40, 46, 52, **54**, 55, 57–58, 64–67, **67**, 68–71, **71**, 72–74, 78, 161, **181**, 182–183
Darmour, Inc. 117
Darwell, Jane 64, 150, **150**
Davies, Marion 78
Davis, Bette 139, 146, 158
Davis, Donald 80
Davis, Jim 169
Davis, Joan 48, 89–91, **90, 91**
Dawson, Frank 106
Day, Hal 74–76
The Dead Father 178
Dean, Margia 167
Death Valley Days 184
de Havilland, Olivia 36
Dehner, John 151
Delgado, Adelaide see Mara, Adele
Del Val, Jean 148
Demarest, William 98, 100
DeNormand, George 163
DeSoto, Henri 150
Destroyer 98, 182
De Toth, André 92, 94–96
Detour 51, 59–66, **60**, **63**, **65**, 68, 70, 75, 77, 110, 117, 120, 128, 134–148,

137, 138, 140, 141, 143, 145, 147, 160, 178, 180
Detour (remake) 75, 148
The Devil's Den see *Satan's Cradle*
DeWolf, Karen 96, 98
Diage, Louis 101
"The Diamond Babe" see *Death Valley Days*
The Dick Van Dyke Show 154
Dieterle, William 36–37
Dietrich, Noah 73
Dinehart, Alan 106
Documentary Channel 172, 178–179
Donlevy, Brian 160, 169–171
Donnell, Jeff **34**, 55, 70, 72, 121–123, 182
Double Indemnity 63, 117, 131–135, 142
A Double Life 64
Dowd, Ross 114
Dracula (1931) 101
Dracula: Pages from a Virgin's Diary 77, 179
The Dragon Murder Case 83
Drake, Claudia 66, 135, 145, 157, **159**, 160
Drake, Ella 145
Dreifuss, Arthur 114
driving 28–31
drugs 58
Duane, Michael 98
Dubin, Joseph 151
Duel in the Sun 160
Dunn, Ralph 155
Dunsmore, Fred 174
Duvivier, Julien 180
Dwan, Allan 169–171

Eagle-Lion Studios see PRC
Earl Carrol's *Vanities* 57
earthquake (1933) 24–25
East Side Kids series 128
Ebert, Roger 142, 144, 180
Eddy, Nelson 171
Edwards, Blake 121
Egoyan, Atom 178
Eisinger, Jo 148
Ellington, Duke 146
Enright, Ray 182
Entertainment Tonight 75
Erdody, Leo 129, 135, 140
Erickson, Steve 178, 180
Esquire magazine 120
Eve of Destruction 172
The Evening Bulletin, Providence 146
Ever Since Venus 52, 60, 83, 98, 114–117, **115, 116**
Everyday Pictures 172

Fairfax High School 29–31, 71
Falkenburg, Jinx 48, 89–91, **90, 91**, 105, 182
Family Films, Inc. 183
Fantl, Richard 83, 96, 121
Farrell, Glenda 49, 52, 70, **71**, 74, 101, 114, 116–117
Feather Your Nest 73
Fehr, Darcy 174, **178**, 180
Feld, Fritz 52, 114, **115**, 116–117
Ferguson, Frank 155–157

Fessier, Michael 169
Fielding, Edward 106
Fier, Jack 109
"*Film Noir*: A Modest Proposal" 131
Fire with Fire 75, 171–172, **173**
Fireside Theatre 183–184
Fisher, Steve 169
fishing 20, **21**, 73, 161
Five Weeks in a Balloon 117
Flagg, Steve 183
Flamingo Hotel 66–68
Flash Gordon series 165
Fleming-Roberts, G.T. 155
Flesh and Leather see *Pier 23*
Flinn, Caryl 140, 146
Florentine Gardens 57
Flournoy, Richard 98
Flower Drum Song 117
flying (as a pilot) 73–75, **74**
The Flying Serpent 134
Flynn, Errol 110
Flynt, Larry 16
Foch, Nina 182
Ford, Glenn 182
Ford, Philip 151
Ford Television Theatre 184
Fort Jackson, South Carolina 17
Foster, Susanna 148
Foulger, Byron 163
Fowley, Douglas 161, **162**, 163
Frankenstein (1931) 101
Freed, Arthur 33, 68, 182
Freeman, Howard 118, 121
Frieze Magazine 179
Fromkess, Leon 59–62, 65, 135, 143–145
Front Page Detective 101, 181, 183
Frye, Dwight 100–101
Fuller, Samuel 66
Funny Girl 101

Gable, Clark 68, 104, 139, 182–183
Galindo, Nacho 169
gambling 23, 46, 50, 52, 57, 69, 71–72
Gang Busters 183
Garfield, John 144
Gargan, Edward 150
Gargan, William 126–127, **128**
Garland, Judy 33
Gateson, Marjorie 114
Gausman, Russell A. 149
General Artists Corp. 146
General Hospital 123
Geray, Steven 165
Getty, J. Paul 39
Gibbins, Duncan 171–172
Gilbert, Billy 52, 114, 116–117
Glasser, Albert 163
Gleason, Pat 135
The Globe and Mail 180
Golden Boy 39–41
Goldfish, Samuel 30
Goldman, Babs 75
Goldman, Jimmie 75
Goldsmith, Martin 75, 135, 139–143
Goldwyn Company 30
Good Luck, Mr. Yates 182
Gorcey, Leo 126–128
The Gracie Allen Murder Case 83
Grant, Jack D. 151, 155

Grant, Johnny 78
Grauman's Chinese Theater 27, 57
Grauman's Egyptian Theater 27, 48, 57, 76–77, 106; American Cinematheque 96, 179
Gravey, Fernand 180
The Great Waltz 30, 180
Green, Alfred E. 182
Green, Howard J. 83
Green Hornet series 165
Greenhalgh, Jack 129, 134, 155, 161, 163, 167
Greenleaf, Raymond 167
Groen, Rick 180
Group Theater (Manhattan) 37
Gruskin, Jerry 151
Guffey, Burnett 118
The Gunfighter 95
Gurdebeke, John 174

Haade, William 155, **156**
Hadley, Reed 169
Hale, Jonathan 96
Haley, Jack 123–125, **123**, **125**
Halfyard, Kurt 179
Hall, Thurston 80, 83, 96, 98, 114
Halliday, Brett 135
Halloween 42, **43**
Halton, Charles 126
Hansard, Helen 163
Happy Birthday 163
Harding, Ann 182
Harlow, Jean 27
Harmon, Julian 167
Harris, David 171
Harris, Enid 171
Harvey, John 148
Havana, Cuba 71
Havier, J. Alex 109
Havlick, Gene 118
The Hawaii Times, Honolulu 146
Hayden, Russell 47–48, 50–51, 86–89, **87, 88**, 112, 114, 160
Hayes, Helen 163
Hayes, Margaret 80
Haymes, Bob 89
Hayward, Susan 139
Hayworth, Rita 50
Hellman, Sam 149
Henley, Jack 98
Henry, O. 163–164
Herbert, Hugh 52, 114, 116–117, **116**, 180
Hicks, Russell 129, **130**
Higher and Higher 106
Hildegarde 64
Hitchcock, Alfred 68
Hitler's Madman 61
Hoberman, J. 180
Holiday, Billie 58
Hollywood Corral 158
Hollywood Forever Cemetery 78
Hollywood Reporter 66–67, 146, 149, 151, 155
Hollywood's Walk of Fame 78
Holscher, Walter 98
Holt, Jack 27, 66, 157, **157**, 160
Homes, Geoffrey 123, 125
Hopalong Cassidy series 88, 145
Hope, Bob 106
Hotaling, Frank 151

House of Frankenstein 111
House of Wax 95
House on Haunted Hill 102
Howard, Esther 135
Hubbard, John 98, 182
Hughes, Howard 73
Hughes, John 172
Hunter, Ross 52, 114, **115**, 117
Huntington, Cleland "Lee" 55, **56**, 63
Huntington, Henry 23
Hurrell, George 41–42
Hurst, Paul 124, 126
Hutchinson, Josephine 43–45
Hutton, Betty 48
Hutton, Ina Ray 52, 114, 116–117
Hygo Television Films 181

I Married Joan 91
I Spy 154
IFC Films 172
Imitation of Life 52, 117
"In Sickness and in Stealth" see *City Detective*
IndieWire Critics' Poll of 2008 180
Infuhu, Teddy 118
Ingram, Jack 86
Inter American Films 163
Invasion of the Body Snatchers 125
Irene, Lilyan 106
Irvine, Richard 148
Isenberg, Noah 148
Ivano, Paul 149
Ivie Anderson's Chicken Shack 58

Jackman, Fred, Jr. 123, 126
Jack's Chicken in a Basket 58
James, Frank 169–171
James, Jesse 169–171
Jason, Leigh 98, 182
Jason, Will 149, 151
Jay, Griffin 109
Jenkins, Allen 64, 150–151
Jenks, Si 150
Jewell, Edward C. 96, 129, 135
jewelry business 17–20, 24, 26, 32, 46, 66, 72
Johnny Guitar 158
Johnson, Rondi 171
Johnson, Tor **104**
Jones, Jennifer 160
Joslyn, Allyn 98, 100–101
Journey to the Center of the Earth 122–123
Juarez 108
Judaism 71
"Judas" see *Fireside Theatre*
Jungle Flight 88, 128, 134, 156, 161–164, **162, 163**
Jungle Jim series 66, 165, 167
Jungle Jim in Pygmy Island see *Pygmy Island*

Kansas Raiders 160, 171
Katzman, Sam 165, 167
The Katzman Corporation 165
Keane, Robert Emmett 123
Keene, Tom 41, 106
Keller, Alfred S. 151
Kendall, Cy 86, 121–123
Kenyon, Charles 118

Kerr, Paul 134
Kessel, Barney 58
Keyes, Evelyn **44**, 98, 100–101, 105, 125, 182
Kier, Udo 179
Kiernan, William 89, 106
"King of the B's: A Retrospective of the Films of Edgar G. Ulmer" 148
Kish, Joseph 91, 98, 118
Kline, Benjamin 60, 86, 114, 135
Klondike Kate 48–50, **49**, 52, 76, 82, 101–106, **103, 104, 106**, 110, 117, 120, 154
Knowles, Patric 184
Korda, Zoltan 182
Korjus, Miliza 180
Korngold, Erich Wolfgang 36
Kosleck, Martin 148
Krasne, Philip N. 163
Kreuger, Kurt 148
Krohn, Bill 148

Labrie, Réjean 174
Lacey, Liam 180
Lady Chaser 134, 145, 155–157, **156**
Laemmle, Carl 61
Lafleur, Stephane 180
Laing, Phyllis 174
Lake, Arthur 78, 96–98
Lamarr, Hedy 65
La Marr Sisters *see* Drake, Claudia
Landers, Lew 61, 83, 86, 109, 112, 181
Landres, Paul 149
Lane, Richard 83, 86
Lang, David 126, 161
Lang, Fritz 144
Lanning, Reggie 169
Lansky, Meyer 71–72
Largay, Raymond 150
Larson, Bobby 118
LaRue (restaurant) 66
LaRue, Frank 86, **87, 88**
Las Vegas 55, 61, 64, 66–69, 71, 73, 75, 78
Lass *see* pets
Lassie 65
The Last Crooked Mile 66, 147, 151–155, **152, 153, 154**, 168
The Last Horseman 66, 89, 112–114, 160, 168
Laszlo, Alexander 123, 126
Lavish, Lea 148
Lawrence, Viola 80
Lazarus, Erna 121
Leave It to Beaver 62, 133, 135, 168
Lee, Connie 96, 98, 114
Lee, Ruth 150
Leipold, John 106
Leo Carrillo State Park 165
Leonard, Sheldon 92, 96, 101, **103**, 151, 153–154
LeRoy, Mervyn 182
Leslie, Joan 169–171
Lester, Ann 41, 55, 64
Levin, Henry 121–122
Lewis, Therese 106
Lindsey, Marilyn 169
Lippert, Robert 168
Lippert Pictures 167
Little, Thomas 148

Littlefield, Lucien 124
Lloyd, Harold 32
Lobay, Jacelyn 174
Loeb and Loeb 72, 74–75
Loew, Marcus 30
Loews theaters (Loews Inc.) 30, 32
Lombard, Carole 27, 181
The Lone Prairie 89
The Lone Wolf (novel) 83
Lone Wolf (series) 45, 47, 80, 82–83, 86, 92
The Lone Wolf in London 83
The Lone Wolf Spy Hunt 83
The Lone Wolf Strikes 83
Long Beach, California 24–25
Lopez, Mario 184
Lord, Phillips H. 183
Los Angeles High School 28–29, 31
Los Angeles Times 75, 142, 146, 180
The Loser 148
Louise, Anita **44**, 98, 182
Lowe, Edmund 50, 68, 91, 98, **99**, 100–101, **100**, 181, 183
Lowery, Robert 155–156, 161, **163**
Loy, Myrna 100
Lubitsch, Ernst 36
Luby, S. Roy 183
Lucas, Dione 73
Lund, John 169–170
Lupino, Ida 144
Lynch, David 178
Lynn, George 109
Lyon, Hugh 17–20, 26, 28, 55
Lyon, Louise Carr Miller 16–20, **17**, 23–29, 31, 45, 52, 61, 65, 72, 74–76, 78
Lytess, Natasha 35, 38, 41

MacArthur, Harold 149
MacBride, Donald 150–151
MacDonald, Edmund 135
MacDonald, Wallace 89, 91, 121
MacLane, Barton 123, 161, 163
MacMurray, Fred 131, 133
MacWilliams, Glen 148
The Mad Monster 134
Maddin, Guy 77, **77**, 96, 174–180
Madsen, Virginia 171–172
"Magic Formula" *see* Ford Television Theatre
Mainwaring, Daniel *see* Homes, Geoffrey
Malyon, Elly 124
Mantz, Paul 163
Mara, Adele **34**, 151, 153–154
Margolis, Herbert 167–168
Marion, Charles R. 149
Marlowe, Faye 148
Martin, Fred B. 149
Martin, Freddy 182
Martino, Marie 155–156
Mason, James 180
Matson, Kathleen "Kitty" Rockwell ("Klondike Kate") 48, 105–106, **106**
Mayer, Louis B. 30, 48
Mazurki, Mike 167
McCarthy, John, Jr. 151, 169
McCool, Mississippi 17
McCrea, Joel 47, 180
McDonald, Frank 123, 125

McGuinn, Joe 86
McGuire, George 135
McKinney, Mark 179
McLeod, Victor 114
McMillan, Meg 174
Medbury, John P. 89
Meehan, George 112
Meet Boston Blackie 84, 86
Meisel, Myron 142
Mercer, Ray 129
Merman, "Doc" 57
Merrick, Lynn **44**, 98
Metro Pictures 30
Meyer, Otto 114
MGM 30–33, 41, 44, 48, 57, 68, 100, 180, 182
Midnight Manhunt 57, 86, 126–128, **127, 128**
A Midsummer Night's Dream 33, 36
Miljan, John 151
Miller, Ann 48, 182
Miller, Don 158
Miller, Eve 167
Miller, Gohar 17
Milo, George 151, 169
Mint Casino 61
The Miracle 33
Mr. Smith Goes to Washington 151
Mix, Tom 27
Mocambo 57
Mohr, Gerald 167
Monogram 133, 143
Monroe, Marilyn 35
Monster 139
The Monster Maker 111
Montgomery, George 80, 109, 121
Moon Over Harlem 144
Mooney, Martin 135, 142
Moore, Don 167
Moore, McElbert 114
Moore, Michael 176
More Than Night: Film Noir in Its Contexts 146–147
The More the Merrier 47, 101, 180–181
Moreland, Mantan 148–149
Morgan, Frank 182
Morgan, Ira H. 165
Morheim, Louis 167–168
Morris, Chester 83–84, 86
Mourning Becomes Electra 108
Mowbray, Alan 114, 117
Muir, Gavin 92, **94**
Muller, Eddie 76
Mummert, Danny 96
Muni, Paul 27
Murder in Times Square 181–182
Murder Is My Business 135
Murder with Apology see Apology for Murder
Murnau, F.W. 36, 61, 144
Murphy, Paul 91
Murray, Noel 180
Museum of Modern Art (New York) 70
Musso and Frank 76
Mutchie, Marjorie Ann 96–97, **97**
My Man Godfrey 27
My Sister Eileen 108
My Winnipeg **76**, 77–78, 96, 172, 174–180, **177, 178**
Myton, Fred 89, 129, 134–135, 155

Naish, J. Carrol 51, 109–111, *111*, 182
The Naked Dawn 144
The Naked Kiss 66
Nardino, Gary 171
Naremore, James 146, 147
Narita, Hiro 171
Nash, Alden 91
National Film Registry 142
Neal, Tom 48, 51–52, 54, 58–62, *60*, *63*, *65*, 68, 101, 103–104, *103*, 106, 109–110, *109*, *111*, *113*, 118–120, *119*, 135, *137*, *138*, 139–140, *140*, *141*, 142, *143*, 144–145, *145*, *147*, 182–183
Neal, Tom, Jr. 148
Negin, Louis 174
Neufeld, Sigmund 62, 114, 117, 129, 134–135, 143, 155
Newberry, Norman 171
Newfield, Sam 62, 129, 134–135, 155–156, 161
Nine Girls 182
Nipp, Eric 174
None Shall Escape 96
Northwest Outpost 171
Nosseck, Max 80
Novak, Eva 129

Oakman, Wheeler 86
Obama, Barack 16, 77
O'Connell, L.W. 80, 83, 89, 91, 94, 121
Odell, Cary 109, 114
Odets, Clifford 39
Of Human Bondage 139, 146
On the Right Side 72, 183
One Dangerous Night *45*, 80–83, *81*, *82*, 86, 98, 101, 139, 167, 181
Orsatti, Frank (agent) 41, 56, 58
Otterson, Jack 149
Oursler, Fulton 148–149
Out of the Past 125
"Out of What Past? Notes on the B Film Noir" 134
Owen, Garry 155

Pabst, G.W. 144
Pacific Electric Railway (Red Car) 23–24, 27
Padden, Sarah 129
Paiva, Nestor 151
Palichuk, Jennifer 174
Palmentola, Paul 165
Palmer, Adele 169
Pantages, Alexander 105
Paramount 30, 56–57, 63, 75, 123, 126, 131, 133, 135, 161, 171
Parker, Charlie 58
Parker, Willard 106, *107*, 108
Parsons, Louella 105
Passport to Suez 47–48, 83, 86, 91–96, *93*, *94*, 139, 154
Pat Novak, for Hire 168
Pathe Laboratories 59, 143
The Pay-Off see *Saddles and Sagebrush*
Peary, Danny 146
Pembroke, George 183
Peterson, Robert 80
pets 25–26, 28, 67, 70, 72, 161
Phillips, Arnold 80

Phillips, Bill 171
Pier 23 68, 135, 160, 167–168
Pierce, William A. 101
Pierson, Carl 167
Pillow Talk 117
Pine, William H. 128, 161
Pine-Thomas Productions 56–58, 123, 126, 128, 144, 161
Pink Panther series 121
pinups *43*, 51, *53*, 120
Pioneertown 88
Polglase, Van Nest 106
Polito, Jon 171–172
"Polly" see *Fireside Theatre*
Powell, Dick 36
Powell, William 27, 100
Powers, Tom 151
PRC 59–63, 65, 117, 120, 129, 133–135, 142–146, 155–156
Preminger, Otto 36
Pride, Ray 180
Priestley, Robert 96, 112
Producers Releasing Corporation see PRC
Profeta, Lou 174
Progressive Pictures Corporation see PRC
Pryor, Roger 123
Pygmy Island 66, 68, 160, 165–168, *166*

Quantrill, William 157–158, 160, 169–171
Quantrill's Raiders 171

Rainer, Luise 180
Ralston, Vera Hruba 64
Randolph, Jane 33, 46, 52
Ray, Nicholas 158
Raymond, Alex 167
"The Red Dress" see *Gang Busters*
Red Ryder series 66, 154
Reid, Kate 171
Reif, Elia see Reif, Elias H.
Reif, Elias H. 129, 155, 161, 167
Reif, Harry see Reif, Elias H.
Reinhardt, Max 32–39, *37*, 41, 44, 46, 52, 61
Reiniger, Lotte 176
Remini, Leah 184
Renaldo, Duncan 161, 163–165
Renegade Girl 66, *67*, 157–161, *157*, *159*, *161*, 164, 168, 171
Repp, Ed Earl 86, 89, 112
Republic Pictures 48, 59, 64, 66, 133, 143, 151, 153–154, 169
Reynolds, Harry 167
Richards, Robert L. 151
Riders of the Northwest Mounted 89
RKO 33, 91
Road to Utopia 106
Roaring City 168
Robinson, Bill 145
Robinson, Edward G. 131, 182
Rogers, Ginger 67
Roland, Gilbert 164
Romero, Cesar 164
Rooney, Mickey 29–30, 33, 36, 58
Roos, Kelley 98
Roosevelt, Eleanor 164
Roosevelt, Franklin Delano 164

Ross, Henry 70, *71*
Rossellini, Isabella 179
Rotsten, Herman 118, 120
Rozsa, Miklos 134
Rubin, Stanley 89
Russ, Tim 171
Russell, Rosalind 106, *107*, 108
Rutherford, Ann 33
Ryan, Tim 135

Sackheim, Jerry 151
The Saddest Music in the World 176, 179
Saddles and Sagebrush 47, 60, 66, 86–89, *87*, *88*, 114, 158, 160, 168, 182
Sahara 182
Salter, Hans J. 149
Salzburg Festival in Austria 36
Samuel Goldwyn Studios 65
San Francisco Film Critics Circle Award 180
Sande, Walter 148
Sanders, George 182
Sands of Iwo Jima 154
Sarris, Andrew 142, 144, 146
Satan's Cradle 163–165
Saturday Evening Post 169
"Savage, Ann" (acting name, how acquired) 41
Saved by the Bell 75, 184
Savlov, Marc 180
Scared Stiff 57, 86, 123–128, *123*, *125*
Scarlett O'Hara's Younger Sister 101
Schaefer, Whitey 57
Schenck, Nicholas 32
Schlitz Playhouse of Stars 184
Schulz, Bruno 177
Scott, Sherman see Newfield, Sam
Sedaris, David 180
Sedway, Moe 78
Seiter, William A. 182
Selwyn, Edgar 30, 32–33
Selwyn, Russell "Rusty" 32–33, 38–39, 45, 47
Selwyn, Ruth 32
Selznick, David O. 63
Seymour, Henry 148
Shane, Maxwell 123
Shannon, Harry 151
Shapiro, Jody 174
Sheffer, Craig 171–172
Shefter, Bert 167
Sheridan, Ann 47, 144
Sherwood, George 129
Shock Corridor 66
Shore, Howard 171
Siegel, Benjamin 66, 68–69, 78
Silva, Mario 114
Silver City Raiders 89
Silvey, Ben 148
Simms, Larry 96
Sinatra, Frank 106
Singleton, Penny 96–98
Sister Kenny 108
Skaaren, Warren 171
Smart, Jean 171
Smith, Alexis 182
Smith, Howard 161
Smith, Perry 118
Snookie see pets

Solomon, Leo 149
Sondergaard, Gale 182
Sosenko, Anna 64
Spartan Productions 167
Spicer, Andrew 147
The Spider 64, 148–149
Stanford, Robert 92, 98
Stanislavsky, Constantin 35, 38
Stanwyck, Barbara 27, 39–40, 131–132
Steele, Barbara 179
Sternbach, Bert 129
Stevens, George 47, 68, 180–181
Stevens, Onslow 182
Stewart, Amy 174
Stewart, Peter *see* Newfield, Sam
Stieffenhofer, Katharina 174
Stoloff, M.W. 80, 83, 89, 91, 96, 98, 101, 106, 109, 121
Stone, George E. 83–84, 86, 123, 125–126
Stone, John 91
Strains of Utopia 140
Strange Affair 101
Strange Illusion 60–61, 120, 144
The Strange Woman 65
Strangers on a Train 68
Strasberg, Lee 35, 37
Strasberg, Paula 35, 37
Strayer, Frank 96, 98
Stuart, Gloria 76
Stulman, Julius 72
Stumar, John 101
Sullivan, James 169
Sullivan's Travels 83
Sully, Frank 98, 100–101, 182
Sunrise 36, 61
Sunset Boulevard (California) 25, 46
Sutton, Grady 106
Swan, Buddy 124
Sweeney, D.B. 171–172
Sylos, Frank Paul 123, 126, 155, 161, 163, 167

Tales from the Gimli Hospital 178–179
"Tango" *see* Schlitz Playhouse of Stars
Tannen, Charles 148
Tannen, William 165
Tannura, Philip 96, 98
Tarzan series 167
Taylor, Dub 86–89, **88,** 112, 114
Tenneson, Clark 29–31
tennis 39, 40, 55, 72, 76
Terrified 112
Terry, Philip 64, 150–151, **150**
Thalberg, Irving 30
Theron, Charlize 139
Thimig, Helene 34, 38
Thin Man series 100
13 Ghosts 102
Thomas, Kevin 75, 142
Thomas, Olive 63
Thomas, William C. 126, 128, 161
Thompson, Glenn P. 135
Thompson, William P. 151

Thoms, Jerome 89, 98, 109, 112, 165
Thorsen, Mel 91, 101
Thrill of Brazil 101
Thundercloud, Chief 66, 157
Time magazine 78, 147, 180
The Tingler 102
Titanic 76
Todd, Holbrook N. 129, 155
Toles, George 174, 178
Tombragel, Maurice 89
Top Hat 83
A Tornado in the Saddle 89
Toronto Film Festival 180
Totter, Audrey 33, 169–171, 182
Travilla, William "Billy" 48, 89, 114
Travis, Richard 167
Treasure of Fear see Scared Stiff
Trevor, Claire 182
Tribeca Film Festival 180
Trivers, Barry 106
Trocadero 66
Turan, Kenneth 180
Turner, Lana 33
Tuttle, Frank 86
TV Guide 146
Twentieth Century 27
20th Century–Fox 40, 64, 148–149
Twilight of the Ice Nymphs 179
Two Latins from Manhattan 91
Two-Man Submarine 51–52, 61, 86, 109–112, **109, 111, 113,** 118, 120, 167
Two Señoritas from Chicago 48, 89–91, **90, 91,** 101

UCLA 75
Ulmer, Edgar G. 59–62, 65, 68, 75, 78, 120, 134–135, 139–146, **144,** 148
Ulmer, Shirley 61, 75, **75,** 78, 144–145
United Artists 65, 145
Universal Studios 52, 61, 64, 144, 149, 151, 167
The Unwritten Code 53–54, 118–121, **119, 120**
Up the Yangtze 180

Vagabond Theatre (tribute to Ann) 147
Valentino, Rudolph 16, 63, 78
Vance, Louis Joseph 80, 83
Van Trees, James 109
Varden, Norma 106
Varela, Nina 169
Variety 146
Varno, Roland 118–119, **119**
Vas, Steven 89
Vaughan, Dorothy **122**
Vendome Liquor and Fine Food 66
Venice Boulevard 30
The Vigilantes Ride 89

Wade, Russell 157, 160, **161**
waitressing 32
Walker, Joseph 106
Warner, Jack L. 36
Warner Brothers 30, 33, 36–37, 46, 55, 57, 144–145

Watkin, Pierre 129
Waxahachie, Texas 20
Wayne, John 154
Webb, Robert 148
Webster, M. Coates 101
Weissmuller, Johnny 66, 165, 167
Welden, Ben 151
Welsch, Howard 149
West, Victor 167
Westmore, Bud 60–61
Westrate, Edwin V. 157
What a Woman! 106–109, **107**
What's Buzzin', Cousin? 48, 182
Wheeler, Lyle 148
White, Leslie T. 109, 118
White, Sam 83
White Pongo 134
The Wife of Monte Cristo 61
Wilder, Billy 131–132, 144
Wilkerson, Billy 66–68
William, Warren 45, **45,** 80–84, **82,** 92, 95, **95**
Williams, Bob 109
Williams, Cara 148
Williams, Charlie 155
Williams, Robert B. 109
Williams, Wade 75, 148
Willis, Norman 129
Wills, Bob (and the Texas Playboys) 86–89, **88,** 112, 114
Wilmot, Robert 118
Wilshire La Brea Bowl 32
Wilson, Stanley 167
Winfrey, Oprah 16
Wisberg, Aubrey 83
Withers, Grant 167
The Wizard of Oz 125
The Wolf Man 83
The Woman from Hell 117
Woman They Almost Lynched 68, 157, 160, 169–171
Wood, Douglas 106
Woodman, Ruth 184
Woodruff, Frank 89–91
World Institute 72
World War I 17
World War II 17, 39, 42, **43,** 45–46, 50–53, 55, 59, 64–65, 69, 84, 89, 92, 98, 109–110, 118–120, 134
Worth, Constance 101
Wright, William 86, 88, 121–122, **122,** 181–182
Wyoming Hurricane 89

Yacula, Kate 174
Yank magazine 120
Yates, Herbert J. 64, 66
Young, Carroll 165
Young, Chic 96, 98
Young, Lee 58
Young, Lester 58
Young Jesse James 171
Younger, Cole 169–171
Younger, Jim 169–171
Yung Chang 180

Zinnemann, Fred 144
Zucco, George 126–127, **128,** 134

www.ingramcontent.com/pod-product-compliance
Lightning Source LLC
Chambersburg PA
CBHW081551300426
44116CB00015B/2835